I0884194

James in Postcolonial Perspective

James in Postcolonial Perspective

The Letter as Nativist Discourse

K. Jason Coker

Fortress Press
Minneapolis

JAMES IN POSTCOLONIAL PERSPECTIVE

The Letter as Nativist Discourse

Cover design: Tory Herman

Cover image: Icon of Saint James the Less (13th c., Greece) / Wikimedia Commons

Library of Congress Cataloging-in-Publication Data is available

Print ISBN: 978-1-4514-7050-5

eISBN: 978-1-5064-0035-8

The paper used in this publication meets the minimum requirements of American National Standard for Information Sciences — Permanence of Paper for Printed Library Materials, ANSI Z329.48-1984.

Manufactured in the U.S.A.

This book was produced using PressBooks.com, and PDF rendering was done by PrinceXML.

Contents

Acknowledgments

Books take time, and over the expanse of time that it took to produce this work, I have been fortunate enough to amass a great deal of gratitude for a great number of people. My scholarly colleagues, who have taught me formally or informally at Drew University, deserve my acknowledgments. While still in course work, I was fortunate enough to take a class on the Letter of James with Leticia Guardiola-Sáenz. She nurtured my interest in the book and gave me far more insight into that little letter than I would have ever had on my own. Because of her passion both for teaching and for the subject matter she taught, my introduction to the Letter of James was profound and spurred me in this direction. For her graciousness as a person and professor, I am deeply grateful. That same semester, Stephen D. Moore taught a class on the Bible, colonialism, and postcolonialism that I also took. The intersection between those classes gave birth to this monograph. Stephen's excitement about my final paper in that class led to my first publication, and it was at that time he suggested I pursue a postcolonial reading of the Letter of James. Rather than encouraging me and sending me on my way, Stephen has offered more help in the process than any one professor should, which is a testimony to what kind of advisor, professor, mentor, and scholar he is. I will always bear the scholarly marks of his fingerprint. Virginia

Burrus, Danna Nolan Fewell, and Otto Maduro were also extremely influential in my growth as a scholar. They exemplify what it means to be renowned scholars and truly great people. My only regret is that I did not finish in time for Otto to read my great appreciation for him—may he rest in eternal peace. To Melanie Johnson-DeBaufre and Althea Spencer-Miller, this work would not be what it is without your help and encouragement. Thank you for all the time you spent with me and my work.

Friends also make books possible. Without overwhelming support from Scott Elliott, Matt Waggoner, Linda Dietch, Eric Thurman, John Schwiebert, and SuJung Shin, I may never have reached this point. They have been with me through this entire journey as good friends and better critics. Beyond their true support, the annual meetings of the Society of Biblical Literature would simply not be as fun or rewarding. You all inspire me to be a better scholar. On a more local level, I want to thank David Graybill and Leah Cohen. Your continual interest in my research topic never ceased to amaze me, and your constant goodwill and companionship made this process much saner and more gratifying than it may have otherwise been.

Without a sabbatical leave during the beginning of 2013, I certainly would have never finished this work, so I would like to thank Wilton Baptist Church for being such an understanding and supportive congregation. You have been a pastor and family to me. Thank you for giving me time and holding me accountable. What Wilton Baptist Church gave me in time, Temple B'nai Chaim gave me in space. Your gift to me of space in your library to function as my desk and office made it possible for me to concentrate my time without any distractions. You will always hold a special place in my heart as my first synagogue.

Finally, I want to thank my family—my mother, Mary, and my father, Kenny, for establishing a work ethic in me as a child and nourishing my sense of independence throughout my life. You made me who I am. My work on this book took more time away from my spouse and children than anybody else—all my children were born during this time period! Without your presence in my life, I would be anchorless. For your love and daily support over all these years, I dedicate this book to you: Pamela, Liam, Owen, and Reyna.

PART I

Constructing the Native

1

Introduction

Who has the authority to constitute authentic identity and mark the boundaries between insiders and outsiders? What is at stake in the process of negotiating identity? Who benefits and who is maligned? These questions understand identity as a mutable construct of negotiations rather than a pure essence, and follow Shirley Anne Tate's interpretation of Stuart Hall: "Identities . . . are positionings that are constantly being transformed. As such, they are never complete as ideas, world-views and material forces interact with each other and are reworked."[1] These questions are important for the Letter of James because James, from beginning to end, is a complex negotiation of Judean identity that confronts both Roman imperialism and Pauline hybridity. The main body of the letter (2:1—5:6) fluctuates between anti-imperial polemic (2:1-13, 3:13-18, and 5:1-6) and anti-Pauline polemic (2:14-26, 3:1-12, 4:1-12, and

1. Shirley Anne Tate, *Black Skins, Black Masks: Hybridity, Dialogism, Performativity* (Hants, UK: Ashgate, 2005), 69. See Stuart Hall, "The Formation of a Diasporic Intellectual: An Interview with Stuart Hall by Kuan-Hsing Chen," in *Stuart Hall—Critical Dialogues in Cultural Studies*, ed. David Morley and Kuan-Hsing Chen (London: Routledge, 1996), 484–503.

4:13-17) as a means to construct the boundary around authentic Judean identity within the early Jesus movement. Identity for James is determined by purity and perfection in contrast to impurity and double-mindedness or two-facedness. The only thing worse than the Roman "world" is anyone who would transgress the pure and perfect boundary that exists between the empire of God and Rome. James calls these boundary crossers "whores," "two-faced," and "transgressors" or "sinners" (4:4, 8).

James, Nativism, and Postcolonial Biblical Studies

James's concentration on an essentialist identity characterized by purity functions as "an organizing principle within a politics of resistance" akin to the Negritude movement inaugurated by Aimé Césaire, Léopold Senghor, and Léon Damas.[2] Negritude as a nativist movement from "below" provided a space and place for those in the African Diaspora, like Césaire, to claim human dignity as a minority living in a European center such as Paris, and to speak back to the center from within an antiracist movement. I do not propose a perfect parallel between James's nativism and negritude, but reading the Letter of James as nativist discourse provides a helpful vocabulary for describing the letter's anti-imperial and antihybrid or antiassimilationist stance, especially in relation to identity negotiation. The postcolonial critique of nativism in general and negritude in particular is also instructive because it shows the vast discrepancies between theories of hybridity and cultural purity. By engaging such cultural theory, the antagonism between James as a cultural purist and Paul as a cultural hybrid becomes clear. James's nativist negotiation against empire ("the world") places him at odds with Pauline hybridity ("double-minded"/"two-faced").

2. Tate, *Black Skins, Black Masks*, 71.

The first part of this book concentrates on nativism as a heuristic tool and offers an analysis of James 1, which begins to construct the native. Chapter 2, which begins this work in earnest, is devoted to an extended definition of nativism and provides a rationale for using such a concept as a lens to read the Letter of James. After defining nativism and answering the question, why use nativism as a lens? I turn to first-century CE Judeanness and focus on what constitutes this as an identity. Who is negotiating Judeanness within Palestine, and how did that differ from negotiating Judeanness within the Diaspora? The Letter of James functions as a form of Judean nativism within Roman Palestine but projects that nativism onto the Diaspora.

Pure and perfect piety is central to James's nativist discourse, which is the controlling topic in chapter 3. Here, I analyze the first chapter of James and pay close attention to the center/margin power dynamic at work within the short, but vitally important, greeting (1:1). At this juncture in the analysis of James 1:1, I agree with many modern commentators on the Letter of James and argue for an early dating of the letter and authentic authorship, which places the letter firmly in Jerusalem. From this standpoint, the Letter of James functions as an official letter from Jerusalem to the Diaspora, or *Diasporabriefe*. It is from this place of authority as the leader of the Jesus movement that James calls for purity and perfection.

In part 2, I follow James's argument in the main body of the letter as he confronts Roman imperialism and Pauline hybridity. Chapter 4 focuses on the anti-imperial passages in James 2:1-13, 5:1-6, and 3:13-18. Since I sense a chiastic structure in James and consider 3:13-18 to be its fulcrum, I exegete it last. In these three pericopae, James confronts: 1) Greco-Roman patronage with God's partiality for the poor (2:1-7) and the Law of God's empire (2:8-13); 2) wealthy landownership that reflected Roman elitism (5:1-6); and 3) "worldly, unspiritual, and evil" wisdom with "wisdom from above" that is "pure" (3:13-18). Here, James divides the universe between the "world" and "God"—"the world" being the Roman world.

In chapters 5 and 6, I exegete the anti-Pauline passages 2:14-26, 3:1-12, 4:1-12, and 4:13-17 after considering a "postcolonial" Paul. I try to emphasize the reasons why James would be anti-Pauline without making these two chapters entirely about Paul. I briefly overview the writings of the New Testament that detail the encounter(s) between James and Paul (Galatians and Acts) and focus on modern scholarship that emphasizes Paul's hybridity in an attempt to produce a postcolonial understanding of Pauline identity. It is through this lens that I read the faith/works binary in the Letter of James as a confrontation against hybridity. James's movement from action to speech in 3:1-12 censures the hybrid teacher whose tongue is like a spring that "pours forth from the same opening both fresh and salty water" (3:12).

Chapter 6 concentrates on the most aggressive argument against hybridity in the Letter of James (4:1-12) and on James's critique of Pauline itineraries. The either/or of "friendship with the world"/"friendship with God" gives James the rhetorical force to call Judean/Roman hybrids "whores" (4:4), "double-minded"/"two-faced" (4:8), and "transgressors" (4:8). Indicative of this kind of friendship with the world is the arrogance and boasting that accompanies (Paul's) travel itineraries. Here, James uses Pauline vocabulary to criticize his missionary activity. Although I understand these four pericopae as anti-Pauline, I do not think that James had any knowledge of Paul's letters. Because of the early dating of James, his critique of Paul must be due to the messages that James received about Paul's preaching and/or the personal encounters between the two—as we see from Paul's perspective in Galatians.

Situating a Postcolonial Reading within Current Scholarship on James

I will briefly situate my reading of James within current scholarship on James; although a more thorough analysis of each issue will follow in the later chapters when these issues are addressed specifically. The primary issues related to the Letter of James for the past thirty years have been dating, authorship, structure, and literary relationship. There continues to be great diversity of opinion on each of these problems, but recently there has been a movement toward a traditional reading that argues for authentic authorship and an early date with a coherent structure that is not dependent on or antagonistic to the Pauline corpus. Each of these items is in direct contradiction to Martin Dibelius's groundbreaking commentary on the Letter of James from 1921.[3] Dibelius systematically unbraided the traditional view on James, which affirmed authorial authenticity and an early date. Dibelius argued that James was written in the early second century CE (anywhere between 80 and 130 CE) and was pseudonymous.[4] In addition to this shift, Dibelius saw no organized structure to the letter, which evidenced the fact that the composition was paranetic in nature. "What one finds," argues Dibelius, "is *paraenesis* in the form of unconnected sayings which have no real relationship to one another. . . . By paraenesis we mean a text which strings together admonitions of general ethical content."[5] For

3. All references to Martin Dibelius's commentary come from the 1976 English translation, *James: A Commentary on the Epistle of James*, trans. Michael A. Williams, Hermeneia (Philadelphia: Fortress Press, 1976).
4. Dibelius dates James after Paul's writings and before Jude; see *James*, 45–46. This late dating provides him evidence for pseudonymity; although, the obvious referent for James is the brother of Jesus and leader of the Jerusalem Church: "Our sources know only one person of reputation in primitive Christianity who could have been suggested by the way in which his name appears in the prescript of our letter: James, the brother of Jesus," 12. For his extended analysis on pseudonymity, see Dibelius, *James*, 17–21.
5. Dibelius, *James*, 3 (emphasis original).

Dibelius, "the entire document lacks continuity in thought."[6] With such a strong view on the lack of structure in James, it is surprising that Dibelius spills so much ink dealing with the issue of literary influence.[7] Specifically, he contends that James's relationship with Pauline writings is important; however, the two authors do not directly influence one another literarily. In other words, James is refuting a misunderstanding of Pauline thought regarding faith and works but not dealing with Paul's writings themselves: "For though the section in Jas 2:14-26 seems to me to presuppose an acquaintance with definite Pauline slogans, it also demonstrates precisely the fact that any penetrating reading of the letters of Paul upon the part of James is out of the question."[8]

Since Dibelius's commentary, most of his arguments have been challenged, but nearly all historical-critical commentaries written on James after Dibelius use him as their reference point. His dominance is only accentuated when reviewing modern German commentaries and works on James.[9] Luke Timothy Johnson's commentary, however, can be credited with changing scholarly opinion about most of Dibelius's theses.[10] Johnson's commentary represents a total

6. Ibid., 2.
7. See Dibelius, *James*, 26–34, for his full analysis of the literary relationship.
8. Dibelius, *James*, 29.
9. See Manabu Tsuji, *Glaube zwischen Vollkommenheit und Verweltlichung: Eine Untersuchung zur literarischen Gestalt und zur inhaltlichen Koharenz des Jakobusbriefes* (Tübingen: Mohr Siebeck, 1997); Christoph Burchard, *Der Jakobusbrief*, Handbuch zum Neuen Testament 15, no. 1 (Tübingen: Mohr Siebeck, 2000); and Gerhard Maier, *Der Brief des Jakobus*, Historische Theologicshe Auslegung (Markgröningen: R. Brockhaus Verlag Wuppertal, 2004) for examples of how Dibelius continues to impact German scholarship on James. Tsuji continually references Dibelius in order to combat Dibelius's refutation of structure in James. In his work, Tsuji goes to great length to show how succinctly organized James is contra Dibelius.
10. Luke Timothy Johnson, *The Letter of James: A New Translation with Introduction and Commentary*, Anchor Bible, 37A (New York: Doubleday, 1995). However, Peter H. Davids's influential commentary, *The Epistle of James: A Commentary on the Greek Text*, NIGTC (Grand Rapids: Eerdmans, 1982), prepared the way for Johnson by persuasively arguing for a definite literary structure throughout the Letter of James, which evidences a plausible *Sitz im Leben*. Davids is also influential in dating James. His development of the two-stage composition theory, *Epistle of James*, 22, was among the first challenges to Dibelius's late dating of James.

break with Dibelius and a return to the traditional view about the letter of James regarding authorship, date, structure, and literary relationship. Johnson regards the authorship to be authentic, the date to be early, the structure to be coherent, and the setting to be real. He also argues forcefully that James and Paul are in harmony with each other and are simply using different meanings of similar words when they appear to disagree. In the process, Johnson makes an appeal to find the "voice" in the text and uses his (re)construction of James's voice as the starting place for examining and (re)constructing everything else related to the text.[11] In the process of defining this "voice," Johnson studies the text, language and style, structure, and genre of James as well as all the possible literary relationships between James and other relevant literature. Johnson turns sermonic in the final analysis of James as he exhorts his audience to hear James's voice: "Such explanation, however, does not yet constitute interpretation in the fullest sense. Interpretation demands not only that the text be described but that its message be engaged."[12]

His persuasive arguments, rooted in the most in-depth historical study of James among modern commentators, have won many adherents.[13] Important departures from Dibelius that predate Johnson, however, must be mentioned. Both Peter H. Davids and Ralph P. Martin mediate the position between Dibelius and Johnson by arguing for a two-stage composition of James, which, by necessity, argues for a later redacted version of the Letter of James.[14]

11. Johnson, *The Letter of James*, 3.
12. Ibid., 162.
13. See Richard Bauckham, *James: Wisdom of James, Disciple of Jesus the Sage*, New Testament Readings (London and New York: Routledge, 1999); William F. Brosend II, *James and Jude*, The New Cambridge Bible Commentary (Cambridge: Cambridge University Press, 2004); and Patrick J. Hartin, *James*, Sacra Pagina, 14 (Collegeville, MN: Liturgical, 2003).
14. See Davids, *Epistle of James*, 12–13, 22, and Ralph P. Martin, *James*, WBC, 48 (Nashville: Thomas Nelson, 1988), lxx–lxxvii. See also Robert W. Wall, *Community of the Wise: The Letter of James* (Valley Forge, PA: Trinity Press International, 1997), 5–11.

This two-stage composition attempts to negotiate the difficulties in dating the Letter of James either early or late by arguing for a later redactor that polished the final version with excellent Greek. Martin and Davids, however, disagree regarding the hostility between James and Paul. Davids does not see any anti-Pauline material in James, while Martin argues for a correction in James to a perversion of Pauline thought.[15]

Johnson's arguments regarding an early date, authentic authorship, and literary structure are convincing, and I agree with his assessment related to all of these issues. The problem with positioning James as early and authentic, however, is Johnson's insistence on *making* James and Paul harmonious. If James is early, and I agree with Johnson that it is, then the rhetoric within the Letter of James is certainly antagonistic to Pauline sensibilities. This is only accentuated when we position James and Paul as first-century Judeans negotiating identity in relation to the Roman Empire—something Johnson and others simply never address. Among commentaries, Martin is the only commentator that seriously addresses issues related to Roman imperialism. I dramatically part ways with the harmonious James and Paul theory and argue that James is specifically critical of Pauline preaching and sensibilities because James and Paul negotiate Judean identity within the Roman Empire differently and in opposition to each other.

Likewise, all of these commentators presuppose a definitive distinction between Christianity and Judaism by the time the Letter of James was written—even while arguing for an early, pre-62 CE date. At this point in the development of the early Jesus movement, the movement itself is still firmly within the boundaries of Judeanness. James characterizes his Judeanness in terms of purity

15. Davids, *Epistle of James*, 21; Martin, *James*, lxxi–lxxii.

and perfection throughout his letter. Paul, however, negotiates a hybrid, interstitial space that blurs the boundaries between purity and impurity. Reading James against Paul in postcolonial terms of nativism and hybridity provides effective vocabulary in describing how they opposed each other as they attempted to manage a subaltern, Judean identity in relation to Roman imperialism. This strange absence among most of these commentaries regarding the place and presence of the Roman Empire as it relates to James, and their concentration on James as a *Christian* document, allows them to focus on James as a theological/ethical letter rather than a letter with explicit political motivation. Focusing on the politics within James, I use a postcolonial biblical hermeneutic to elucidate the relationship between James and Paul and show them to be two competing voices within first-century Judeanness.[16]

16. I describe other pertinent postcolonial readings of the Letter of James later when I provide a rationale for nativism as a lens for reading.

2

Nativism

According to John Higham, one of the preeminent authorities on nativism in American history, "Nativism has been hard for historians to define."[1] Besides the fact that nativism "is distinctly American," Higham's questions reveal the difficulty in definition: "Does nativism consist only of the particular complex of attitudes dominant in the antiforeign crusades of the mid-nineteenth century [in the U.S.]? Or does it extend to every occasion when native inhabitants of a country turn their faces or raise their hands against strangers in their midst?"[2] Higham traces the "antiforeign spirit" in American nativism in the middle of the nineteenth century to show how this movement was a reaction to the unprecedented immigration that the United States was experiencing from Europe.[3] Peter Schrag describes one anti-

1. John Higham, *Strangers in the Land: Patterns of American Nativism, 1860–1925* (New Brunswick, NJ and London: Rutgers University Press, 2002 [1955 original]), 3.
2. Ibid., 3.
3. Ibid., xi. For specific information on Irish and German immigration to the United States from 1830 to 1860, see Tyler Anbinder, *Nativism and Slavery: The Northern Know Nothings and the Politics of the 1850s* (Oxford: Oxford University Press, 1992), 9–10; and Peter Schrag, *Not Fit for Our Society: Nativism and Immigration* (Berkeley: University of California Press, 2010), 24–25.

Catholic, American nativist reaction in Boston during this period: "In August 1834, a nativist mob, many with Indian-style faces, broke into the Ursuline convent and school in Charlestown, near the site of the battle of Bunker Hill across from the Charles River in Boston, and torched it. . . . In the days following, they returned to torch what was left of the Ursuline property, while other rioters roamed through Boston."[4] This nativist reaction to "foreigners" eventually led to the founding of organizations like the Native American Democratic Association (NADA), which was organized in New York City in 1835, and the Order of the Star Spangled Banner, better known as the Know Nothing party, in the 1850s. Tyler Anbinder describes the growth of the Know Nothings in particular: "None attained greater prominence than the . . . Know Nothing party. Vowing to reduce the influence of immigrants and Catholics, the Know Nothings burst onto the American political scene in 1854, and by the end of the following year they had elected eight governors, more than one hundred congressmen, the mayors of Boston, Philadelphia, and Chicago, and thousands of other local officials."[5] More recently, some scholars have focused on the "New Nativism" in America regarding current issues related to immigration, specifically Proposition 187.[6] Within this new nativist movement, the emphasis on speaking English and the fear of terrorist threats from U.S. borders rhetorically function to create an "us"/"U.S." versus "them"/"foreigner" mentality. In both the historical and modern versions of nativism, there is an appeal to authenticity and purity regarding identity.

4. Schrag, *Not Fit for Our Society*, 26.

5. Anbinder, *Nativism and Slavery*, ix.

6. See Robin Dale Jacobson, *The New Nativism: Proposition 187 and the Debate over Immigration* (Minneapolis: University of Minnesota Press, 2008); and Juan F. Perea, ed., *Immigrants Out!: The New Nativism and the Anti-Immigrant Impulse in the United States* (New York: New York University Press, 1997).

While these observations regarding the origins of "nativism" in the United States are helpful in situating my argument, this is not the sort of nativism that I describe for the purposes of my reading of the Letter of James. What is described as American nativism is what I understand as a "nativism from above" or a "nativism from the center." Higham's second question regarding a definition of nativism is more appropriate for my purposes: "Or does it extend to every occasion when native inhabitants of a country turn their faces or raise their hands against strangers in their midst?"[7] How does the nature of this question shift when the "strangers in their midst" are not immigrants seeking a better life, but colonial forces that seek to destroy native culture, steal natural resources, and take native land? This is what I describe as "nativism from below" or "nativism from the margins." In this sense, instead of maintaining a dominant culture, nativism is an attempt to preserve or rehabilitate indigenous culture in opposition to assimilating imperial/colonial culture. Nativism from the margins confronts and resists, then, both imperialism and cultural hybridity. This idea of nativism, however, is a contested issue within postcolonial theory and needs to be positioned in the complex postcolonial debate.

Within the larger field of postcolonial studies, nativism functions as a broad category that encompasses liberation movements such as Negritude, Pan-Africanism, and Negrismo. What all these movements have in common is their anticolonial stance from the perspective of a colonized culture. Nativism looks to a nostalgic past that was unencumbered and untouched by the cultural collision birthed by colonialism. While constructing this past, nativists attempt to recuperate, resuscitate, and rejuvenate this historic identity as a unifying force in order to fight for independence from colonial

7. Higham, *Strangers in the Land*, 3.

control. This had a profound impact on the rationale for nationalist movements throughout the colonized world during the 1960s and 1970s and continues to have ramifications for many postcolonial nations today.[8] The possibility or probability of resurrecting a pure native identity, however powerful it is for nationalist movements, has been challenged by many cultural theorists including, but not limited to, Frantz Fanon, Edward Said, and Homi Bhabha. One of the most difficult issues related to nativism concerns the material results.[9] In many independence movements, nativism favors "a single dominant cultural group" within the larger movement.[10] By favoring

8. It should be noted here that the concepts of nation and nationalism are modern constructions rather than essentialist foundations. Nation is a European product that functioned to galvanize large groups of people for the benefit of a dominant and controlling elite. The ideology of nation or myth of nation constructs a nationalism that hegemonically functions to homogenize a group of heterogeneous people. Due to this hegemonic discourse, nation is always unstable and prone to deteriorate without strong emphasis on "national" symbols, language, traditions, etc. in order to mask the arbitrariness of the construct. The European construction of nation coalesced fully only during the early modern expansionist movements, i.e., modern imperialism and colonialism, due to the necessity of defining "nation" in relation to "other," that is, colonized people. It is in this interaction between European nation and non-European native that anticolonial or decolonization movements happened. In this sense, nativism is a reaction to (European) nationalist expansion that uses nationalistic ideology only to turn it on its head. See further Bill Ashcroft, Gareth Griffiths, and Helen Tiffin, *Post-Colonial Studies: The Key Concepts* (London and New York: Routledge, 2000), 149–55; and Homi K. Bhabha, ed., *Nation and Narration* (London and New York: Routledge, 1990).
9. I use "material" here in a classic Marxist fashion, i.e., historical materialism, rather than "cultural materialism," which is more common in literary and cultural studies. Understanding the material results of imperialism as historical realities places a historical problem at the fore rather than politics. Rather than uncritically revert to classical Marxist material history, Benita Parry offers a blistering critique of theory while viewing material history through the lens of colonial violence. In her critique, colonial violence demands a materialist approach to history. The violence of nativism and other liberation theories, then, is understood as a reaction to the violence of colonialism. I use "material results" here based on Fanon's insistence on violence as purification and Parry's insistence on keeping the material effects of colonialism in the fore rather than allowing them to be muddled underneath a palimpsest of theory. See Benita Parry, *Postcolonial Studies: A Materialist Critique* (London and New York: Routledge, 2004), 75–92; Frantz Fanon, *The Wretched of the Earth*, trans. Constance Farrington (New York: Grove, 1963 [French original, 1961]), 35–106; Robert Young, *White Mythologies: Writing History and the West* (London and New York: Routledge, 1990), 21–47.
10. Ashcroft, Griffiths, and Tiffin, *Post-Colonial Studies*, 160. See also Seri Inthava Kau'ikealaula Luangphinith, "Nativism," in *Encyclopedia of Postcolonial Studies*, ed. John C. Hawley (Westport, CT: Greenwood, 2001), 321–22.

a dominant cultural group, critics argue that nativism replaces one oppressive hierarchy with another.

Benita Parry challenges this postcolonial, theoretical critique of nativism. She shows that what postcolonial theorists either willfully ignore or simply disdain

> is that notions of communal ethnic identity were invoked in the interests of mobilizing populations against their foreign rulers, while cultural heritages denigrated and despised by colonialism were affirmed as authentic traditions. Such recuperations, however, were not made in the interest of discovering uncontaminated origins or claiming ethnic purity, and were remote from any attempt to retrieve a past known to be irrecoverable.[11]

Parry not only forces postcolonial theorists to pay attention to the material/real results of colonialism, but also critiques a too-simple notion of nativism that many postcolonial theorists reify. For instance, the negritude movement that promoted a unified identity in a "transnational blackness" resists simple binarisms and essentialisms. Based on the work of Léopold Senghor, one of the founders of the negritude movement, Chike Jeffers argues that "*Négritude* is part of a cultural exchange through which all peoples are meant to be unified but not made uniform."[12] Senghor's negritude was not only an attempt to independently define identity/self in opposition to an other, but it was also an attempt to understand civilizations as complementary. Through Senghor's concept of *métissage*, negritude would help/develop Europe. For instance, "the spiritual wisdom and vitality of negritude would have to supersede the materialistic emphasis in Europe," but through this encounter both civilizations

11. Parry, *Postcolonial Studies*, 10.
12. Chike Jeffers, "Black Civilization and the Dialogue of Cultures: Senghor's Combination of Cultural Nationalism and Cosmopolitanism," in *Negritude: Legacy and Present Relevance*, ed. Isabelle Constant and Kahiudi C. Mabana (Newcastle upon Tyne, UK: Cambridge Scholars Publishing, 2009), 55.

would flourish.[13] The first step, however, in negritude, for Senghor, was to be "rooted in the virtues of black people," and only after "blossoming" there could negritude move toward *métissage*.[14] Negritude as a particular form of nativism from the margins forces critics of nativism to at least be more specific in their assessment. Mikela Lundahl takes simple critiques of nativism and negritude to task by asking the questions "why certain Western thinkers choose to emphasize this legacy [of essentialism and particularism] instead of the liberating aspects of Negritude" and "why [do] so many commentators choose to ignore the intentions of the Negritude movement?"[15]

Even early scholars of decolonization, however, were aware of the capacity within nativism to reproduce colonial constructions refashioned as native. Albert Memmi writes with sympathy about nativist reproduction of colonial structures, describing it as nearly a historical inevitability:

> The important thing now is to rebuild his people, whatever be their authentic nature; to reform their unity, communicate with it and to feel that they belong. This must be done no matter what the price paid by the colonized. Thus he will be nationalistic but not, of course, internationalistic. Naturally, by so doing, he runs the risk of falling into exclusionism and chauvinism, of sticking to the most narrow principles, and of setting national solidarity against human solidarity—and even ethnic solidarity against national solidarity. But to expect the colonized to open his mind to the world and be a humanist and internationalist would seem to be ludicrous thoughtlessness. He is still regaining possession of himself, still examining himself with astonishment, passionately demanding the return of his language.[16]

13. Frederick Ochieng'-Odhiambo, "Negritude: The Basic Principles and Appraisal," in *Negritude: Legacy and Present Relevance*, ed. Constant and Mabana, 73.
14. Léopold Sédar Senghor, *Liberté 3: Négritude et Civilization de l'Universel* (Paris: Éditions du Seuil, 1977), 469–70.
15. Mikela Lundahl, "Negritude—An Anti-Racist Racism? (Or Who Is the Racist?)," in *Negritude: Legacy and Present Relevance*, ed. Constant and Mabana, 83–84.

The exclusionism and chauvinism to which Memmi refers is always present in "the colonized's self-assertion" because the identity politics at work within nativism are always in reaction to colonial epistemology and, therefore, are always related to colonial epistemology. Due to its continual association with colonial constructs, nativism always has the capacity—or it is an essential characteristic of nativism—to recreate oppressive hierarchies.

Aimé Césaire may have been the first "nativist from the margins" when he coined the term *négritude* as an identity that attempted to unite French-speaking African descendants. While studying with Léopold Sédar Senghor (from Senegal) and Léon Damas (from Guiana) in Paris during the 1930s, Césaire began publishing the journal *L'Étudiant noir* (*The Black Student*). In the March 1935 issue of *L'Étudiant noir*, Césaire wrote a passionate article against assimilation to Francophone culture. It was in this article that he used the term *négritude* for the first time.[17] It was a call to all descendants of Africa in a diasporic setting to reclaim an authentic African identity. Césaire states this plainly in an interview with Haitian poet and militant René Depestre in 1967: "This, for me, was a call to Africa. I said to myself: it's true that superficially we are French, we bear the marks of French customs; we have been branded by Cartesian philosophy, by French rhetoric; but if we break with all that, if we plumb the depths then what we will find is fundamentally black."[18] This fundamental sentiment of a pure and authentic native identity is what defines nativism from the margin. In creating and ascribing to this identity, practitioners create an antiassimilationist stance against a colonial

16. Albert Memmi, *The Colonizer and the Colonized*, trans. Howard Greenfeld (Boston: Beacon, 1965 [French original, 1957]), 135.
17. R. D. G. Kelley, "A Poetics of Anticolonialism," in Aimé Césaire, *Discourse on Colonialism*, trans. Joan Pinkham (New York: Monthly Review Press, 1976 [French original, 1955]), 12.
18. Aimé Césaire, *Discourse on Colonialism*, trans. Joan Pinkham (New York: Monthly Review Press, 1976 [French original, 1955]), 84.

cultural identity. In this way, nativism adamantly confronts colonialism on a cultural level, which leads to and empowers independence movements. This confrontation is necessary due to the violence that colonialism enacts on native people. Césaire surmises, "Every day that passes, every denial of justice, every beating by the police, every demand of the workers that is drowned in blood, every scandal that is hushed up, every punitive expedition, every police van, every gendarme and every militiaman, brings home to us the value of our old societies."[19]

Césaire's sentiments are profound and understandable, but his critics expose the inadequacy of his idealism, which also exposes some inadequacies of nativism. In an attempt to confront imperial power, nativism fails to consider the ramifications of its narrow definitions of identity. In other words, in the attempt to create an antiassimilationist culture, nativism eventually casts off colonial cultural contours only to reproduce the same hierarchical structures of power with new, native faces in charge. The minority voices within the postindependence nation continue to fall victim to hierarchical oppression. Frantz Fanon warns of this outcome in his 1961 masterpiece *The Wretched of the Earth*. In Fanon's manifesto, he calls the colonized to arms with the conviction that only violence can purify the national consciousness: "The colonized man finds his freedom in and through violence."[20] This violence has three stages: (1) nativist assimilation to colonial cultural norms, (2) nativist rejection of colonial cultural norms in lieu of precolonial native culture, and, finally, (3) the establishment of a national culture with a strong social consciousness.[21] In many ways, Fanon agrees with

19. Ibid., 44.
20. Fanon, *Wretched of the Earth*, 86.
21. See Chidi Amuta, "Fanon, Cabral and Ngũgĩ on National Liberation," in *The Post-Colonial Studies Reader*, ed. Bill Ashcroft, Gareth Griffiths, and Helen Tiffin (London and New York: Routledge, 1995), 158–59, for an extended discussion about Fanon's three phases of violence.

Césaire in the first two stages of violence, but he makes a definitive break with his teacher in the third stage:

> The mobilization of the masses, when it arises out of the war of liberation, introduces into each man's consciousness the ideas of *a common cause, of a national destiny, and of a collective history.* In the same way the second phase, that of the building-up of the nation, is helped on by the existence of this cement which has been mixed with blood and anger. . . . During the colonial period the people are called upon to fight against oppression; after national liberation, they are called upon to fight against poverty, illiteracy, and underdevelopment.[22]

It is at this point that Fanon moves away from simple racial unity found in nativism to a social consciousness that brings the populace together around common values that contradict colonialism.[23] In a radical departure from looking to the past for a set of precolonial values, Fanon exhorts, "The Third World ought not to be content to define itself in the terms of values which have preceded it. On the contrary, the underdeveloped countries ought to do their utmost to find their own particular values and methods and a style which shall be particular to them."[24] In this process of developing a social consciousness for the nation, Fanon is adamant about the people keeping the bourgeois elite accountable to the nation instead of allowing them to become puppets of a past colonialism. Kwame Anthony Appiah recognizes Fanon's failed predictions: "The national

22. Fanon, *Wretched of the Earth*, 93–94 (emphasis mine).
23. Edward Said, *Culture and Imperialism* (New York: Vintage, 1993), 267, brilliantly comments on Fanon's transition from national to social consciousness: "His notion was that unless national consciousness at its moment of success was somehow changed into a social consciousness, the future would hold not liberation but an extension of imperialism."
24. Fanon, *Wretched of the Earth*, 99. For a similar, yet blistering, critique, see Chielozona Eze, *Postcolonial Imagination and Moral Representations in African Literature and Culture* (Lanham, MD: Lexington, 2011), 30–33. Regarding nativist self-definition in relation to Europe, Eze disdainfully says, "The West always looms large in Africa's engagement with reality. Once Europe is interjected in any African discourse, the African is rightly on his guard and quickly scuttles to his imaginary cocoon to retrieve his [*sic*] pure self that supposedly neuters European influence," 33.

bourgeoisie that took on the baton of rationalization, industrialization, bureaucratization in the name of nationalism, turned out to be a kleptocracy."[25]

Edward Said echoes Fanon and Appiah in his critique of nativism. One of the most difficult problems Said sees with nativism is how it recapitulates colonial ideology. In other words, in a colonial relationship, there will always be a "clear-cut and absolute hierarchical distinction" between ruler and ruled.[26] Nativism only reinforces the colonial distinction, even when it inverts the binary and gives the greater position to the native. Said's resistance to nativism parallels his resistance toward imperialism:

> But we have evidence of [nativism's] ravages: to accept nativism is to accept the consequences of imperialism itself. To leave the historical world for the metaphysics of essences like négritude, Irishness, Islam, or Catholicism is to abandon history for essentializations that have the power to turn human beings against each other.[27]

Concentrating on "the metaphysics of essences" creates an identity that cannot be self-critical or negotiated. Ultimately, what is placed on the old throne of imperialism is simply another dictatorial regime, as Said maintains:

> In countries like Algeria and Kenya one can watch the heroic resistance of a community partly formed out of colonial degradations, leading to a protracted armed and cultural conflict with the imperial powers, in turn giving way to a one-party state with dictatorial rule and, in the case of Algeria, an uncompromising Islamic fundamentalist opposition.[28]

25. Kwame Anthony Appiah, "The Postcolonial and the Postmodern," in *Post-Colonial Studies Reader*, 121.
26. Said, *Culture and Imperialism*, 228.
27. Ibid., 228–29.
28. Ibid., 229–30.

Said is simply unwilling to include a nativist phase in his search for liberation, which is where he differs from Fanon.

Along with Said, Homi Bhabha sees another option for liberation other than nativism.[29] Bhabha's complex cultural analysis takes a radically different approach to confronting colonialism. For Bhabha, colonialism was born with the seeds of its own destruction. In his work on colonial hybridity, mimicry, and ambivalence, Bhabha cultivates these seeds of de(con)struction. For Bhabha, hybridity can be liberating for the colonized because it "intervenes in the exercise of authority not merely to indicate the impossibility of its identity, but to represent the unpredictability of its presence."[30] As colonial discourse attempted to constrain the native, both the colonizer and the colonized were changed by their interaction. Through this ambivalent relationship, the colonized native began to take on the characteristics of the colonizer, which performed as mimicry. Hybridity is then not simply the interaction between the colonizing and colonized cultures, but it is an identity that threatens the authority of the colonizer as one who controls representations. The colonizer's authoritative representation of the native as something *other* begins to disseminate as the native mimics/mocks the identity of the colonized. Ania Loomba reiterates this point, saying, "The converted heathen and the educated native are images that cannot entirely or easily be reconciled to the idea of absolute difference. While at one level they represent colonial achievements, at another they stand for impurity and the possibility of mixing, or to use a term that has become central to postcolonial theory, 'hybridity.'"[31]

29. Said and Bhabha, however, are very different in what they consider valid options to nativism. Said's exposé of representation regarding the West/Orient binary shows how colonial epistemological structures supported the absolute devastation of colonized cultures. Bhabha critiques Said's suppositions, arguing that colonial representation is always unstable. See Edward Said, *Orientalism* (New York: Vintage, 1978), and Homi K. Bhabha, *Location of Culture* (London and New York: Routledge, 1994).

30. Bhabha, *Location of Culture*, 114.

Hybridity, in this case, not only threatens the colonizer's identity and authority, but also notions of "pure" native identity. Identity in the colonial interactions between the colonizer and the colonized, then, is constantly shifting. In the liminal space of the colony, there is no possibility of pure identity for either the colonizer or the native. There is only hybridity. As an intermingled identity, hybridity poses a problem and a threat to both the imperial power and the nativist. Since the cultural borderline between center and margin is blurred, the ambiguity of *othering* becomes exposed as representational power. The colonized can no longer be categorized as the ultimate other; therefore, a space is opened for manipulating the sociocultural systems established by imperial power by means of mimicry that slips into mockery. In this way, hybridity not only threatens imperial rule, it also threatens any sense of native identity that is ideologically free of imperial influence.

If hybridity characterizes colonial identity, then mimicry characterizes colonial action. Specifically, it is the action taken by the colonized, yet initiated by the colonizer, where the colonized imitates the life and culture of the colonizer. This action is most pronounced through language, that is, when the colonized begins to speak/write the language of the colonizer. The problem with this action is that the mimetic product is never a perfect reproduction of the imperial power. The eventual product is a hybrid that is incapable of being an identical twin. Memmi provides a chilling account of this failure to authentically duplicate identity:

> To that end, they endeavor to resemble the colonizer in the frank hope that he may cease to consider them different from him. . . . But if the colonizer does not always openly discourage these candidates to develop that resemblance, he never permits them to attain it either. Thus, they live in painful and constant ambiguity. Rejected by the

31. Ania Loomba, *Colonialism/Postcolonialism* (London and New York: Routledge, 1998), 119.

> colonizer, they share in part the physical conditions of the colonized and have a communion of interests with him; on the other hand, they reject the values of the colonized as belonging to a decayed world from which they eventually hope to escape.[32]

At best, mimicry is a mirror image—almost the same, but not quite.[33] By means of manipulation, however, mimicry becomes mockery and can function as resistance to colonial authority. Ashcroft, Griffiths, and Tiffin make this point abundantly clear: "This is because mimicry is never very far from mockery, since it can appear to parody whatever it mimics. Mimicry therefore locates a crack in the certainty of colonial dominance, an uncertainty in its control of the behaviour of the colonized."[34] This slippage in mimicry reveals the instability of colonial representation. In Bhabha's view, this slippage is always present in colonial discourse. In other words, the colonial endeavor "inevitably embodies the seeds of its own destruction."[35] This mimetic action that Bhabha outlines only exists in an ambivalent relationship between the colonizer and the colonized. Ambivalence, then, is the context for mimicry and hybridity.

Hybridity, as the state of identity flux and interchange, and mimicry, as the resistant actions of the hybrid that destabilizes colonial power, are both characterized, for Bhabha and Loomba, as ambivalent. Bhabha contends, "Consequently, the colonial presence is always ambivalent, split between its appearance as original and authoritative and its articulation as repetition and difference."[36] In another chapter, Bhabha describes this ambivalent relationship of love and hate, compulsion and revulsion as follows:

32. Memmi, *The Colonizer and the Colonized*, 15–16.
33. Bhabha, *Location of Culture*, 86.
34. Ashcroft, Griffiths, and Tiffin, *Post-Colonial Studies: The Key Concepts*, 139.
35. Ibid., 140.
36. Bhabha, *Location of Culture*, 107.

> Two contradictory and independent attitudes inhabit the *same place*, one takes account of reality, the other is under the influence of instincts which detach the ego from reality. This results in the production of multiple and contradictory belief. The enunciatory moment of multiple belief is both a defense against the anxiety of difference, and itself *productive* of differentiations. Splitting is then a form of enunciatory, intellectual uncertainty and anxiety that stems from the fact that disavowal is not merely a principle of negation or elision; it is a strategy for articulating contradictory and coeval statements of belief.[37]

In this paragraph Bhabha deals specifically with the deep psychological impact that postcolonial ambivalence has on the postcolonial hybrid. Based on Bhabha's definition, ambivalence characterizes hybrid identities. Ambivalence colors both the colonizer and the colonized as *less than one and double*.[38] The colonized do not fit into tight categories of those who desire colonial comfort and those who resist colonial rule. This desire and disgust happen simultaneously in everyone involved in the colonial project. Postcolonial ambivalence, then, "describes this fluctuating relationship between mimicry and mockery, an ambivalence that is fundamentally unsettling to colonial dominance."[39] Bhabha also points out that ambivalence has the capacity to subvert imperial power: "The ambivalence at the source of traditional discourses on authority enables a form of subversion, founded on the undecidability that turns the discursive conditions of dominance into the grounds of intervention."[40] This poststructuralist subversion of hierarchy to which Bhabha alludes provides the foundation for his concept of ambivalence as resistance. This resistance, however, is problematic in the same way hybridity and mimicry are; that is, it is firmly theoretical.

37. Bhabha, *Location of Culture*, 132.
38. Ibid., 102–22.
39. Ashcroft, Griffiths, and Tiffin, *Post-Colonial Studies: The Key Concepts*, 13.
40. Bhabha, *Location of Culture*, 112.

While most forms of nativism are rooted in the material struggle for liberation, much postcolonial theory is conceived in the hallowed halls of the academy. On this point, R. S. Sugirtharajah criticizes Bhabha's theoretical opposition to nativism:

> Hybridity in the postmodern lexicon is defined as possessing emancipatory potential and an antidote to the virulent form of nativist thinking. While nativism seeks to eradicate any form of impurity in the indigenous culture, postmodern notions of hybridity tend to sweep under the carpet the cultural and political impact of colonialism. Such a notion of hybridity is oblivious to the economic hardship, helplessness, and marginalization which are ongoing realities.[41]

Sugirtharajah captures the harsh divide and opposition between nativism and postcolonial theory as competing forms of resistance. Parry offers a more nuanced intervention, highlighting the fact that "it remains important to urge more historically grounded directions and greater discrimination in the enquiries of an ecumenical and proliferating field where the material impulses to colonialism, its appropriation of physical resources, exploitation of human labour and institutional repression, have receded from view."[42] Her attempt to reconceptualize nativism in order to remember the devastation of colonialism acts as a constant critique of the theoretical formations of Bhabha. Parry's insistence on the historical (f)act of violence enacted by colonialists on natives pushes the ethical edges of postcolonial theory. Even if "post-independence regimes blind [postcolonial] critics to the import of liberation struggles conducted in the name of nationalism," Parry argues that "valorizing hybrid, deterritorialized and diasporic forms of consciousness that are apparently uninflected and untroubled by ethnicity or class" is not a suitable solution.[43]

41. R. S. Sugirtharajah, *Postcolonial Criticism and Biblical Interpretation* (Oxford: Oxford University Press, 2002), 194.
42. Parry, *Postcolonial Studies*, 3.
43. Ibid., 10.

In her final analysis, Parry concludes that in their "scorning emancipatory expectations as naïve and self-righteous, and liberation movements as self-interested," postcolonial critics "have rendered nugatory the joining of intelligible and still viable indigenous resources and age-old traditions of colonial resistance with the ethical horizons and utopian reach of socialism."[44] Loomba critiques this line of thought while siding with Bhabha, maintaining that "colonial identities—on both sides of the divide—are unstable, agonized, and in constant flux. This undercuts both colonialist and nationalist claims to a unified self, and also warns us against interpreting cultural difference in absolute or reductive terms."[45] Although Sugirtharajah and Parry are sympathetic to nativism, the evidence of Bhabha and his allies' analysis of cultural hybridity cannot be denied or overlooked. Nativism's desire for purity with the exclusion and expulsion of colonial influence is made impossible precisely because of postcolonial hybridity. These theoretical concepts, then, are at odds with one another, and when theoretical concepts become material reality, there is serious conflict between the involved parties.

This conflict between the postcolonial concepts of ambivalence, mimicry, and hybridity, on the one hand, and nativism on the other is the main lens through which I will read James. I understand the Letter of James as a nativist document that promotes "pure and undefiled piety" as an essentialist identity that opposes Roman imperial oppression and any form of hybridity/assimilation with Roman imperialism. The Letter of James intervenes in the Diaspora—a highly contested space of hybridity—in an attempt to prevent "double-mindedness." The nativist strategy involved in opposing Roman imperialism is at odds with any form of strategy involving hybridity as resistance. In fact, the entire Letter of James

44. Ibid., 10.
45. Loomba, *Colonialism/Postcolonialism*, 178.

fluctuates between opposing empire and opposing hybridity. Where the Letter of James attacks hybridity—dead faith (2:14-26), diabolical dialogue (3:1-12), double-mindedness (4:1-12), and deceptive business dealings (4:13-17)—there is, as we shall see, a correlation to certain Pauline sensibilities. The capacity in certain Pauline writings to assimilate otherness rather than reject it—especially otherness in relation to Roman imperialism—would certainly be at odds with the sort of piety prescribed by the Letter of James. The nativism in the Letter of James functions as a biting critique of the hybridity found in the Pauline corpus.

Why Nativism?

Now that nativism has been positioned in postcolonial studies, there are at least two questions left to ask and answer, however provisionally, before approaching the text of James. As a critical apparatus, is postcolonialism a legitimate mode of inquiry for biblical studies; and more specifically, why nativism for the Letter of James? This interdisciplinary endeavor warrants an explanation and/or apologia. Many critics within the biblical studies guild chide attempts to introduce postcolonial theory into the realm of biblical studies. The primary concern for such critics is the alleged "anachronistic" nature of the interdisciplinary enterprise. Within the historical-critical tradition, it is more acceptable to be labeled a heretic, atheist, or agnostic than anachronistic. It is important, nonetheless, to acknowledge the vast differences between Roman imperialism in the first century and European imperialisms dating from the sixteenth century to the twentieth century. R. S. Sugirtharajah points out, however, that postcolonial theory has the capacity to go beyond modern forms of imperialism: "There were other forms of colonialism before and after European expansion and withdrawal."[46] At every level, this process involves using a modern methodology or reading strategy to access ancient texts, which in many ways is no different than using the historical-critical method. The questions that postcolonial theory asks are simply different than historical-critical questions, but they are equally valid and important. Sugirtharajah sees postcolonial biblical criticism as one way, among others, to bring the field of biblical interpretation into dialogue with the "problems of the contemporary world."[47] He argues that

> the greatest single aim of postcolonial biblical criticism is to situate colonialism at the centre of the Bible and biblical interpretation. ... What postcolonial biblical criticism does is to focus on the whole issue of expansion, domination, and imperialism as central forces in defining both the biblical narratives and biblical interpretation. . . . Postcolonialism's ongoing battle for emancipation, and continuing attempt to dismantle imperial institutions and dominating structures offers a valuable field for collaboration.[48]

Sugirtharajah exemplifies what Stephen D. Moore classifies as a form of postcolonial biblical criticism that comes from the liberation/contextual/vernacular hermeneutics arena.[49]

46. Sugirtharajah, *Postcolonial Criticism*, 3.
47. Ibid., 26.
48. Ibid., 25. For his most recent introduction to the field of postcolonial biblical criticism, see R. S. Sugirtharajah, *Exploring Postcolonial Biblical Criticism: History, Method, Practice* (Oxford: Wiley-Blackwell, 2012).
49. Stephen D. Moore, *Empire and Apocalypse: Postcolonialism and the New Testament* (Sheffield: Sheffield Phoenix Press, 2006), 3–23. In Moore's mapping of the postcolonial biblical criticism field, he plots three overlapping clusters: liberation/contextual/vernacular hermeneutics, "X and Empire" work, and work that draws on extrabiblical postcolonial studies. Prominent examples of the first cluster are R. S. Sugirtharajah, *The Bible and the Third World: Precolonial, Colonial and Postcolonial Encounters* (Cambridge: Cambridge University Press, 2001); Fernando F. Segovia, *Decolonizing Biblical Studies: A View from the Margins* (Maryknoll, NY: Orbis, 2000); Fernando F. Segovia, ed., *Interpreting Beyond Borders*, The Bible and Postcolonialism, 3 (Sheffield: Sheffield Academic Press, 2000); Gerald West, ed., *Reading Other-Wise: Socially Engaged Biblical Scholars Reading with Their Local Communities*, Semeia Studies, 62 (Atlanta: Society of Biblical Literature, 2007); David Sanchez, *From Patmos to the Barrio: Subverting Imperial Myths* (Minneapolis: Fortress Press, 2008); David Joy, *Mark and Its Subalterns: A Hermeneutical Paradigm for a Postcolonial Context* (London: Equinox, 2008); and Musa W. Dube, Andrew M. Mbuvi, and Dora Mbuwayesango, eds., *Postcolonial Perspectives in African Biblical Interpretations*, Global Perspectives on Biblical Scholarship, 62 (Atlanta: Society of Biblical Literature, 2012).

Moore and Fernando F. Segovia also recognize another trend in postcolonial biblical criticism that they call "X and Empire." They remark that "whereas the more traditional biblical scholar has tended to peer through [the] lens [of empire] intermittently, the particular authors in the cluster we are considering [X and Empire] tend to gaze through it unrelentingly."[50] Although the most distant cluster from postcolonial theory proper, X and Empire sharply brings empire into focus as the main lens to read biblical texts. In the process, it has been the most palatable form of postcolonial biblical criticism for the larger field of mainstream biblical studies.[51] Because of its close connection to mainstream biblical studies, X and Empire—for better or worse—grants postcolonial biblical studies a more legitimate seat at the table of biblical studies. In fact, the rationale for the use of X and Empire as an analytical tool for biblical interpretation warrants much less argument than other, more theoretical explications in spite of the fact that the former "would offer significant conceptual and practical resources for focusing, sharpening, and nuancing such analysis."[52]

These "theory heavy" modes of postcolonial biblical criticism are described by Moore as drawing on extrabiblical postcolonial studies,

50. Stephen D. Moore and Fernando F. Segovia, "Postcolonial Biblical Criticism: Beginnings, Trajectories, Intersections," in *Postcolonial Biblical Criticism: Interdisciplinary Intersections*, ed. Stephen D. Moore and Fernando F. Segovia (London and New York: T. & T. Clark International, 2005), 7–8.

51. See, for example, Richard Horsley, ed., *Paul and Empire: Religion and Power in Roman Imperial Society* (Harrisburg, PA: Trinity Press International, 1997); Warren Carter, *Matthew and Empire: Initial Explorations* (Harrisburg, PA: Trinity Press International, 2001); Richard Horsley, *Jesus and Empire: The Kingdom of God and the New World Disorder* (Minneapolis: Fortress Press, 2003); Warren Carter, *John and Empire: Initial Explorations* (London: T. & T. Clark, 2008); Neil Elliott, *The Arrogance of Nations: Reading Romans in the Shadow of Empire* (Minneapolis: Fortress Press, 2008); Ingeborg A. K. Kvammen, "Imperial Presence in the Assembly: An Interpretation of Jas 2:1-13 with a Postcolonial Optic" (Ph.D. diss., School of Mission and Theology, 2008); David Rhoads, David Esterline, and Jae Won Lee, eds., *Luke-Acts and Empire: Essays in Honor of Robert L. Brawley*, Princeton Theological Monograph Series (Eugene, OR: Pickwick, 2011); and Stanley E. Porter and Cynthia Long Westfall, eds., *Empire in the New Testament*, McMaster New Testament Studies Series (Eugene, OR: Pickwick, 2011).

52. Moore, *Empire and Apocalypse*, 9–10.

and are indicative of the kinds of postcolonial readings Moore and others like him practice. These postcolonial biblical critics engage the theories of Edward Said, Gayatri Spivak, and Homi Bhabha—to name only the most (in)famous—and use their conceptual frameworks as reading strategies.[53] To that end, Moore argues that "[p]ostcolonial criticism is not a method of interpretation (any more than is feminist criticism, say) so much as a critical sensibility acutely attuned to a specific range of interrelated historical and textual phenomena."[54] Turning that sensibility to biblical texts is at the heart of this form of postcolonial biblical criticism. In his introduction to his own essay that uses this type of reading strategy, Moore describes this way of reading: "What I am about, then, in this essay is not so much applying the postcolonial theory of Homi Bhabha or Gayatri Spivak to John's representations of empire as replicating Bhabha's and Spivak's signal strategy: that of deploying a deconstructive sensibility to tease out the tortuous complexities and contradictions of life under colonialism and imperialism."[55]

53. See, for example, Tat-siong Benny Liew, *Politics of Parousia: Reading Mark Inter(con)textually*, Biblical Interpretation Series, 42 (Leiden: Brill, 1999); Erin Runions, *Changing Subjects: Gender, Nation and Future in Micah*, Playing the Texts, 7 (Sheffield: Sheffield Academic Press, 2002); Eric Thurman, "Looking for a Few Good Men: Mark and Masculinity," in *New Testament Masculinities*, ed. Stephen D. Moore and Janice Capel Anderson, Semeia Studies, 45 (Atlanta: Society of Biblical Literature, 2003); Christopher A. Frilingos, *Spectacles of Empire: Monsters, Martyrs, and the Book of Revelation*, Divinations: Rereading Late Ancient Religion (Philadelphia: University of Pennsylvania Press, 2004); Laura E. Donaldson, "Gospel Hauntings: The Postcolonial Demons of New Testament Criticism," in *Postcolonial Biblical Criticism*; Robert Paul Seesengood, *Competing Identities: The Athlete and Gladiator in Early Christianity* (London: Continuum, 2007); Joseph A. Marchal, *The Politics of Heaven: Women, Gender, and Empire in the Study of Paul*, Paul in Critical Contexts (Minneapolis: Fortress Press, 2008); Stephen D. Moore and Mayra Rivera, eds., *Planetary Loves: Spivak, Postcoloniality, and Theology*, Transdisciplinary Theological Colloquia (New York: Fordham University Press, 2011); and Christopher D. Stanley, ed., *The Colonized Apostle: Paul through Postcolonial Eyes*, Paul in Critical Contexts (Minneapolis: Fortress Press, 2011).

54. Moore, *Empire and Apocalypse*, 7.

55. Stephen D. Moore, *The Bible in Theory: Critical and Postcritical Essays* (Atlanta: Society of Biblical Literature, 2010), 327–28.

I outline Moore and Segovia's threefold division of postcolonial biblical criticism, however malleable, in an attempt to show the legitimacy of this form of criticism as a field of inquiry within biblical studies and to recognize the vast diversity of what can be considered postcolonial biblical criticism. The primary question related to the allegedly anachronistic nature of this interdisciplinary pursuit is determined by the capacity for postcolonial theory to be transhistorical and/or transcultural. Can social and cultural theory based on Western empires from the sixteenth to the twentieth centuries elucidate anything about Roman imperialism in the first century and how it relates to biblical texts? Those who advocate for and practice postcolonial biblical criticism understand the "imperial-colonial formation" as "recurring historical phenomena."[56] Moore concludes the preface to *Empire and Apocalypse* with an autobiographical flourish—not uncommon and not unwelcomed in Moore's work—that embodies these recurring imperial-colonial phenomena:

> The "truth" of this construal of the colonial condition—and the postcolonial condition besides—is one that I internalized long before encountering Homi Bhabha. It is a construal that perfectly captures the convoluted manner in which the postcolonial Ireland of the 1950s and 1960s in which I was raised related to British cosmopolitan culture. Either I am guilty, then, of projecting my own ambivalence toward empire onto early Christian texts themselves innocent of that trait, or else my cultural formation has sensitized me to elements in these texts that I might otherwise have overlooked. But that is to articulate two overly stark poles of what is, in fact, a complex spectrum. And to attempt to do justice to such complexities is, as indicated earlier, the prime exegetical aim of this book.[57]

56. Fernando F. Segovia, "Mapping the Postcolonial Optic in Biblical Criticism: Meaning and Scope," in *Postcolonial Biblical Criticism*, 71.
57. Moore, *Empire and Apocalypse*, x.

In Moore's case, there is a transhistorical and transcultural aspect to postcolonial theory, which is precisely the argument that Fernando F. Segovia echoes:

> I subscribe to the view that imperial-colonial formations represent long-standing and wide-ranging phenomena, present across historical periods and cultural contexts. I see no reason why postcolonial analysis should be limited to the modern and capitalist formations of the West; I see comparative analysis as justified and in order. Such analysis can thus be gainfully extended to the world of antiquity in general and to the Roman formation in particular.[58]

According to Segovia, postcolonial biblical criticism is at its highest level of academic prowess when it strikes "a balance of general principles or common elements and unique details or distinct components."[59]

It is at this level that I read James as a nativist reaction to the Roman Empire. As has been discussed above, nativism fetishizes purity, specifically racial, national, and ethnic forms of purity. One of the primary reasons I read the Letter of James as a nativist reaction to Roman imperialism is its concentration on and repetition of the theme of purity and perfection. Purity in both nativism and in the Letter of James functions within the realm of imperial/colonial identity negotiation. The antithesis between Rome and Jerusalem or Rome and the empire of God, although veiled in hidden discourse, runs alongside the theme of purity and perfection. Reading the complexities of this discourse through the lens of the complexities of nativism highlights James's dual attack against both empire and hybridity. Once this dual attack is foregrounded using nativism as a conceptual framework, two rivals appear in the background: Roman imperialism (empire) and Pauline sensibilities (hybridity).

58. Segovia, "Mapping the Postcolonial Optic," 75.
59. Ibid., 70.

To date, there are only two chapters and one monograph that use a postcolonial optic to read the Letter of James. Sharon Ringe's chapter on James in *A Postcolonial Commentary on the New Testament Writings* and my contribution to *Reading James with New Eyes: Methodological Reassessments of the Letter of James* were both published in 2007, and were the first publications that brought the weight of postcolonial theory to bear on the Letter of James.[60] The next year (2008), Ingeborg A. K. Kvammen finished her dissertation, which focused a postcolonial optic on James 2:1-13.[61] There has not been a sustained postcolonial reading of the entire Letter of James, a gap this monograph attempts to fill.

Nativism and Judeanness in the First Century CE

The Letter of James represents only one example of Judean identity negotiation within the sociopolitical environment of Roman Palestine.[62] The Dead Sea Scrolls; the writings of Josephus, Philo, and Paul; the Gospel of Matthew; and other such texts all represent other forms of negotiating a Judean identity within this same time period, but with a broader geographical reach. All of these authors and texts are firmly positioned within the realm of what Shaye Cohen calls "Jewishness." For Cohen, this realm of identity encompasses religious, political, and geographical identity, but he also acknowledges the fluidity and subjectivity of determining identity: "In most places and most of the time, individual Jews were not distinctive; it was easy for a gentile to pass as a Jew, and for a

60. Sharon H. Ringe, "The Letter of James," in *A Postcolonial Commentary on the New Testament Writings*, ed. Fernando F. Segovia and R. S. Sugirtharajah (London: T. & T. Clark, 2007), 369–79; K. Jason Coker, "Nativism in James 2.14-26: A Post-Colonial Reading," in *Reading James with New Eyes: Methodological Reassessments of the Letter of James*, ed. Robert L. Webb and John S. Kloppenborg (New York: T. & T. Clark, 2007), 27–48.

61. Kvammen, "Imperial Presence in the Assembly." Her revised dissertation is forthcoming from Brill.

62. I argue for a Palestinian provenance for the Letter of James in the next chapter.

Jew to pass as a gentile—if that is what you wanted to do and if you knew what to do."[63] The fluidity of Jewishness, however, was problematic for those who would police the boundary between "us" and "them," whether in Palestine or in the Diaspora. In the sociopolitical environment of Roman Palestine leading up to the first Jewish Revolt, this sort of identity politics was a matter of great importance. Issues of assimilation and association ultimately determined if you were for or against Rome. In this case, Cohen is certainly right to conclude that "[i]t is not the boundary that makes the group; it is the group that makes the boundary."[64] Cohen attempts to "understand how the Jews of antiquity drew the boundaries between themselves and the gentiles, and thus to understand their conceptions of 'Jewishness.'"[65] Policing the boundary between insiders and outsiders is a major preoccupation in the Letter of James, and the boundary within an imperialist context usually concentrates on identity.

Theorizing Judeanness

Caroline Johnson Hodge revises Cohen's language of Jewishness because she feels it obfuscates rather than clarifies the historical referent of the term. Rather than using the terms Jewish and Jewishness, Hodge proposes Judean and Judeanness. This situates the referent geographically and religiously, that is, in terms of the temple and cult. Although her translation of *Ioudaios/oi* and *Ioudaismos* is not totally satisfying, Hodge prefers Judean/Judeanness for strategic reasons: "to encourage us to think carefully about the multiplicity

63. Shaye Cohen, *The Beginning of Jewishness: Boundaries, Varieties and Uncertainties* (Berkeley: University of California Press, 2001), 3. He later adds: "Jewishness will remain a social construct—a variable, not a constant. In this book I hope to illuminate the beginnings of Jewishness," 10.

64. Cohen, *Beginning of Jewishness*, 6.

65. Ibid., 8.

and flexibility of ethnic labels."[66] Hodge explains how multiple and flexible identities, or nested identities, could be used and emphasized depending on a particular circumstance. To use Hodge's primary example, Paul of Tarsus freely uses his nested identities for strategic purposes. Focusing on Paul's autobiographical statements in his letters, Hodge argues that "[t]hese lists exemplify this notion of nested identities: while all of these components—circumcised, descendant of Abraham, of the tribe of Benjamin—belong under the larger umbrella of Judeanness, each item is also a distinct identity itself, which could be emphasized or de-emphasized depending on the context."[67] Throughout Paul's identity negotiations, Hodge understands his "work as a teacher of gentiles" as "a part of the larger story of Israel, not a break from it."[68] From her perspective, Paul is firmly within the complex and shifting "umbrella of Judeanness." Hodge's approach challenges traditional notions of identity as fixed and rigid. In fact, one of her primary critiques of Cohen's work on Jewishness is that his differentiation between "Jew" and "Judean" considers "Jew" an identity that is open and mutable while "Judean" is fixed and immutable.[69] Hodge's view of identity as mutable, fluid, and nested is helpful when analyzing identity negotiation within the realm of Judeanness in the first century.[70]

Both Hodge and Cohen understand Judean identity as a social construct rather than a predetermined essence. Their work is helpful

66. Caroline Johnson Hodge, "Apostle to the Gentiles: Constructions of Paul's Identity," *Biblical Interpretation* 13, no. 3 (2005): 272.
67. Ibid., 275.
68. Ibid., 276.
69. Ibid., 272, n. 5.
70. I use Hodge's "Judeanness" throughout my analysis although Hodge, herself, reassesses her terminology in her book *If Sons, Then Heirs: A Study of Kinship and Ethnicity in the Letters of Paul* (Oxford: Oxford University Press, 2007). Here, Hodge, 13, does not want to ignore the "broad cohesion shared by different groups of Jews throughout history," which the terms Judean and Judeanness obviously problematize. In the end, Hodge simply leaves the terms *Ioudaios/Ioudaioi* untranslated.

when considering the agonizing existential situation of Judeanness under Roman imperialism both in Palestine and in the Diaspora. The nested identities available within the realm of Judeanness offered multiple opportunities to resist and/or assimilate Roman ideals. The ambivalence within negotiated Judeanness in the crucible of the imperial-colonial encounter is reflected in the multifarious responses to Roman imperialism by Judean authors and communities. The spectrum of Judeanness ranges from sectarians in Qumran who denounced the Temple in Jerusalem as totally corrupted (by Rome), to a highly educated and assimilated elite in Egypt who committed themselves to local patriotism within the Diaspora. This diversity has led John M. G. Barclay to conclude that "Jews lived in many different geographical locations, in social conditions which varied over time, and at differing social levels. We can expect to find an almost infinite variety in the ways they reacted to their variant milieux."[71] Within these "complex and variegated social phenomena" called Judeanness, "heterogeneity and fluidity . . . were some of the overriding characteristics."[72] Although the vast diversity within Judeanness offered tremendous room for negotiating identity depending on local circumstances, this also led to conflict within Judeanness on what was determinative for the identity. Siân Jones and Sarah Pearce's work on identity formation within this context is instructive: "[C]onceptions of the Land, and loyalty towards it, were constantly shifting as representations of 'pure' and 'orthodox' Judaism, and by extension Jewish identity, were created. Through such processes, whereby idealized constructions of identity and land are produced, power relations were established and contested both within Jewish

71. John M. G. Barclay, *Jews in the Mediterranean Diaspora: From Alexander to Trajan (323 BCE–117 CE)* (Edinburgh: T. & T. Clark, 1996), 3.

72. Sarah Pearce and Siân Jones, "Introduction: Jewish Local Identities and Patriotism in the Graeco-Roman Period," in *Jewish Local Patriotism and Self-Identification in the Graeco-Roman Period*, ed. Sarah Pearce and Siân Jones (Sheffield: Sheffield Academic Press, 1998), 26.

communities and between Jews and non-Jews."[73] Questions like, who had the capacity to determine Judeanness and where was the locus of authority that authorized authentic Judeanness, became sites of conflict and turmoil, especially when the answers to these questions put Judeans in conflict with Roman authorities. As is indicated in the preceding scholarship, the answers to these questions were different in different locations, that is, in Palestine and in the Diaspora.

Negotiating Judeanness in Palestine

Questions of authority and authenticity in relation to identity, although specific to each epoch, inevitably arise in imperial-colonial contexts. The vast diversity within Judeanness in Palestine alone attests to these negotiations. Herodians, Pharisees, Sadducees, Essenes, the Fourth Philosophy, Zealots/Sicarii, Samaritans, and Galileans all negotiated identity in relation to Roman imperialism differently, and most of these subgroups would fit easily within the rubric of Judeanness. In the period that led up to the revolt against Rome, issues of self-determinacy and independence created a reverse discourse laden with nativist rhetoric not entirely dissimilar to anticolonial independence movements in modernity: "Nativism emerges from this milieu of the psychology of colonialism as a reverse-discourse seeking to subvert and undermine colonial ideologies through mobilization of decentered African identity and culture."[74] Josephus's description of Judas the Galilean, who led a revolt against Rome, shows—however negatively—Judas and his

73. Ibid., 44.
74. Sabelo J. Ndlovu-Gatsheni, "Nativism and the Debate on African Public Sphere in Postcolonial Africa: Reflections on a Problematic 'Reverse-Discourse'" (paper, Council for the Development of Social Science Research in Africa's [CODESRIA] Twelfth General Assembly: Governing the African Public Sphere, Yaoundé, Cameroon, December 7–11, 2008), 6. The paper was presented under a panel called "Nationalism, Public Sphere and Citizenship in Africa."

followers' self-determined rejection of Rome: "They said that the assessment [by Rome] carried with it a status amounting to downright slavery, no less, and appealed to the nation to make a bid for independence."[75] Those who followed Judas the Galilean, followers whom Josephus calls the Fourth Philosophy, "did not shrink from the bloodshed that might be necessary."[76] Josephus will say later that their "passion for liberty" cannot be dissuaded since "they are convinced that God alone is their leader and master."[77] As is evidenced by the Fourth Philosophy, Roman imperialism had a radicalizing effect on certain areas of Judeanness where independence was understood as divine right. In relation to this Judean revolt, Ndlovu-Gatsheni's assessment of nativism is all too appropriate: "Nativism struggles for an African public sphere in which Africans have a right to self-definition, where Africans own the state, and where Africans are free from interference of colonial matrix of power and where they are allowed to determine their political and economic destiny. Defined and read from this perspective, nativism is a form of reverse-discourse with its own agency and status rooted in discourse of decolonization."[78]

A self-determined rejection of Roman occupation equally meant a self-determined rejection of Roman assimilationists or hybrids. As Ndlovu-Gatsheni instructs us, "Nativism is about who belongs to the political community, who has the right to rule, what has legitimacy to determine public discourse and who has a right to constitute the African public sphere."[79] In the context of first-century Judeanness within Roman Palestine, this applied to both the Roman and Roman-Judean leaders. The quintessential paradigms for Judean/Roman

75. Josephus, *Ant.* 18.1.4 (Feldman, LCL).
76. Josephus, *Ant.* 18.1.5 (Feldman, LCL).
77. Josephus, *Ant.* 18.1.6 (Feldman, LCL).
78. Ndlovu-Gatsheni, "Nativism," 27–28.
79. Ibid., 28.

hybridity in Palestine were Herod the Great and his successors, most of whom are negatively constructed by ancient sources. Herod the Great was a Roman citizen and was recognized by Rome as king of Judea. When Rome conferred this title on Herod, it most likely renewed a treaty of friendship and alliance between Judea and Rome that was first established by Hasmonean leaders in an attempt to "free themselves from the yoke; for they saw that the kingdom of the Greeks was enslaving Israel completely."[80] This renewal made Judea a "*socius et amicus populi romani*, an ally and friend of the Roman people."[81] This "friendship with Rome" extended to Herod's successors, especially the two tetrarchs Herod Antipas and Philip. Herod Antipas "fortified Sepphoris to be the ornament of all Galilee, and called it Autocratoris."[82] Autocratoris (Imperator) was one of the official titles of Augustus; as the name of the city, it could be translated as Imperial City. Philip, likewise, revitalized one of the cities in his tetrarchy and renamed it Caesarea (Caesarea Philippi) in honor of the Caesars. These are some examples of how interconnected Herod and his heirs were to Rome.[83] This close connection with Rome and Herod's maniacal behavior are some of the reasons ancient Judean authors doubted Herod's Judeanness. In fact, Herod had his pedigree cleansed of his Idumaean background in order to support his Judeanness and authorize/legitimize his rule.[84] According to Cohen, "Herod may have been a Jew, but he was also a 'bad' Jew. Most forms of ancient Judaism, I think, would

80. 1 Macc. 8:18. Reading 1 Maccabees alongside Josephus's construal of Judas the Galilean is interesting, since both consider the foreign rule at their respective times to correspond with slavery.
81. Samuel Rocca, *Herod's Judea: A Mediterranean State in the Classical World* (Tübingen: Mohr Siebeck, 2008), 53.
82. Josephus, *Ant.* 18.2.1 (Feldman, LCL).
83. See Peter Richardson, *Herod: King of the Jews and Friend of the Romans* (Minneapolis: Fortress Press, 1999), 139–59, for an extended discussion regarding Herod's connection to Rome.
84. See Cohen, *Beginning of Jewishness*, 13–24.

have disapproved of Herod's murder of his wives and children. The largesse he bestowed on pagan temples, cities, and festivals, and his other violations of the ancestral laws, provoked hostile comment in antiquity."[85] One example of that "hostile comment" is from Josephus, who criticized Herod's gifts toward "foreign" or "Greek" cities: "It was generally admitted that he was on more friendly terms with Greeks than with Jews. For instance, he adorned the cities of foreigners by giving them money, building baths and theatres, erecting temples in some and porticoes in others, whereas there was not a single city of the Jews on which he deigned to bestow even minor restoration or any gift worth mentioning."[86] At this point in his *Antiquities*, Josephus seems so adamantly opposed to Herod that he completely fails to mention Herod's enormous renovation of the Temple in Jerusalem—a contribution so large that Peter Richardson says one "needs a book in itself" to describe it.[87] The Judean leadership of Roman Palestine was so thoroughly romanized that their Judean identity was questioned—that is, no "real" Judean would ever assimilate to that degree. Their economic and cultural amalgamation with Rome eventually became untenable for some Judean factions, as Roberto U. Maynard-Reid suggests:

> The Zealot party, which was representative of the Palestinian, mainly Judean, peasant piety, showed hostility toward the rich of the city, the upper priesthood of the Temple, and the foreign rulers; the Zealots led the drive toward social change. In their overall strategy of achieving a more just order in society, they took up arms against the establishment in the first part of the first century. The Jewish War amply illustrates the tensions in the social structure in the Roman Empire during that century.[88]

85. Ibid., 23.
86. Josephus, *Ant.* 19.7.3.
87. Richardson, *Herod*, 171.
88. Pedrito U. Maynard-Reid, *Poverty and Wealth in James* (Maryknoll, NY: Orbis, 1987), 23.

Negotiating Judeanness in the Diaspora

Within the Judean diaspora, negotiating Judeanness in the Roman Empire was equally complex and fluid. In an important collection of essays, John M. G. Barclay describes three interlinked themes that permeate Judean diasporic communities within the Roman Empire: 1) Diaspora is a site of "*both local and translocal identities*"; 2) its "*cultural self-expression*" is always ambiguous; and, 3) "[u]nderlying both the features just [mentioned] is the persistent question of *power and politics*."[89] Negotiating diasporic Judeanness was contentious because it entailed belonging to two places at one time: both the local existence and a translocal existence "in" the homeland/Promised Land. Since one lived in the Diaspora, the Land lived in them rather than them living in the Land. The reality of Diaspora created a crisis of identity for Judeans. What constituted their Judeanness? How was it authorized or authenticated? In every locale of Judean diaspora, these questions were answered differently at different times. In spite of the fact that Josephus is one of our best resources for Judeanness in Roman Palestine, all of his writing took place in the imperial center: Rome. In this sense, Flavius Josephus is a quintessential diasporic Judean and his writings, at some level, reveal an anguished identity. At every turn, Josephus is justifying Judean existence both in Roman Palestine and Rome. Almost all of the heroes in the writings of Josephus are Judeans performing great acts of Roman patriotism. Almost all of the antagonists perform acts that are both un-Judean *and* un-Roman. In this sense, cultural self-expression is always ambiguous in a diasporic setting. As Barclay argues: "It is characteristic of a diaspora group to refuse the simple binary options of becoming

89. John M. G. Barclay, "Introduction: Diaspora Negotiations," in *Negotiating Diaspora: Jewish Strategies in the Roman Empire* (London and New York: T. & T. Clark International, 2004), 2–3 (original emphasis).

wholly like *or* remaining wholly unlike the host culture, of assimilating into the 'majority' culture or preserving its 'distinct' traditions in a cultural enclave. Like the postcolonial notion of 'hybridity,' this complex strategy of multiple cultural identities defies neat categories."[90] It is here that Barclay and Hodge intersect. Saul/Paul of Tarsus is an exemplar of this sort of ambiguous self-expression within Judean diaspora.[91] The nested identities that Paul displays for specific sociopolitical reasons are the primary way he was able to travel as widely as he did. In some contexts, he would appeal to his Roman citizenship (if the author of Acts is to be credited). In other contexts, he would argue for his deep Judean connections. In other contexts, still, he would give all those things away in order to identify with the Judean messiah, Jesus of Nazareth. This ambiguous identity leads to Barclay's third theme of diaspora: power and politics. There are internal conflicts within diasporas, there are conflicts with the local population, and there are conflicts with other diasporas. Is there enough cultural power within the diasporic community to self-identify both locally and translocally? Since Paul's form of diaspora was more transient than local, his writings are replete with references to power struggles with other leaders—both local and centered in the homeland. Where did Paul receive his source of authority? Who legitimized Paul's message? In other words, from where does Paul derive power? Is his power equal to, less than, or greater than that of his opponents? A more pressing question, for the purposes of this study, related to power and politics is how did Paul's "power" relate to the "power" of the Jesus movement headquartered in Jerusalem? At every level, then, Judean diaspora is characterized by issues of hybridity and power.

90. Ibid., 2.

91. I discuss Paul's self-expression within the Judean diaspora in chapter 4.

James as a Form of Judean Nativism in Roman Palestine

Nativism and nativist rhetoric, as previously mentioned, are produced under the sociopolitical atmosphere of empire. The value of this lens for reading the Letter of James becomes increasingly relevant when the sociopolitical environment that gave rise to the letter is historically (re)constructed. As I will argue later, the Letter of James was most likely written by James of Jerusalem, the brother of Jesus, approximately in the middle of the first century CE. Due to its Palestinian provenance before the destruction of the Temple in Jerusalem, the Letter of James stands as one of the earliest writings of the New Testament from that geographic location. Concentrating on the sociopolitical environment that gave rise to the Letter of James is important in understanding James's voice (to use the vocabulary of Luke Timothy Johnson).[92]

During the Roman Period, Palestine was a terribly contested area. From the time of Herod the Great (37–4 BCE) to the first Jewish-Roman Wars (66–70 CE), Roman Palestine—Jerusalem in particular—struggled under extreme sociopolitical turmoil. Although economic conditions improved under Augustus and his successors, these improvements only benefited a small group of elites in Palestine, which is one reason the general populace was so angered by Herod's building campaigns.[93] As Herod introduced an incredible period of architectural production, Judea experienced draught and famine. Due to the massive economic gap between the wealthy elite and the impoverished masses—accentuated by Roman economic policies—the seeds of revolt and revolution were sown. Herod's assimilation with Roman practices coupled with his ruthless ruling

92. See Luke Timothy Johnson, *The Letter of James: A New Translation with Introduction and Commentary*, Anchor Bible, 37A (New York: Doubleday, 1995), 162–64, for his concentration on James's voice.

93. See Josephus, *J.W.* 7.172-77, 7.285-303, and 7.394, for Herod's architectural achievements.

tactics contributed to this rising tide of sociopolitical instability. As bad as Herod was, the period after his reign only saw Palestine suffer worse atrocities, as Josephus explains:

> Indeed, that period had, somehow, become so prolific of crime of every description amongst the Jews, that no deed of iniquity was left unperpetrated. . . . So universal was the contagion, moreover, to outdo each other in acts of impiety towards God and of injustice towards their neighbor; those in power oppressing the masses, and the masses eager to destroy the powerful. These were bent on tyranny, those on violence and plundering the property of the wealthy.[94]

Because of the economic calamity, "it becomes more and more evident that it was not merely political dissatisfaction or religious fanaticism that brought unrest throughout the empire. The root cause of the misery was economic."[95]

After Herod's death, Palestine was divided into tetrarchies. The administration of these areas was so poorly managed that Roman procurators were eventually given rule over the entire area. The cruelty and poverty that these procurators meted out eventually led to the first Jewish Revolt in 66 CE. During the time of the procurators, there were several sects that rose in rebellion that led to revolution. Groups such as the Zealots and the Fourth Philosophy would eventually rise up to confront both Rome and Rome's minions. Josephus blames the first Jewish-Roman War on the combination of the procurators' ineptness and the rebels' thirst for blood. During this time, identity became an important part of one's posture toward Roman imperialism. As the seeds of revolution were being sown, issues of identity became increasingly bifurcated. One was either for Rome or against Rome, and life and death balanced on that line. If

94. Josephus, *J.W.* 7.259-62 (Thackeray, LCL).
95. Maynard-Reid, *Poverty and Wealth*, 18.

Josephus's account of James's death is correct (circa 62 CE), then it was in this hostile environment that the Letter of James was written.

The Letter of James, then, functions as a counter-imperial decree from the center of Judeanness. Within the content of the letter, James sets up a dichotomy between the "world" and those who ascribe to James's worldview. The "world" is literally the Roman Empire and all those who assimilate and conspire with it.[96] Although James may not be directly related to the Dead Sea Scrolls and other writings like it, these texts certainly share a cultural frustration with the "world."[97] In this way, James represents a Judeanness that positions itself against the Roman Empire. Scholars who do not take this view tend to represent James as a Christian document and emphasize the "fact" that "Christianity" left Palestine after the destruction of Jerusalem by Rome in 70 CE. Analyzing James as a document of early Judeanness, however, demonstrates its intimate connectedness with the identity politics of first-century Roman Palestine—a time that saw what Seth Schwartz calls the "shattering" of Judaism.[98] Although Luke Timothy Johnson argues for this same sociopolitical environment as the setting for the Letter of James, he never adequately explores how this environment affected James or the Letter of James. Throughout his work, Johnson concentrates on James's ethical and theological propositions. Nowhere does Johnson allude to the larger political setting as an impactful circumstance in the composition of the Letter of James. This omission is only accentuated by the fact that Johnson emphasizes how the Letter of James contradicts common Roman

96. I devote special attention to this issue in chapter 3.

97. See Josephus, *Ant.* 18.11-22, *J.W.* 2.119-61; Philo, *Good Person* 12, *Hypothetica* 11.1–11.8 for their accounts of the Essenes as well as the Dead Sea Scrolls (especially 1QS 6:13—7:8, 1QS 3:12-24, and CD 6:11—7:6a), which may or may not have been authored by the Essenes.

98. Seth Schwartz, *Imperialism and Jewish Society, 200 B.C.E to 640 C.E.* (Princeton and Oxford: Princeton University Press, 2001), 15, states "I suggest that under the combined impact of the Destruction and the failure of the two revolts, the deconstruction of the Jewish 'nation,' and the annexation of Palestine by an empire at the height of its power and prosperity, Judaism shattered."

social norms. By acknowledging that the Letter of James diametrically opposes social concepts that characterized a Roman worldview, and nowhere connecting those points of conflict with a political agenda, Johnson misses what may be the most important aspect of the Letter of James: it is an anti-imperial text that was produced in an atmosphere of severe political opposition. In this sense, the ethics and theology that Johnson "finds" in the Letter of James are more accurately political interventions.

These political interventions manifest themselves as nativist discourse that calls for purity and perfection in the face of imperial oppression and assimilation. In this fragmented space, James attempts to create rigid boundaries around a certain type of identity within Judeanness. The conflicts in Jerusalem during 30–66 CE as evidenced in Josephus's writings; the different schools of Jewish thought found in the writings of Philo and Josephus; the beheading of John the Baptist; the crucifixion of Jesus as a Roman rebel; and James as heir to a rebellious throne all heighten the likelihood that the Letter of James was, in fact, an anti-imperial document. In such a contentious environment as Jerusalem in the mid-first century CE, where would James fall on the spectrum of Judeanness? James's insistence on action, purity, justice, and the law would have placed him firmly in what postcolonial critics call the "nativist" camp. The remarkable similarities of this short letter with the Dead Sea Scrolls and Josephus's and Philo's descriptions of the Essenes places James squarely in the rubric of Judeanness that opposed both the Roman world and other Judeanness that colluded with it—possibly Judeanness such as that of the Sadducees and Herodians. The degree of James's refutation of empire and hybridity, however, shows its degree of similarity with other, more radical forms of Judeanness, notably that of the Zealots.

By the end of the first century, there was not yet a clear distinction between Christianity and Judaism as two definable religions.[99]

According to Daniel Boyarin, they are twins wrestling in the womb until the fourth century, when the rise of imperial Christianity ultimately determined the lines of orthodoxy.[100] The Letter of James textually represents one small, early part of that prolonged wrestling match. In other words, the letter is evidence of identity negotiation within the realm of Judeanness in the first century. The overarching context of this struggle was the Roman Empire. The Letter of James evidences a site of contention where Judeanness is being negotiated specifically within a Roman Palestine context, but certainly for a broader audience than Judeans living in the Land. Judeanness, according to James, is radically distinct from the Roman world. In this narrowing vision of Judeanness, multiplicity is distinctly condemned as double-mindedness and Judean identity becomes singular. This concentration on singularity, purity, and perfection confronts any form of Judeanness that is multiple, intentionally nested, and variable. In this way, James, who is at *home* in the homeland (indeed, in the *center* of the homeland, Jerusalem), disciplines all forms of Judeanness that do not conform to his insistence on purity and perfection in Roman Palestine, but especially in the Diaspora. Pauline hybridity, described by Hodge as a form of nested identities, would be an example of diasporic Judeanness that embodies what James considers "friendship with the world." The rhetoric involved in this disciplining, the critique of both empire

99. In fact, the term "religion" as we know it in modernity did not carry our modern connotations during this time. Daniel Boyarin contends that religion in the modern sense germinated in the fourth century. See Boyarin, *Border Lines: The Partition of Judaeo-Christianity* (Philadelphia: University of Pennsylvania Press, 2004), 202–25.

100. Daniel Boyarin, *Dying for God: Martyrdom and the Making of Christianity and Judaism* (Stanford: Stanford University Press, 1999). Hodge, "Apostle to the Gentiles," 271, agrees with Boyarin, arguing that "[a] major limitation of the traditional approach (which posits the dichotomy of Judaism and Christianity) is that it assumes a rigid understanding of identity, in which one is either X or Y. I propose that we conceptualize identity in a more complex way. Instead of understanding ethnic identity as monolithic and fixed, imagine it to be multi-faceted and flexible."

and hybrid, and the positioning in the homeland all contribute to the rationale for reading the Letter of James as a nativist reaction to empire within the variegated forms of Judeanness under Roman imperialism. As is evident from the political context of first-century Roman Palestine, a postcolonial optic is warranted.

3

Pure and Perfect Piety: Nativist Discourse in the Letter of James

Now that a heuristic map of Judeanness in the first century has been drawn, it is important to situate the Letter of James within this landscape. The debate regarding authorship and addressees within scholarship on James is instructive in this cartographical endeavor. I will begin with the historical issues regarding James's position within Judeanness and use the category of nativism to shed new light on this topic. The epistolary opening, the overarching theme, the nature of the rhetoric, and the structure of the letter itself all conspire to position the Letter of James as a nativist reaction to empire.

The language of purity and perfection that pervades the Letter of James establishes an abiding dichotomy throughout the letter. The way in which James employs this rhetoric of purity and perfection creates an essentialist identity that is reminiscent of nativist discourse. This essentialist identity calls those in the Diaspora to return to a place of belonging, which is defined by the "new" center, and critiques both the "other" and the "hybrid" while using the master's tools. Nativism seeks to maintain the essentialist categories of colonizer/colonized but turns that binary upside down, whereby the "native" is the most civilized, honorable, and dignified, and the colonizer is the most uncivilized, dishonorable, and undignified. A provocative example of this inversion comes from one of the founders of nativism, Aimé Césaire:

> First we must study how colonization works to *decivilize* the colonizer, to *brutalize* him in the true sense of the word, to degrade him, to awaken him to buried instincts, to covetousness, violence, race hatred, and moral relativism; and we must show that each time a head is cut off or an eye put out in Vietnam and in France they accept the fact, each time a little girl is raped and in France they accept the fact, each time a Madagascan is tortured and in France they accept the fact, civilization acquires another dead weight, a universal regression takes place, a gangrene sets in, a center of infection begins to spread; and that at the end of all these treaties that have been violated, all these lies that have been propagated, all the punitive expeditions that have been tolerated, all these prisoners who have been tied up and 'interrogated,' all these patriots who have been tortured, at the end of all the racial pride that has been encouraged, all the boastfulness that has been displayed, a poison has been distilled into the veins of Europe and, slowly but surely, the continent proceeds toward *savagery*.[1]

In this instance, Césaire claims that Europe has become the savage through colonialism by erasing the civilizations of its colonial subjects and exposing its own uncivilized barbarity. Inverting this binary reifies the lines drawn by the colonial interaction and simultaneously creates another monster besides the colonizer. The other monster is the native that assimilates colonial culture. This cultural hybrid blurs the lines of any essentialist identities and threatens to destabilize the boundaries that nativism establishes.

1. Aimé Césaire, *Discourse on Colonialism*, trans. Joan Pinkham (New York: Monthly Review Press, 1976 [French original, 1955]), 35–36.

The dual front indicative of nativist rhetoric is evidenced in the Letter of James in the way purity and perfection function throughout the letter. Purity and perfection firmly establish and demarcate the impermeable boundaries that James draws. In order to support this thesis, I will analyze James 1:1 in order to see how James creates a "center" in Jerusalem to which he calls the Diaspora. Situating James in Jerusalem within the cultural matrix of Judeanness emphasizes Jerusalem as a conceptual center for James's nativist discourse. Since identity is the focus of the rhetoric of the letter, James's identity is important; therefore, the first part of this chapter will be devoted to (re)constructing James. Following this analysis, I will turn my attention to the identity of "the twelve tribes of the diaspora." Once the identity of these "brothers and sisters" (2:15) in the Diaspora has been contextualized, I will focus on the rhetorical force of the letter and see how James uses the rhetoric of purity and perfection to define the center and create impenetrable boundaries that highlight the total contrast between what is pure and impure, that is, between James and empire. In the process of policing this boundary, James also takes aim at the border crossers. Those who would transgress this strategic essentialism mix and mingle with the world; thus they become impure and stained by the world. These cultural hybrids take a tongue lashing (3:1-12) and are characterized as having an impure piety and dead faith. The rhetoric of purity and perfection in James, then, functions to demarcate empire and discipline would-be border crossers.

James 1:1 as Center/Margin Power Dynamic

The Letter of James is contextualized in Jerusalem by virtue of the fact of authorship—whether authentic or not. The only "James" with enough authority to write with such imperatival force to which this text could belong or to which it would be attributed would be the leader of the "Jerusalem Church." There is, as we shall see, a growing consensus in scholarship to understand the letter as authentic to James, who was the leader of the church in Jerusalem.[2] In this case, the text originates from a place in the *center* of pious life within Judeanness. Jerusalem maintained its place as the center of Judean, exilic, and diasporic piety until the destruction of the Temple in 70 CE, with the exception of sectarian communities like that at Qumran, which took a different view of Jerusalem and its Temple. The influence and authority of James of Jerusalem is evidenced in other first-century texts like Galatians, Acts, and Josephus's *Jewish Antiquities*. According to Galatians, Paul goes to Jerusalem to meet with this James and defers to him to see if his preaching was legitimate or not, and in that encounter, Paul describes James as one of the "acknowledged pillars" of the Jesus movement (Gal. 2:9). Paul would later describe his powerful opposition in Antioch as "certain people from James" (Gal. 2:11-12). Another encounter between James and Paul is described in Acts, which was written much later, but affirms the same kind of authority resting with James (Acts 15, 21). Apparently, James of Jerusalem had the authority to legitimize or render illegitimate the content of Paul's message. James's influence in Jerusalem is further affirmed by Josephus's account of James's death. According to Josephus, James's death created discontent within Jerusalem that only added to the instability of the city just before the beginning of the Jewish Revolt.[3] In all three of these accounts, James is connected to a strong seat of leadership within Jerusalem.

2. I will duly review all of the main arguments concerning authorship later in this chapter under the heading, "James and Jerusalem Provenance." See Luke Timothy Johnson, *The Letter of James: A New Translation with Introduction and Commentary*, Anchor Bible, 37A (New York: Doubleday, 1995), 89–121; Patrick J. Hartin, *James*, Sacra Pagina, 14 (Collegeville, MN: Liturgical, 2003); William F. Brosend II, *James and Jude*, New Cambridge Bible Commentary (Cambridge: Cambridge University Press, 2004), 1–5; Ralph P. Martin, *James*, WBC, 48 (Nashville: Thomas Nelson, 1988), xxxi–xli, for an extended argument for James's authenticity.
3. Josephus, *Ant.* 20.200.

The identity of the James of 1:1 has been a contested question that has preoccupied much of modern scholarship on the Letter of James. In the "quest for the historical James," there are at least two major issues that complicate the process: limited sources and scholarly approach. First, the material at the disposal of modern scholars to (re)construct a historical James is sparse at best. The Letter to the Galatians and 1 Corinthians 15, the Synoptic Gospels, the Acts of the Apostles, and Josephus's *Jewish Antiquities* are the only extant documents from the first century that explicitly mention James, the brother of Jesus.[4] Of these sources, Galatians, Acts, and the *Jewish Antiquities* say more about the person of James than any of the other texts, including the Letter of James itself. Within the Letter of James, there is very little autobiographical information regarding the attributed author; however, the letter clearly evidences the author's worldview. Second, the way scholars use "James" obscures the referent. In other words, James has been used to identify both the person and the letter. For instance, when Luke Timothy Johnson determines the "voice of James," he specifically identifies the voice of the *text* not the *person*.[5] Timothy B. Cargal provides the best analysis of this issue by showing how scholars either concentrate on history (an outside-in approach) or linguistics (an inside-out approach).[6] Scholars who focus on history begin "outside the text (with the extra-textual phenomena of tradition, socio-historical setting, etc.)" and then use that construction to interpret the text.[7] Johnson is extremely

4. The other extant literature attributed to James comes from the second century and only adds to the difficulty and complications involved in (re)constructing a historical James. See Luke Timothy Johnson, *Brother of Jesus, Friend of God: Studies in the Letter of James* (Grand Rapids: Eerdmans, 2004), 2, n. 10.
5. Johnson, *Brother of Jesus*, 2.
6. Timothy B. Cargal, *Restoring the Diaspora: Discursive Structure and Purpose in the Epistle of James* (Atlanta: Scholars, 1993), 5–8.
7. Ibid., 6. See John Painter, *Just James: The Brother of Jesus in History and Tradition*, 2nd edition (Columbia: University of South Carolina Press, 2004), as a prime example of this type of "outside-in" scholarship.

critical of this type of scholarship: "A puzzling feature of all these reconstructions of the historical James is the minor role played by the letter ascribed to him. . . . But this is a mistake. With the exception of the evidence in Paul, Acts, and Josephus, the letter is the historically most certain evidence we have concerning James."[8] Other scholars who concentrate on "linguistic" readings start with the text and determine "the author's convictions as expressed within the text and other communication processes at work within the text" and move out "to the relationship with extra-textual traditions, social conditions, etc."[9] Those who concentrate on the text tend to minimize the extent to which one can construct a historical James. Darian Lockett, a proponent of the textual emphasis, does an excellent job describing the author of the letter but his focus does "not rest upon identifying the historical author of the text."[10] Likewise, Johnson, who argues that the letter is early and authentic, goes so far as to say that he "will not try to do the impossible and demonstrate beyond the possibility of cavil that James of Jerusalem was indeed the author of James."[11] The focus of these scholars has more to do with the letter than the person of James. In what follows, I will start with the Letter of James and use the text as a way to identify the person in an attempt to position James within first-century Palestinian Judeanness, and I will consult the other available resources to see what kind of light, if any, they shed on the person, James of Jerusalem.

The Letter of James begins with a simple greeting that bifurcates all that follows and therefore is worth all the detailed attention it has received in scholarship. In this short greeting, the person of James is positioned as the author of the letter and the center of the

8. Johnson, *Brother of Jesus*, 2.
9. Cargal, *Restoring the Diaspora*, 7.
10. Darian Lockett, *Purity and Worldview in the Epistle of James* (London: T. & T. Clark, 2008), 66.
11. Johnson, *Brother of Jesus*, 3.

discourse. The letter literally comes from James and is sent to the Diaspora. This directional language creates a sense of center and margin. James represents the center from whom the letter comes and the Diaspora represents the margins to which the letter is sent. This center/margin binary between sender and receiver characterizes the entire letter and creates a sense of authority and hierarchy that is important throughout. The center/margin binary is accentuated by the imperatival and prophetic force that resonates throughout the letter.

James of Jerusalem, Brother of Jesus

Although the Letter of James does not have many autobiographical glosses, the self-referential passages are helpful in understanding the identity of the author. In addition to these scant passages, the language and style of the letter also speak to the identity of the author. In light of Luke Timothy Johnson's justified frustration with scholarship that attempts to "uncover" the authentic identity of James by consulting all of the available ancient sources *besides* the Letter of James itself, I will begin with the Letter of James and then move to the other ancient sources. Compiling the evidence from all of these sources may help "position" James the person and James the letter.

James in the Letter of James

Many scholars have noted that the simplicity of the prescript (1:1) demands a well-known figure. The absence of an extended prescript that elaborates and justifies the author's position of authority evidences a place of power that was neither defensive nor self-promoting. This stands in marked contrast to other letters within the New Testament where the author attempts to legitimize and assert authority with an extended prescript in the face of opposition that seems to be challenging the writer's authority. Paul's opening prescript in the Letter to the Galatians provides an example of this type of posturing: "Paul, apostle not from human or through human authority but by Jesus Christ and God the father, who raised him from the dead" (Gal. 1:1). In total contrast, the Letter of James opens with a simple prescript: "James, slave of God and of the Lord Jesus Christ." The "James" of this prescript must be a notable figure whose identity is taken for granted. That lack of additional information regarding the author's identity and authority clearly shows that the author enjoys some level of fame among the addressees.

"Slave" (δοῦλος) as the main description of the author places James in a lineage of leadership and authority. It is not so much the identity as a slave but as "a slave of God" that warrants the banner of leadership. Throughout the LXX, this image of God's slave is applied to historic leadership: Abraham (LXX Ps. 104:42), David (2 Sam. 7:8, 25, 29; 1 Chron. 17:4), Moses (LXX Ps. 104:26, 42; Mal. 3:24), Joshua (Judg. 2:8), and other prophets (Amos 3:7; Joel 3:2; Jon. 1:9; Jer. 7:25; Ezek. 38:17). Slave of God, then, is a description of one who is under the authority of God and acts with the authority commissioned by God. James, then, stands in a long history of "slaves of God," but he is also a "slave of the Lord Jesus Christ." Other New Testament authors used this construction but dropped θεοῦ: Rom. 1:1, Phil. 1:1, and 2 Pet. 1:1. With the addition of κυρίου Ἰησοῦ Χριστοῦ, James not only places himself under the authority of God but also under the authority of the "Lord Jesus Christ." James places himself (and the audience) squarely within the messianic movement related to Jesus of Nazareth. Within this movement, James exudes a confidence in his authority by placing himself in a lineage of "slaves of God." The litany of imperatives that follows provides additional proof of James's place of authority in relation to the recipients of the letter.

In addition to the prescript, James is self-referential in three other passages: 1:18, 2:1, and 3:1. In James 1:18 and 2:1, the author uses first-person plural pronouns that bring the author and audience together in shared belief. In James 1:18, the author speaks of a shared birth ("God gave us birth") and a shared identity as "first fruits." This shared birth is placed within cultic terminology that refers to the Judean sacrificial system. This shared birth, then, is within the boundaries of Judeanness as a source of identity for both the author and audience. The common birth (ἀπεκυέω) in verse 18 is contrasted to the antithetical birth (ἀπεκυέω) in verse 15, where human desire conceives and births sin, and sin, when it is finished, gives birth (ἀπεκύει) to death. The common birth of the author and audience, then, stands in total distinction to another "worldly" birth that is characterized by sin and death. Their shared origins and shared identity as first fruits firmly place the author and audience within the overall rhetoric of purity and perfection.

In James 2:1, the author employs another first-person plural pronoun with regard to the common faith that the author shares with the recipients. In addition to this common faith, fictive kinship is also employed in order to strengthen the rhetoric and the common ties. What they hold in common in 2:1 is the faith of "our" Lord Jesus Christ of glory. The translational difficulties in this passage are evidenced by the textual variants in the earliest manuscripts as well as the diversity of scholarly opinion. Whether the author and audience share *in* the faith of their Lord Jesus Christ of glory or whether they share *the* faith of their Lord Jesus Christ is inconsequential to their shared *beliefs*. Lockett agrees, arguing that "faith in Jesus Christ is a foundational characteristic of both the author and the audience. Thus along with the reference to Jesus Christ in 1.1, in 2.1 the author indicates that the prime component of both the author's and audience's identity is defined by servanthood to and faith in Jesus

Christ."[12] They hold common beliefs regarding Jesus Christ that have implications for the entire community. In the overall schematic of 2:1-13, the implications have to do with showing partiality to the poor rather than the wealthy. Here we find another classic binary opposite when James employs first-person plural pronouns. In both instances where James speaks autobiographically in common with the recipients, the rhetoric is employed within a system of stark dualism that simultaneously pairs the recipients with James and separates them from another domain or set of relationships. Later in 2:21, James speaks of Abraham as *our* father, which refers to a common origin and functions as a call to faith that works rather than a dead faith.

The final self-referential passage in the Letter of James is 3:1, where James calls himself a teacher (διδάσκαλος). The importance of this identity reference is highlighted by David Hutchinson Edgar since the term "occurs 49 times in the canonical gospels, 42 of which refer to Jesus as teacher, including the direct address διδάσκαλε 30 times."[13] In other parts of the New Testament, the term is applied to those in strong leadership positions (Luke 2:46; 3:12; John 3:1, 10; Acts 13:1; Rom. 12:7; 1 Cor. 12:29; Eph. 4:11; 1 Tim. 1:10; 2:7; 4:13, 16, 5:17; 6:1, 3; 2 Tim. 1:11; 3:10; Titus 1:9; 2:1, 7; Heb. 5:12). According to Edgar, "[I]t can be asserted that apostles, prophets and teachers were generally recognised as authorities under the special commission of God."[14] In the overall passage of 3:1-12, James deals with the main prerogative of a teacher: speaking. Those who cannot control the tongue should not pursue the office of teacher. In this instance, it seems like James is effectively silencing a contradictory

12. Ibid., 171.

13. David Hutchinson Edgar, *Has God Not Chosen the Poor?: The Social Setting of the Epistle of James* (Sheffield: Sheffield Academic Press, 2001), 50–51.

14. Ibid., 54. Edgar agrees with Martin, *James*, 108; Peter H. Davids, *The Epistle of James: A Commentary on the Greek Text*, NIGTC (Grand Rapids: Eerdmans, 1982), 136; Lockett, *Purity and Worldview*, 173.

voice. In fact, an uncontrollable tongue is not only evidence of a false teacher, it is evidence of worthless piety (1:26). It is from the office of teacher that James writes with such imperative force. The coupling of διδάσκαλος with δοῦλος as the only self-referential titles used by the author indicates one who is in a position of power in relation to the recipients of the letter. As the teacher begins to teach, the language and style that James employs bear witness to his identity.

It is commonly noted among scholars that the *koine* Greek with which James writes is among the most polished in the New Testament. James's use of "complex and persuasive wordplay" reveals an author who is at home in the Greek language.[15] The language alone has caused scholars to dismiss James, the brother of Jesus, as the author of the text. Werner Georg Kümmel specifically argues that "the fluent Greek is hardly to be attributed to James the brother of the Lord."[16] How could an Aramaic-speaking peasant have written Greek with such fluency? Arguing for James's authenticity, Johnson shows that "[t]he entire thrust of recent research has been to demonstrate how pervasive and long-standing was the Hellenization of Palestine, shown above all by the use of the Greek language."[17] Sepphoris's proximity to Nazareth would only add to the likelihood that James, and Jesus for that matter, would have been familiar with the Greek language as Johnson argues: "There is every reason to think, moreover, that the family of Jesus would have some acquaintance with Greek culture."[18] Johnson finally, and flatly, states

15. Johnson, *Letter of James*, 8.

16. Werner Georg Kümmel, *Introduction to the New Testament*, trans. Howard Clark Kee (Nashville: Abingdon, 1975), 406. See also Martin Dibelius, *James: A Commentary on the Epistle of James*, trans. Michael A. Williams, Hermeneia (Philadelphia: Fortress Press, 1976), 17.

17. Johnson, *Letter of James*, 117. See also Martin Hengel, *The "Hellenization" of Judaea in the First Century after Christ*, trans. John Bowden (London: SCM, 1989).

18. Johnson, *Letter of James*, 117. See also Martin Hengel, "Jakobusbrief als antipaulinische Polemik," in *Tradition and Interpretation in the New Testament*, ed. Gerald F. Hawthorne and Otto Betz (Grand Rapids: Eerdmans, 1987), 251, for his concentration on Sepphoris as the

that "[t]here is, in short, no linguistic reason why James of Jerusalem could not have written this letter."[19] Beyond James actually writing the letter himself, Martin Hengel proposes that James certainly would have had scribes at his service as the leader of the Jesus movement in Jerusalem: "Jak konnte in Jerusalem einen rhetorisch geschulten Sekretär dazu herangezogen haben."[20] These two possibilities adequately settle the language question.

The introductory chapter of James alone illustrates the author's comfort and ease with the Greek language. James uses a string of catchwords that systematically and rhetorically link one section to the other, which only adds to the persuasiveness of James's rhetoric. For instance, verses 4-5 are linked by the catchword *lack* (λειπόμενοι/λείπεται) and the thematic verses for the entire letter are linked by *piety* in verses 26-27 (θρησκὸς/θρησκεία). In addition to using catchwords as a means to link passages, James also uses alliteration throughout the letter. In 1:12-14, James alliterates π as he plays on the root for temptation (πειρασμόν): πειρασμόν (v. 12); πειραζόμενος, πειράζομαι, ἀπείραστος, πειράζει (v. 13); and πειραζέται (v. 14). The rhythm that James creates throughout his letter by using alliteration provides a powerful mnemonic style that adds flavor to James's invectives. Besides these rhetorical conventions, James also uses homoioteleton (1:6, 14; 2:12; 3:17; 4:8), parechesis (1:24), and paronomasia (1:1-2; 2:4, 20; 3:17; 4:14). It is clear by James's language and style that he is intentional with how he writes so as to be as persuasive as possible.

Many scholars also recognize James's familiarity with Greco-Roman diatribe. James, as a teacher, uses diatribe as a pedagogical tool by using standard literary tropes associated with diatribe style.

"langjährigen Hauptstadt Galiläas," and a possible place where James would have encountered and learned Greek.

19. Johnson, *Letter of James*, 118.

20. Hengel, "Jakobusbrief," 251.

Vocative address, rhetorical questioning, an appeal to an exemplum, the use of comparisons, an imaginary interlocutor, and the fluctuation between second-person singular to second-person plural and back all fit within the diatribe conventions, and James uses all of these devices in his letter.[21] More than James's language, style, and conventions, however, Johnson argues "that James uses the *topoi* of Greco-Roman moral instruction in order to develop his argument."[22] The *topoi* of envy, friendship, and taciturnity are all developed and used to organize the structure of the letter.[23]

It is clear from the linguistic and stylistic evidence in the Letter of James that the author is thoroughly familiar with Greco-Roman literary conventions. What is also clear from the content of the letter is that the author finds as his primary source of authority the LXX. Following Johnson's work, Lockett determines that "where Greco-Roman literary devices and moral topics are taken up by James, his intellectual heritage rests firmly in the Jewish scriptures."[24] The LXX provides the foundation for all of James's arguments. Johnson shows that the worldview of James is more reflected in "the power of God to create and to judge," which comes from the LXX, rather than the common Greco-Roman cultural convention of honor and shame.[25] References to the heroic figures of Abraham and Rahab (2:21ff.), multiple references to the Decalogue (2:11ff.), use of νομός (1:25, 2:8, and so on), quotations from Leviticus 19 (2:8; 5:4), and the use of Isa. 40:6-7 (1:11) all testify to the indebtedness James has to the LXX as his source of authority.

James's appeal to the LXX as a source of authority, however, is refracted through the lens of the Jesus tradition that runs deeply

21. See Johnson, *Letter of James*, 8–11; Lockett, *Purity and Worldview*, 166–68.

22. Johnson, *Brother of Jesus*, 18.

23. Johnson, *Brother of Jesus*, 18.

24. Lockett, *Purity and Worldview*, 169.

25. Johnson, *Brother of Jesus*, 18–19.

through the ethos of the entire letter. There is broad consensus among scholars regarding James's use of the Jesus tradition. Scholars such as Dean B. Deppe show that James alludes to the Jesus tradition at least eight times in the letter, while others like Patrick J. Hartin argue that the entire letter is influenced by the Jesus tradition, specifically the Q source.[26] The range of scholarly opinion regarding James's use of the Jesus tradition varies greatly; as Bauckham surmises, "one person's verbal allusion is another person's verbal coincidence."[27] This diversity of opinion is due in large part to the fact that James never quotes Jesus directly. Johnson and Bauckham use this fact to argue for an early dating of the letter since James "does not repeat it [the Jesus tradition]; he is inspired by it."[28] After providing at least seven additional parallels between passages in James with the Synoptic Gospels beyond Deppe's analysis, William F. Brosend contends that "when one tallies not only allusions but parallels of content and/or terminology and common references, Deppe's list grows from eight to thirty-six, and this does not include nine themes common to the preaching of Jesus and the letter of James."[29] What is most important for the discussion of the identity of the author of the Letter of James is the fact that the author shows a deep knowledge of the Jesus tradition, which guides the interpretation of the LXX. The

26. Dean B. Deppe, *The Sayings of Jesus in the Epistle of James* (Chelsea, MI: Bookcrafters, 1989); Patrick J. Hartin, *James and the Q Sayings of Jesus* (Sheffield: JSOT Press, 1991). See also John S. Kloppenborg, *Q, the Earliest Gospel: An Introduction to the Original Stories and Sayings of Jesus* (Louisville and London: Westminster John Knox, 2008), 98–121. For a brief and succinct overview of the Jesus tradition in the Letter of James, see John S. Kloppenborg, "The Reception of the Jesus Tradition in James," in *The Catholic Epistles and the Tradition*, ed. Jacques Schlosser (Leuven: Leuven University Press, 2004), 93–141. For a concentrated analysis of the way in which the Jesus tradition functions in the rhetoric of the letter see Wesley Hiram Wachob, *The Voice of Jesus in the Social Rhetoric of James* (Cambridge: Cambridge University Press, 2000), where Wachob concentrates on how James uses the Jesus tradition in the pivotal first argument within the letter, 2:1-13.

27. Richard Bauckham, *James: Wisdom of James, Disciple of Jesus the Sage*, New Testament Readings (London and New York: Routledge, 1999), 82.

28. Ibid., 82.

29. Brosend, *James and Jude*, 11.

author, then, is firmly embedded in an environment that is immersed in Greek language, Judean scripture, and the Jesus tradition, all of which are taken for granted by the author. This "slave" and "teacher" masterfully writes a letter interpreting the LXX with the authority of Jesus in order to affect the recipients—the Diaspora—in a way that would cause them to practice pure and perfect piety.

The amalgam of cultural influences within such a short letter is staggering, especially considering the force of the letter toward purity. Lockett's analysis is instructive because he shows that James has "a high degree of acculturation, while showing a low degree of accommodation."[30] Unlike other literature of Judeanness that uses "acculturation for greater cultural accommodation" such as Philo and *The Letter of Aristeas*, James functions more like 4 Maccabees, which shows "a high degree of acculturation" but "uses its sensibilities to promote cultural antagonism."[31] Although James is at home within cultural diversity, there is a pious purity that cuts through all of it and puts him and his recipients at odds with the larger Greco-Roman world. In spite of the evidence within the letter that points to an author of multifarious cultural allegiances, James vividly demands purity and perfection as he constructs a world divided along the axis of God/purity and the world/impurity.

James in the Rest of the New Testament

By scouring through the rest of the New Testament for a "James" that could fit this description, scholars have narrowed their options regarding James's identity to at least three "historical" personalities: James the son of Zebedee, brother of John (Matt. 10:2; Mark 1:19, 29; 3:17; 5:37; 9:2; 10:35, 41; 13:3; 14:33; Luke 6:14; Acts 1:13), James the son of Alphaeus (Matt. 10:3; Mark 3:18; Luke 6:15; Acts 1:13),

30. Lockett, *Purity and Worldview*, 169.
31. Ibid., 168.

or James of Jerusalem, the brother of the Lord (Gal. 1:19; 2:9, 12; 1 Cor. 15:7; Matt. 13:55; 27:56; Mark 6:3; 15:4; 16:1; Luke 24:10; Acts 12:17; 15:13; 21:18; Jude 1). Since James the son of Zebedee, brother of John, was "killed with the sword" by Herod Agrippa I according to Acts 12:2, most scholars discredit the notion that he is the possible author. It seems unlikely that he could have had the authority to write with the brevity found in the Letter of James by the time of his death around 44 CE. James the son of Alphaeus simply does not feature prominently enough or carry enough authority in other first-century literature produced by Jesus-followers to warrant candidacy as author. James of Jerusalem, the brother of the Lord, then becomes the primary option. Besides the weakness of the evidence for the other two James, James of Jerusalem, brother of Jesus, has strong support in both canonical and extracanonical texts as the probable author of the letter. Paul writes about James of Jerusalem as the "Lord's brother" in one of his writings (Gal. 1:19) and it is clear from his letter that James is a powerful figure in Jerusalem among Jesus-followers. This notion of James being a leader among Jesus-followers in Jerusalem is corroborated by the accounts in Acts 15 and 21 regarding the Jerusalem Council. In Acts, James has the capacity to make the final decision relating to how gentiles will be incorporated into the new movement: "Therefore I have reached the decision that we should not trouble those Gentiles who are turning to God" (Acts 15:19). Josephus also writes about the death of James of Jerusalem in his *Jewish Antiquities* 20:200, which has tremendous implications for the dating of the letter. For these reasons, there is a growing scholarly consensus around the identity of "James" in James 1:1. Concluding that James of Jerusalem and brother of Jesus was the person to whom this letter was attributed does not, however, indicate scholarly consensus around authorial authenticity versus pseudonymity.

Authentic, Composite, Pseudonymous

There are three prevalent options concerning the authorship of James.[32] According to Martin Dibelius, the letter is pseudonymous and uses the authority of the leader of the Jerusalem Church, James of Jerusalem, who was also identified as the brother of Jesus.[33] Others such as Luke Timothy Johnson support the notion that the letter was authentically written by the same James of Jerusalem.[34] Peter H. Davids offers a third option, which argues that the letter was a composite work that has some original content written by James of Jerusalem, but was edited, annotated, and enlarged by his followers at a later stage.[35] This two-stage hypothesis gathered some momentum after Davids's commentary was published, but has since lost its appeal in recent scholarship.

The debate between authentic, composite, and pseudonymous authorship relies on cumulative data rather than any single factor. Commentators who argue for pseudonymous authorship usually emphasize the letter's disparate structure, linguistic style, late date, reception history, and anti-Pauline polemic. Others who argue for authentic authorship generally emphasize the nascent sayings of Jesus in the letter, the social realities reflected, the assumption of identity in the letter, an early date, and harmony with or ignorance of Pauline thought.

Since I agree with Johnson and argue throughout for authentic authorship and an early date, I need to provide extended

32. Although somewhat dated, Davids, *Epistle of James*, 4, charts the commentators that take these different positions.

33. Dibelius, *James*, 11–21. See also Sophie Laws, *The Epistle of James*, Harper's New Testament Commentary (San Francisco: Harper & Row, 1980), 32–42, and François Vouga, *L'Épître de Saint Jacques* (Genève: Labor et Fides, 1984), 17–18.

34. Johnson, *Letter of James*, 89–123. See also Hartin, *James*, 16–25; Brosend, *James and Jude*, 2–5; Bauckham, *James*, 16–17.

35. Davids, *Epistle of James*, 9–22.

argumentation for this option. In the most recent commentaries on the Letter of James, authentic authorship and early dating have become common. There are several criteria for this assertion, but none of them functions alone as a definitive reason for authorship and dating; rather, their cumulative effect provides enough evidence to make the argument.

First, the greeting in the letter lacks any attempt to expound on exactly who James is. It is taken for granted that the recipients would know that this is the leader of the Jerusalem Jesus movement and one "who needed no further introduction."[36] The identity of the "James" in 1:1 is presumed.[37] The quantity of imperatives within the short letter also attests to someone who wrote with assumed authority.

Another major factor in understanding James as an early letter is the way the Jesus tradition is appropriated. The name of Jesus is invoked only twice in the letter and Jesus is never specifically quoted. As we will see below in the exegesis of specific passages, there has been a tremendous amount of scholarship detailing James's engagement with Jesus sayings in general and the Q tradition in particular. Johnson argues that "the actual shape of the sayings [of Jesus] in James is closer to that associated with the hypothetical gospel source called Q than to the redacted versions in the Synoptics."[38] James's close connection to these pre-Synoptic sayings of Jesus would certainly place the Letter of James in the middle of the first century.

Historically, the lack of anything particularly "Christian" in the letter besides the two references to Jesus has caused some scholars to argue that James was a Jewish document that was Christianized. While this has never fully gained any consensus within scholarship on James, it is important to notice how closely connected the letter

36. Brosend, *James and Jude*, 4.

37. See Hartin, *James*, 21.

38. Johnson, *Letter of James*, 119.

is to Judeanness. The LXX is the main source of citation throughout the letter and is usually engaged via the Jesus tradition, as we will see specifically in James 2:1-13. Hartin argues that "[t]he author is heir above all to the Hebrew wisdom tradition."[39] The lack of "ethnic reasoning" in the letter also attests to its Judean nature. Unlike Paul, who is specifically writing to a gentile audience and trying to incorporate gentiles into the historic Judean covenant with God through ethnic reasoning, James assumes the ethnicity of "the twelve tribes of the diaspora" (1:1) and so appeals to them differently.[40]

While nearly all of the proponents of an early date and authentic authorship deny that James had an anti-Pauline polemic, they recognize that the two used similar language and were most likely from the "first generation Jewish Christians [who were] deeply affected by Greco-Roman moral traditions yet fundamentally defined by an allegiance to the symbols and story of Torah."[41] This close linguistic connection to Paul, who was one of the earliest writers of the Jesus movement, could also indicate an early date.

One of the main arguments against the Letter of James being early and authentic is the high level of proficiency in Greek in which the letter was written. This has led scholars to either argue for a later date, since it is presumed that a Galilean could not write such sophisticated Greek, or argue for a "two-level hypothesis," where a later redactor compiled the letter in its final form.[42] Jan Nicolaas Sevenster, however, persuasively argues that the Greek found in the letter of James in particular could have certainly come from a first-century Palestinian provenance, so does not necessarily nullify

39. Hartin, *James*, 21.
40. See "A Postcolonial Paul" below for an extended discussion of this topic.
41. Johnson, *Letter of James*, 120.
42. See Davids, *Epistle of James*, 12; Martin, *James*, lxxvii; and Robert W. Wall, *Community of the Wise: The Letter of James* (Valley Forge, PA: Trinity Press International, 1997), 9, for an extended argument for a two-stage development for the Letter of James.

authentic authorship or an early date for the letter.[43] Additionally, Johnson concludes, "[T]here is also the strong likelihood that the first Christian community in Jerusalem was itself at least bilingual if not exclusively Greek-speaking from the beginning. There is, in short, no linguistic reason why James of Jerusalem could not have written this letter."[44]

Although I follow the above scholars and argue for an early date and authentic authorship, the cumulative nature of the argument precludes any definitive evidence for either an early or late date, much less the issue of authorship. In fact, my overarching postcolonial reading of the Letter of James could very well fit within a later dating. In other words, my thesis does not rest exclusively on dating or authorship.[45]

James and Jerusalem Provenance

What all of these options do not dispute is that, whether authentic or not, the letter was written with the authority of James of Jerusalem, the brother of Jesus. It is important that all three options point to the same source of authority because it connects the Letter of James to Jerusalem literally and figuratively. On all accounts, then, James is writing from the center of Judeanness geographically and embodying the center of Judeanness personally as he relates to his audience, that is, the Diaspora. Excluding the final word of greeting (*chairein*), the opening of the letter begins with *Iakōbos* and ends with

43. Jan Nicolaas Sevenster, *Do You Know Greek? How Much Greek Could the First Jewish Christians Have Known?* Supplements to Novum Testamentum, 19 (Leiden: Brill, 1968), 3–21.
44. Johnson, *Letter of James*, 117–18.
45. In a conversation, Melanie Johnson-DeBaufre challenged my early dating/authentic authorship argument. She thought there was potential in taking my larger reading of James and placing it at the end of the first century or beginning of the second century because it could evidence a strong Judean identity within the Jesus movement at a date that would challenge assumptions regarding the dating of the "parting of the ways." Although her suggestion is provocative, I find the arguments listed above for an early date convincing.

diaspora. There is no question about the direction of authority from the greeting. James is the center and the margins are the Diaspora. The volume of imperatives that follow this greeting is fitting for the center/margin binary that has been constructed.

According to Darian Lockett, the Letter of James fits within the category of a "letter to the diaspora from Jerusalem."[46] Following this tradition, James's identity and location exudes authority over "the twelve tribes of the diaspora." Within the context of Jerusalem, however, James's seat of authority is much more nuanced. In relation to the high priest, it is clear that James was powerless if Josephus correctly narrates James's demise. According to Josephus, it seems as though Ananus assumed the Sanhedrin would not object to stoning James "and certain others" based on his accusation of them as "having transgressed the law" (*Ant.* 20:201). The commotion this caused in Jerusalem among "the most fair-minded" and "strict in observance of the law" was based on Ananus's convening the Sanhedrin without the permission of the Roman procurator Albinus, which indicates another layer of power discrepancy that also interpolates the client king Herod Agrippa. Although Josephus's account of James's accusation and death is fraught with difficulties in trying to decipher James's exact political position in Jerusalem, it helps to show that James certainly was not in a position of power in relation to the Roman procurator, the client king, the high priest, the Sanhedrin, and possibly even the "fair-minded" in Jerusalem. In other words, the power center created in the epistolary opening of James was relative to James's audience. The power he enjoys in Paul's letter to the Galatians and the Acts of the Apostles does not translate to other

46. Lockett, *Purity and Worldview*, 73–76. See Donald J. Verseput, "Genre and Story: The Community Setting of the Epistle of James," *CBQ* 62 (2000): 96–110 (99–100). See also Bauckham, *James*, 19–21; Manabu Tsuji, *Glaube zwischen Vollkommenheit und Verweltlichung: Eine Untersuchung zur literarischen Gestalt und zur inhaltlichen Koharenz des Jakobusbriefes* (Tübingen: Mohr Siebeck, 1997), 18–27; Vouga, *L'Épître de Saint Jacques*, 24–27, 35–37.

demographics in Jerusalem. James may be the leader of an emerging movement within Judeanness, but he certainly was not among the powerful elite in Jerusalem. We are left to conjecture whether or not Ananus felt threatened by the new movement that James represented, but this event had to warrant some significance in order for Josephus to narrate Ananus's fall from the position of high priest. The story functions as a way to explain Ananus's removal, but James, as a named and explained figure—one who was the brother of a so-called messiah—is prominent in the explanation. The recording of James's death by Josephus begs the question of James's relation to the high priest and the Sanhedrin. Was the interim between procurators the best opportunity to get rid of rivals, opponents, or critics? Josephus goes to lengths to paint a picture of an unwise Ananus who was "rash in his temper and unusually daring" and who was also from the "school of the Sadducees, who are indeed more savage than any of the other Judeans."[47]

In light of Josephus's portrayal, Ananus was the antagonist who acted in ways that jeopardized peace within Jerusalem. The "fair-minded" (ἐδόκουν ἐπιεικέστατοι), whether advocates of James or not, certainly opposed Ananus's actions. His action of convening the Sanhedrin to exercise capital punishment incited the "fair-minded" to petition King Agrippa to force Ananus to desist from his actions and to bring their frustration to Albinus while he was on his way to Jerusalem from Alexandria. The "fair-minded," then, had enough influence to send a delegation to both King Agrippa and Albinus, and they also had enough power to eventually have Ananus removed from the high priesthood. This short excerpt from Josephus evidences the fact that James did not enjoy power at the level of the high priest or Sanhedrin, but was a sufficiently prominent figure to lead

47. Josephus, *Ant.* 20.199 (my translation).

to the removal of a high priest. Whatever his precise position of power, James was certainly in the middle of the political atmosphere in Jerusalem when he was accused and killed by Ananus.

In the years immediately preceding the Jewish revolt, it is not difficult to imagine a letter that criticized preferential treatment to the wealthy, faith without action toward the most vulnerable in society, slander, earthly wisdom, friendship with the world, arrogant business plans, and the wealthy creating frustration among the political elite in Jerusalem. If Josephus can be trusted at all in relation to his narration of the murders and killings he records during this period of time, then the positions expressed in the Letter of James provide enough reason for the political elite to plot James's death. James, although the leader of the emerging Jesus movement, is positioned as a subaltern voice within the political leadership in Jerusalem—the same leadership that had John the Baptist (possibly his relative) killed. James's concentrated use of purity/pollution rhetoric throughout his letter only accentuates his relationship to the high priest and Sanhedrin.[48]

As a subaltern voice, James defines what pure and undefiled piety is and implores the Diaspora to resist all forms of dead and worthless faith. The universe, for James, is divided between good and bad, God and the world. Identity, for James, paradoxically reflects Gayatri Spivak's notions of the "true" subaltern as "defined as a difference from the elite."[49] The fact that James writes/speaks, however, contradicts Spivak's own notion of the subaltern: "If the subaltern

48. See Elsa Tamez, *The Scandalous Message of James: Faith Without Works Is Dead* (New York: Crossroad, 1990), 21–26; Pedrito U. Maynard-Reid, *Poverty and Wealth in James* (Maryknoll, NY: Orbis, 1987), 1–13; Davids, *Epistle of James*, 28–34; Frantz Fanon, *The Wretched of the Earth*, trans. Constance Farrington (New York: Grove, 1963 [French original, 1961]), 52–57; Albert Memmi, *The Colonizer and the Colonized*, trans. Howard Greenfeld (Boston: Beacon, 1965 [French original, 1957]), 90–118, to see rationale for the colonized turning to internal violence.

49. Gayatri Chakravorty Spivak, "'Can the Subaltern Speak?' Speculations on Widow Sacrifice," *Wedge* 7/8 (Winter/Spring 1985). Cited in *The Post-Colonial Studies Reader*, ed. Bill Ashcroft, Gareth Griffiths, and Helen Tiffin (London and New York: Routledge, 1995), 27.

can speak then, thank God, the subaltern is not a subaltern any more."[50] Although Spivak's definition of the subaltern is "thoroughly theorized," according to Stephen D. Moore, she constantly defines it as a negative or negation: "The subaltern is all that is not elite, but the trouble with those kinds of names is that if you have any kind of political interest you name it in the hope that the name will disappear."[51] This erasure of imperial oppression is a major part of James's strategy. Within the realm of the empire of God that is governed by the imperial law (cf. James 2:8, νόμον βασιλικὸν), love of neighbor erases systemic oppression (cf. James 2:6, "Is it not the rich who oppress you?").[52] James's subalternity is finding its voice in his nativist rhetoric that resists Roman imperialism. The radical disconnection between the subaltern and Roman imperialism is precisely what James is urging on his recipients. James's implicit representation of Jerusalem and, more importantly, the empire of

50. Gayatri Chakravorty Spivak, "The New Historicism: Political Commitment and the Postmodern Critic," in *The Post-Colonial Critic: Interviews, Strategies, Dialogues*, ed. Sarah Harasym (London and New York: Routledge, 1990), 158.

51. Spivak, "The New Historicism," 158. For Moore's analysis of Spivak, see "Situating Spivak," in *Planetary Loves: Spivak, Postcoloniality, and Theology*, ed. Stephen D. Moore and Mayra Rivera (New York: Fordham University Press, 2011), 13–30 (20).

52. Understanding James as a subaltern, however, does not fully correlate to Spivak's notion of subaltern. Bill Ashcroft, Gareth Griffiths, and Helen Tiffin, "Subaltern," in *Post-Colonial Studies: The Key Concepts* (London and New York: Routledge, 2000), xx, show that Spivak's "point is that no act of dissent or resistance occurs on behalf of an essential subaltern subject entirely separate from the dominant discourse that provides the language and the conceptual categories with which the subaltern voice speaks." The way in which I use the term subaltern for James and his recipients is closer to the definition provided by Spivak's cohorts in the Subaltern Studies collective. Specifically, Ranajit Guha, "On Some Aspects of the Historiography of Colonial India," in *Selected Subaltern Studies*, ed. Ranajit Guha and Gayatri Chakravorty Spivak (Oxford: Oxford University Press, 1988), 35, describes the subaltern as "the general attribute of subordination in South Asian society, whether this is expressed in terms of class, caste, age, gender and office or in any other way." Spivak's enduring contribution to the continued use and transformation of the term pertains to her concentration on the gendered nature of the subaltern, specifically subaltern women. Stephen Morton notes: "By engaging with the historical knowledge of such disempowered women, Spivak expands the original definition of the subaltern, developed by Ranajit Guha and others, to include the struggles and experiences of women," in *Gayatri Chakravorty Spivak*, Routledge Critical Thinkers (London and New York: Routledge, 2003), 59.

God as the center/metropolis has a counter-imperial valence, that is, it de-centers Rome. James's letter, then, is a nativist call to the Diaspora to come home to the "real" center.

The Diaspora Identity

Now that James has been located on the map of first-century Judeanness, I will turn my attention to the recipients of the letter, "the twelve tribes of the diaspora." If James is the subaltern center, then "the twelve tribes of the diaspora" collectively represent the subaltern periphery. The emerging field of diaspora studies has had a tremendous impact on how ancient historians have (re)constructed the Judean diaspora. Engaging this scholarship provides another way of analyzing the recipients of the Letter of James and highlights issues of nativism within the text. Nativism and diaspora are closely related in many of the writings of anticolonialist scholars. This connection between diaspora and nativism within the Letter of James in relation to the author and audience emphasizes the anti-imperial discourse that runs throughout the letter. In order to situate the subaltern periphery, I will start by establishing a theoretical framework for diaspora, then turn to the issues related to the Letter of James as a *Diasporabriefe*. I will then focus on the Letter of James and see how the recipients are characterized in the letter while using the analytical tools provided by current diaspora studies.

Theoretical Framework

Diaspora existence is always defined by both lack *and* doubleness or, to use the term Homi K. Bhabha has popularized to describe the colonial encounter, by hybridity. Diaspora is the situation of being split away from a homeland. In this case, it is an identity of lack or an identity that is missing something of an essential essence. The missing part of diasporic existence is home or homeland.[53] The importance of place in diasporic existence cannot be overstated. Where do those who live in the diaspora fit? Where do their allegiances reside? Diaspora and home/homeland are co-constitutive realities. The doubleness of diaspora is represented by the current place/residency or the place of "not home"/"homeland." Negotiating authentic existence in diaspora necessitates an experience of betrayal in which another identity is accepted or imposed. The cultural interaction within diaspora, then, creates a new identity that is informed by the current locale and, by necessity, it is a hybrid identity; therefore, identity is doubled. The wide spectrum of assimilation, accommodation, acculturation, and enculturation is brought to bear on diasporic existence. What parts of homeland culture are negotiable and what parts are not? Whether modern or ancient, these are some of the cultural issues that arise in diaspora settings and they all have political consequences. Philo of *Alexandria*, *Flavius* Josephus, and Paul of *Tarsus* were all diaspora Judeans who negotiated their diasporic existence in different ways for different reasons. Philo's embassy to Gaius, Josephus's Rome-loyal account of the Jewish revolt, and Paul's frequent imprisonments all exemplify the politics of negotiating diaspora. By addressing the letter to "the twelve tribes in the diaspora," the Letter of James seeks its home within the politics of negotiating diaspora.

53. Although John M. G. Barclay, "Introduction: Diaspora Negotiations," in *Negotiating Diaspora: Jewish Strategies in the Roman Empire* (London and New York: T. & T. Clark International, 2004), 2, argues that "[t]he current intellectual mood is not to regard 'diaspora' as failure or lack, but to celebrate its power to challenge the modernist ideal of the nation-state and to critique its desire for ethnic homogeneity." By "current intellectual mood," Barclay means postcolonial theorists who support the idea of hybridity as subversive rather than critics of such theory, that is, those who wage materialist critiques on such theory from a nativist standpoint like Benita Parry, *Postcolonial Studies: A Materialist Critique* (London and New York: Routledge, 2004).

Diasporabriefe

Labeling the recipients as "the twelve tribes of the diaspora" places the addressees at the margins of Judeanness while at the same time it reifies James's position as the center, which authorizes and authenticates everything that follows. "Diaspora," then, holds more meaning than what most commentators give it. It is not simply a metaphor for "the new Israel worldwide" or "Christians everywhere."[54] Darian Lockett advances a description of the Diaspora here in James beyond the mere metaphorical. He argues that "the ascription of sender and audience in 1.1 must be taken as a significant clue for determining the *world of concerns* and *view of reality* into which this text spoke."[55] Following the "tradition of official letters sent from Jerusalem to diaspora communities," Lockett understands the Letter of James as "a work addressed from a leader in Jerusalem to those living outside Palestine with the intent of bringing exhortation and encouragement to persevere in the face of trial."[56] The *Diasporabriefe* subgenre was fairly common within the experience of Judeanness. According to Donald J. Verseput, "This prevalent notion that Israel's dispersion would one day be overcome by divine deliverance following national repentance echoed repeatedly throughout Second Temple Judaism and beyond and became the occasion for a peculiar subgenre of Jewish epistolary literature to which we may attach the label 'covenantal letters to the Diaspora.'"[57] These "letters to the Diaspora" generally consoled the diasporic communities for having to live among gentiles outside of Jerusalem. From the examples Verseput cites, he concludes that "the diasporic

54. See Davids, *Epistle of James*, 63–64; Johnson, *Letter of James*, 169; Hartin, *James*, 50–51.
55. Lockett, *Purity and Worldview*, 70 (emphasis mine). See also Verseput, "Genre and Story," 99.
56. Lockett, *Purity and Worldview*, 73–74.
57. Verseput, "Genre and Story," 100. See also Lockett, *Purity and Worldview*, 73–76; Bauckham, *James*, 19–21; Tsuji, *Glaube zwischen Vollkommenheit und Verweltlichung*, 18–27; Vouga, *L'Épître de Saint Jacques*, 24–27; 35–37.

existence of the addressees is associated with affliction, while the author of the letter offers instruction and encouragement in the hope of a coming salvation."[58] It is clear from the opening verses of James's introduction that endurance (ὑπομονήν) is a primary subject for James (v. 3). The struggle between God/purity and the world/impurity that characterizes the rhetoric of James is to be endured so that those in the Diaspora may be found pure and undefiled by the world, which is characteristic of *Diasporabriefe*.[59] Purity and its counterpart, perfection, become central themes throughout the Letter of James and function as evidence for the empire of God. In his book *Diasporas*, Stéphane Dufoix argues that "[p]romoting purity is an effective argument, since the community operates on an ideal of continuity with its origin. But traditions are never transplanted in exactly the same way. . . . [T]he purity that must be maintained depends on the near-total absence of 'crossbreeding.'"[60] The δίψυχος, the double-minded, are not the evil empire of the world, but represent those in the Diaspora who have transgressed the boundary between home (the empire of God) and other (the empire of the world). Purity and pollution is the boundary that the whole letter of James polices and patrols.

Beyond this thematic similarity, James also fits within the ethos of other letters to the Diaspora in the sense that it is sent from "an authoritative center, typically Jerusalem."[61] Although the subgenre to which the Letter of James belongs does not identify the *specific* audience of the letter, it helps to contextualize the relationship between author and audience. Homeland, in this relationship

58. Verseput, "Genre and Story," 101.

59. See Tsuji, *Glaube zwischen Vollkommenheit und Verweltlichung*, 18–27; Martin Klein, *"Ein vollkommenes Werk": Vollkommenheit, Gesetz und Gericht als theologische Themen des Jakobusbriefes* (Stuttgart, Berlin, Köln: Kohlhammer, 1995), 185–90.

60. Stéphane Dufoix, *Diasporas*, trans. William Rodarmor (Berkeley: University of California Press, 2008 [French original, 2003]), 74.

61. Verseput, "Genre and Story," 100–101.

between author and addressees, is always Palestine—and the center of that would be Jerusalem. Geography, although it plays an important part in positioning James and his audience, is not the only aspect of the homeland/diaspora binary. Dufoix explains that "[i]n creating a geography without physical territory, dispersion is never so unified as when the local is able to give meaning to the global, and vice versa."[62] For James, this extraterritorial place where the local (represented by James) gives meaning to the global (represented by the Diaspora) is the empire of God, which is governed by the pure and perfect imperial law and mediated through the sayings of Jesus that pepper the entire letter. This extraterritorial place—the empire of God—is the homeland to which James calls the Diaspora.

Subaltern Periphery

Understanding the subgenre of the Letter of James as *Diasporabriefe* fixes James as *the* authoritative center in relation to the diasporic recipients. James's position in the homeland speaks to the lack or loss of culture/piety in the Diaspora and calls the audience to purity and perfection, which is at the core of the center. By confronting the empire of this world as the "non-self," James asserts a "purity in contexts where the prospect of mixing threatens one's uniqueness."[63] The force of the subgenre along with the rhetoric of James may betray its intent. Is there a need for such aggressive rhetoric if those in the Diaspora actually "longed" for a homeland? Were those in the Diaspora comfortable within a heterogeneous cultural situation? James's authority indicates a view from the center. This does not mean the recipients agreed. Social-scientific readings of the Letter of James have certainly contributed to identifying the social situations of the recipients of the letter; however, there continues to be

62. Dufoix, *Diasporas*, 75.
63. Ibid., 93.

considerable disagreement regarding the capacity of scholars to locate the recipients with much specificity.

Recent scholarship concerning the ancient Jewish diaspora may shed some light on this issue. How "at home" were those who lived in the Diaspora? How much did they long for Jerusalem during the period around the time the Letter of James was produced? According to scholars of early Judaism, the sociocultural circumstances of the multifarious diasporic communities were extremely complex. The experience of diasporic communities in Rome was quite different from other communities in areas like Alexandria, so the desire or longing for the homeland varied from one site of diaspora to the next. This challenges scholarly notions about the diaspora as punishment for disobedience, which characterizes diaspora as a site of struggle.[64] Although the Letter of James reflects this sentiment, this does not mean those living in the Diaspora understood themselves in the same way. Sarah Pearce and Siân Jones make this point abundantly clear:

> An important aspect of charting the varieties of Jewish experience and perspective in antiquity is exploring the extent to which our sources reflect identification and affiliation with the Land and, at the same time, to consider the evidence for their expressing a sense of patriotism towards local authorities and communities. This enterprise requires careful attention to the effect of ideological presuppositions which assume, whether from benign motives or not, the controlling influence of Jerusalem on the Diaspora.[65]

While the subgenre *Diasporabriefe* evidences the importance of Jerusalem for the Diaspora, it must be understood as a voice *from the center* in Jerusalem, which includes the Letter of James. The voices

64. See Bauckham, *James*, 11–28; Lockett, *Purity and Worldview*, 70–75; Verseput, "Genre and Story," 99–100.

65. Sarah Pearce and Siân Jones, "Introduction: Jewish Local Identities and Patriotism in the Graeco-Roman Period," in *Jewish Local Patriotism and Self-Identification in the Graeco-Roman Period*, ed. Sarah Pearce and Siân Jones (Sheffield: Sheffield Academic Press, 1998), 16.

from the periphery may sound markedly different, as Pearce and Jones argue: "The existence, however, of other Jewish temples and of forms of Judaism which did not require or even rejected the Temple, together with the lack of evidence for explicit Diaspora reaction to the destruction of the Temple in 70 CE, raise significant questions as to the importance or universal significance of the Jerusalem Temple for Jews."[66]

Philo of Alexandria, for example, considered Alexandria as his *patris* and Jerusalem as his *metropolis*.[67] In this context, "The diaspora Jews, Philo affirms explicitly, live at a distance through no transgression but through the need of an overpopulated nation to send out *apoikiai*."[68] The Diaspora as colonies connects them to Jerusalem as the *metropolis* and constitutes an identity with agency rather than an identity characterized by lack. According to Pearce, Philo's use of ἀποικία is completely indebted to the way in which it was used in Greco-Roman literature: "Greek colonies were indeed independent, but their independence was from their mother-city; they did not think of the mother-city as the true home to which they would ultimately return."[69] At least for Philo, then, Jerusalem was not a homeland that necessitated a return in order to have an authentic identity as a Judean. Pearce concludes that she does "not believe, however, that Philo's mother-city/colony language expresses any sense that Jerusalem is the only genuine home for Jews in contrast with temporary fatherlands or colonies outside Judea."[70] Philo nowhere constructs a "doctrine of return."[71] Although Philo cannot represent

66. Pearce and Jones, "Introduction," 18.
67. *Flacc.* 46; *Legat.* 281.
68. Erich S. Gruen, *Diaspora: Jews amidst Greeks and Romans* (Cambridge, MA and London: Harvard University Press, 2002), 242.
69. Sarah Pearce, "Jerusalem as 'Mother-City' in the Writings of Philo of Alexandria," *Negotiating Diaspora: Jewish Strategies in the Roman Empire* (London and New York: T. & T. Clark International, 2004), 26.
70. Pearce, "Jerusalem as 'Mother-City,'" 36.

the entire Diaspora, he does provide strong evidence that the Diaspora was a much more complex situation than simply a place of "not home." The capacity in the Diaspora for dual allegiance, in fact, may be the rationale for James's aggressive rhetoric of purity and perfection. James's concentration on pure and perfect piety in opposition to double-mindedness and friendship with the world diametrically opposes the local patriotism found in instances like Philo and other forms of diaspora identity negotiation. Assimilation with the world is not tolerated in James's rhetoric of purity, which aggressively confronts any form of cultural hybridity.

The Diaspora in the Letter of James

Within the Letter of James, the recipients are not described in detail, but it is important to see how James constructs his recipients' identity. Besides the prescript that is addressed to "the twelve tribes of the diaspora," James uses the vocative ἀδελφοί repeatedly throughout the letter, which creates fictive kinship. According to Pierre Keith, the use of ἀδελφοί creates a "collective identity" that is characterized by "equality" and reflects a "common belonging to the chosen people," which evokes "reciprocal links of loyalty and solidarity."[72] James often modifies ἀδελφοί with μου ἀγαπητοί, which strengthens the familial ties between the author and recipients. The recipients are not simply "brothers and sisters," they are "deeply loved" by James himself. Statistically, James uses ἀδελφοί more than almost all of the other New Testament writers, which indicates a rhetorical attempt on the part of James to pull his audience close or to call them home.[73] This type of fictive kinship is important in nativist discourse.

71. Gruen, *Diaspora*, 243.

72. Pierre Keith, "Les Destinataires de l'Épître de Jacques," *Foi et Vie* 102, no. 4 (2003): 23.

73. James uses ἀδελφοί fifteen times in 108 verses. Only 1 Corinthians (twenty-two times in 437 verses) and Acts (twenty-six times in 1,002 verses) uses ἀδελφοί more, based on the ratio of usage per verse.

Rhetorically, it creates a close relationship and normalizes it. Although the Negritude movement spanned disparate locations throughout the French-speaking world, Césaire remarks upon the solidarity he found within it: "It was also an affirmation of our solidarity. That's the way it was: I have always recognized that what was happening to *my brothers* in Algeria and the United States had its repercussions in me. I understood that I could not be indifferent to what was happening in Haiti or Africa. Then, in a way, we slowly came to the idea of a sort of black civilization spread throughout the world."[74] In Césaire's case, it did not matter if he knew specific details of what was happening to his "*nègre*" brothers and sisters within the "black civilization spread throughout the world."[75] What mattered for Césaire is that they stood and fought together with a single, unified identity: *négritude*. Césaire found/finds his brothers and sisters in universal negritude. Not dissimilar to Césaire's rhetoric, James uses ἀδελφοί fifteen times. It is coupled with imperatives eleven times (1:2, 16, 19; 2:1, 5; 3:1; 4:11; 5:7, 9, 10, 12), with rhetorical questions three times (2:14; 3:12; 5:19), and with an infinitive construction with imperatival force once (3:10). The solidarity created by fictive kinship is used by James to sternly direct the Diaspora toward a teaching from the center, which may indicate some knowledge about the social situation of the Diaspora on the part of James.

What is clear from James's rhetoric of fictive kinship is that the ἀδελφοί are to be pure and undefiled by the world. According to Keith, this call to separate from the world evidences the fact that "the difficult circumstances imposed by external factors, are presented in the letter primarily in economic terms. . . . It is concluded that at least the strong criticism of the rich is partly based on knowledge of the

74. Césaire, *Discourse on Colonialism*, 92 (emphasis mine).

75. Ibid., 89, adopts "the word nègre, as a term of defiance. . . . There was in us a defiant will, and we found a violent affirmation in the words nègre, and négritude."

situation."[76] Gerd Theissen agrees with Keith and specifies the target of James's rhetoric, however indirect, as the Roman imperial elite: "The attacks against the wealthy, who are outside the community, are indirect attacks against the Roman political elite. A direct attack was impossible, but it is quite possible to do so indirectly because it was easier to blame the wealthy than the representatives of the Empire."[77] The diasporic social situation, according to Theissen's argument, is a contested set of circumstances as evidenced from the rhetoric of James. When James's argument transitions from anti-imperial rhetoric (2:1-13; 3:13-18; and 5:1-6) to focus on the recipients themselves, James drops the ἀδελφοί terminology and addresses the Diaspora in castigating terms: adulteresses (4:4), sinners (4:8), and double-minded (4:8).[78] This transition in address from ἀδελφοί to μοιχαλίδες, ἁμαρτωλοί, and δίψυχοί indicates a transition from anti-imperial rhetoric focused on outside opposition to antihybrid rhetoric focused on inside opposition. The only thing worse than the Roman Empire is those from within the Diaspora who would assimilate imperial culture. Darian Lockett follows Johnson by arguing for a much more cautious analysis of James's rhetoric: "This language does not reflect the social-historical character of the audience, rather it is affective rhetoric."[79] While affective rhetoric does not have the social location of an audience as its main priority, it can provide social data that aids in constructing a "social-historical" location. Lockett's caution, however, raises the question about how

76. Keith, "Les Destinataires," 25.

77. Gerd Theissen, "Éthique et communauté dans l'épître de Jacques: réflexions sur son Sitz im Leben," *Études Théologiques & Religieuses* (2002): 172. Davids, *Epistle of James*, 28–34, and Maynard-Reid, *Poverty and Wealth*, 5–11, portray a similar *Sitz im Leben* for the Letter of James but they do not specify Roman imperialism as the main target of James's invectives against the wealthy.

78. See Lockett, *Purity and Worldview*, 153–54; Johnson, *Brother of Jesus*, 103.

79. Lockett, *Purity and Worldview*, 158.

well James knew his audience and how well scholars can determine that scenario.

This begs the question: How much *did* James know about the diasporic recipients? Richard Bauckham answers this question quite simply: "[L]iving in Jerusalem and in constant contact with Jewish pilgrims from the Diaspora, he [James] will not be ignorant of conditions in the Diaspora or of the Jewish Christian communities in the Diaspora."[80] Bauckham's comment is supported by Paul's account of meeting James and other leaders in Jerusalem in his Letter to the Galatians. Additionally, Paul speaks about a collection for the "poor" in Jerusalem throughout his epistles.[81] This collection has Paul traveling between Jerusalem and the Diaspora throughout his ministry. The connection between James and Paul via Galatians and Paul's collection would be enough to evidence the fact that James received word on the conditions in the Diaspora at least periodically. If the "men from James" in Galatians were officially from James in Jerusalem, then there is additional evidence that James responds to certain circumstances that the Diaspora faced. The evidence in Acts, of James authorizing a letter to the Diaspora in response to Paul's problems, may also contribute to the strength of this argument. In both accounts in Galatians and Acts, James is positioned in Jerusalem as the center of authority and responds to issues in the Diaspora.

Theorizing Diaspora

What is clear from the Letter of James is that the "twelve tribes in the diaspora" were faced with critical identity issues within the larger Roman Empire "where internal and external boundary lines are either ill-defined or precariously weak."[82] John M. G. Barclay

80. Bauckham, *James*, 26.
81. See 1 Cor. 16:1ff.
82. Lockett, *Purity and Worldview*, 76.

agrees: "The multi-locale attachments of diaspora—belonging both *here* and *there*—create an ambiguity of identity, whose particular configurations vary, of course, from case to case."[83] Diaspora is always a highly probable site for cultural assimilation. In fact, Jana Evans Braziel and Anita Mannur argue, "Diasporic subjects are marked by hybridity and heterogeneity—cultural, linguistic, ethnic, national—and these subjects are defined by a traversal of the boundaries demarcating national and diaspora."[84] As a letter to the Diaspora, James attempts to utterly clarify those boundaries and clean up the ambiguities for the Diaspora. In order to clearly define the boundaries, James uses the rhetoric of purity and perfection to define a piety that connects the Diaspora to the homeland and separates them from the world. James uses the authority of the LXX filtered through the Jesus tradition to call the Diaspora to the homeland. In this sense, the "ingathering" of the Diaspora is not to a place as much as to an ideology, that is, to Jesus' interpretation of the Law.[85] This home within the tradition has a *perfect law* that sets the Diaspora *free* from the *world* in which they live (1:25). James places his claim on the Diaspora through this letter. In this sense, Barclay's work is informative: "Diaspora communities are typically sites of contested power, both internal contests over the interpretation of 'tradition,' and contests with the 'host' community or with other diasporas. The power of communities to define themselves and their place within the larger society is tied to their ability to resist the dominant political forces and challenge the cultural power which categorizes them as 'alien.'"[86] James is interpreting the tradition *for* the Diaspora in a way that marks them as "other" in relation to the pervading Greco-Roman

83. Barclay, "Introduction," 2.
84. Jana Evans Braziel and Anita Mannur, "Nation, Migration, Globalization: Points of Contention in Diaspora Studies," *Theorizing Diaspora: A Reader* (Oxford: Blackwell, 2003), 5.
85. See Gruen's discussion of Temple versus Torah, *Diaspora*, 240.
86. Barclay, "Introduction," 3.

culture; thus for James, the Diaspora is the subaltern periphery. James is systematically attacking "Romano-Jewish Identity" not only as "double consciousness" but as "double-mindedness."[87] Rather than celebrating hybridity as cultural leverage, James levels a nativist attack on all forms of assimilation by using the rhetoric of purity and perfection. The way "diaspora" is used in relation to the authorship of the letter, then, creates a binary that signals an anti-imperial decree similar to the cultural antagonism found in other writings such as 4 Maccabees. Closer to the Letter of James, of course, are the references in other New Testament writings to James of Jerusalem writing or authorizing letters to the Diaspora and sending an embassy to the Diaspora, as stated earlier. The politicized geography between Jerusalem and the Diaspora firmly creates a center/margin dichotomy where James functions as the "center" that produces pure and perfect piety.[88] James, then, becomes the model for piety in a reimagined world where Rome has been displaced by the empire of God that now functions as the center.[89]

Purity and Perfection as Characteristic of the Center

After James quickly establishes his center in 1:1, he narrates an annotated table of contents by briefly deliberating on every major theme developed in the letter. Johnson calls verses 2-27 an "*epitome* of the work as a whole" that establishes the polar oppositions that characterize James.[90] Although James 1 may not be a formal epitome

87. Ibid. See also Paul Gilroy, *The Black Atlantic: Modernity and Double Consciousness* (Cambridge, MA: Harvard University Press, 1993).
88. A possible example of this social situation may be found in 1 Corinthians.
89. On the pietàs of the emperor, see Carlos F. Noreña, *Imperial Ideals in the Roman West: Representation, Circulation, Power* (Cambridge: Cambridge University Press, 2011), 73–74.
90. Johnson, *Letter of James*, 175, 83. See also Lockett, *Purity and* Worldview, 93–105; Klein, *"Ein volkommenes Werk,"* 43–45, 119–21; John Hall Elliott, "The Epistle of James in Rhetorical and Social Scientific Perspective: Holiness-Wholeness and Patterns of Replication," *Biblical Theology Bulletin* 23 (Summer 1993): 71–81.

as Johnson proposes, there is a growing consensus among scholars to understand 1:2-27 as an introduction to the letter.[91] However one describes 1:2-27, it is clear that James begins to characterize the center and demarcate it from the ideological other. Throughout James 1:2-27, there are a series of binary opposites that culminate in verses 26-27, which functions as the thematic focus of the entire letter, that is, pure and undefiled piety (θρησκεία καθαρὰ καὶ ἀμίαντος) as opposed to worthless piety (μάταιος ἡ θρησκεία). The rhetoric of purity within this thematic verse that controls the entire letter is significant because it creates the axis on which the entire letter turns. All the oppositions that precede and follow verses 26-27 fall within this rhetorical bifurcation between purity and pollution.

James 1:2-27 Analysis

As James 1:2-27 develops, Manabu Tsuji sees a twofold division "whereby both parts are formally parallel (1:2-12 parallels 1:13-27), since they begin with the topic of temptation and close with a blessing."[92] Tsuji maintains that verses 2-12 create the *Grundmotiv* (primary motive) of the entire letter and verses 13-27 function as the explanation of this primary motive. Within the introductory chapter, James separates the world between worthless piety (v. 26) and pure and undefiled piety that is unstained by the world (v. 27). Recognizing the diaspora as a place of temptation and testing (v.

91. Bauckham, *James*, 72, flatly denies Johnson's use of epitome to describe 1:2-27: "Unfortunately this is inaccurate." Bauckham argues that an epitome circulated as an independent work, which systematically summarized the larger work. The correspondence between 1:2-27 and the rest of the letter is too loose for Bauckham to consider it a formal epitome, but is close enough thematically and structurally to consider it an introduction.

92. Tsuji, *Glaube zwischen Vollkommenheit und Verweltlichung*, 63. Vouga, *L'Épître de Saint Jacques*, 18, agrees with the exception of the division coming between verse 11 and verse 12 rather than between verse 12 and verse 13: "Les deux sections [vv. 2-11 and vv. 12-27] sont construites en parallèle: v. 2-4//12-18, les épreuves et l'endurance; v. 5-8//19-21, reproches sur la sagesse et la parole; v. 9-11//22-25, attitudes face aux riches et aux pauvres." Davids, *Epistle of James*, 22–28, calls it a "double-opening statement." See also Lockett, *Purity and Worldview*, 67–68.

2), James calls his audience to endure (v. 3) the diaspora because this leads to perfection and wholeness (v. 4). In other words, pure piety is characterized as perfect works. The antitheses to the perfect works of pure piety are lack (vv. 4-5), doubt (twice in v. 6), double-mindedness and instability (v. 8), wealth (vv. 9-11), desires, sin and death (v. 14), variation and shadowy change (v. 17), anger (vv. 19-20), filthiness and evil (v. 21), delusion (v. 22), and forgetfulness (v. 24). All these characteristics describe a worthless piety (v. 26) that opposes the pure piety of perfect works that are unstained by the world (v. 27). By the time the reader of James gets to the thematic passages in verses 26-27, it is clear that the rhetoric of verses 2-25 is calling on the Diaspora to make an obvious choice for pure and perfect piety. In every section that follows in the Letter of James, this rhetorical bifurcation is relentlessly employed, that is, pure and perfect piety versus worthless piety stained by the world. With the introduction of ὁ κόσμος in verse 27, the ultimate antithesis is finally revealed. The world and pollution function as the rhetorical other that stands against God and purity. This is the line that separates pure piety from worthless piety.

Postcolonial Analysis

Within the landscape of Roman imperialism, Frantz Fanon's characterization of the colonial world is instructive:

> The colonial world is a Manichean world. . . . As if to show the totalitarian character of colonial exploitation the settler paints the native as a sort of quintessence of evil. Native society is not simply described as a society lacking in values. It is not enough for the colonist to affirm that those values have disappeared from, or still better never existed in, the colonial world. The native is declared insensible to ethics; he represents not only the absence of values, but also the negation of values.[93]

93. Fanon, *The Wretched of the Earth*, 41.

Fanon's disciple, Abdul R. JanMohamed, "uses the uncompromisingly dualistic aspect of the concept [Manichean] to describe the process by which imperial discourse polarizes the society, culture and very being of the colonizer and colonized into the Manichean categories of good and evil."[94] JanMohamed argues that Fanon's definition is "not a fanciful metaphoric caricature but an accurate representation of a profound conflict."[95] The colonial conflict is the utter conquering of natives and native lands as well as the destruction of their culture. By describing natives as morally inferior and in need of colonial help, the Manichean rhetoric provides the "moral" rationale for the colonial endeavor. JanMohamed explains, "If such [colonial] literature can demonstrate that the barbarism of the native is irrevocable, or at least very deeply ingrained, then the European's attempt to civilize him can continue indefinitely, the exploitation of his resources can proceed without hindrance, and the European can persist in enjoying a position of moral superiority."[96] In nativist rhetoric, this Manichean world is affirmed yet upended so that the native gazes back at the colonizer with the same intense disdain. James firmly establishes this nativist reaction to empire by creating immutable differences between worthless piety, that is, the false piety of those who transgress the boundary between God/world, and pure and perfect piety in verses 2-27. James's essentialism does more than simply invert colonial binaries. Benita Parry's appraisal of JanMohamed's positive use of nativism shows how nativist intervention goes beyond inversion of essentialist categories:

94. Ashcroft, Griffiths, and Tiffin, *Post-Colonial Studies: The Key Concepts*, 134.

95. Abdul R. JanMohamed, "The Economy of Manichean Allegory: The Function of Racial Difference in Colonialist Literature," *Critical Inquiry* 12, no. 1 (1985): 59–87 (60).

96. Ibid., 62.

> JanMohamed maintains that each [colonial and nativist] fulfills a different ideological function, the one 'solving' contradictions in order to secure a coherent colonialist world and thereby justify the established ascendency, the other making known the conflicts afflicting this world and through realist representations of Africa's cultures, wiping out the negative and derogatory images purveyed by European literature.[97]

Rather than give in to the temptations of the world and assimilate imperial values, James calls the Diaspora to endure these tests (1:2-4) and shows that it is, in fact, ὁ κόσμος that is utterly polluted and a contaminating force.[98] The call to pure and perfect piety in James is a call to regain an identity of dignity that is being threatened, which is indicative of nativist rhetoric. Parry argues for the strength of this aspect of nativism:

> For colonized and postcolonial cultures traumatized by colonialism, subjected to a "peripeteia of values" culminating in "historical catalepsy," a fiction that recuperates Africa's autonomous resources and reconstitutes the fragmented colonial subject makes an active contribution to the collective aspiration of regaining a sense of direction and identity. Such remembrance does not encourage a passive yearning for reinstalling an unrecoverable past, but is an intercession winning back a zone from colonialist representation.[99]

97. Parry, *Postcolonial Studies*, 28.
98. I explicitly argue for ὁ κόσμος as synonymous with the Roman Empire later in chapter 5. Although the Johannine usage of ὁ κόσμος cannot be folded into the way James uses the term, Adele Reinhartz, "The Colonizer as Colonized: Intertextual Dialogue Between the Gospel of John and Canadian Identity," in *John and Postcolonialism: Travel, Space and Power*, ed. Musa W. Dube and Jeffrey L. Staley, The Bible and Postcolonialism, 7 (London and New York: Sheffield Academic Press, 2002), 179, argues that the connection between the Roman Empire and "the world" in the Fourth Gospel is "slim" and only by "implication." Stephen D. Moore, *Empire and Apocalypse: Postcolonialism and the New Testament*, The Bible in Modern World, 12 (Sheffield: Sheffield Phoenix Press, 2006), 73, takes issue with Reinhartz's "too tentative" analysis and argues for a more explicit connection between "the world" and Rome in the Fourth Gospel: "This assertion depends on a certain assumption, namely, that Rome can reasonably be construed as a major, if unspecified, component of 'the world' (*ho kosmos*) to which the gospel incessantly refers: if 'the world' does not contain Rome—is not, indeed, permeated by Roman power, and for all intents and purposes coextensive with it—then what weight, freight, or purchase could the term possibly have in John's own world?"
99. Parry, *Postcolonial Studies*, 29.

Purity and Perfection

James's "intercession" or intervention revolves around the rhetoric of purity and perfection. By focusing on received tradition from the LXX through the Jesus tradition, James authenticates "the past in producing a counter-discourse."[100] Tsuji's analysis is informative because it not only shows the importance of verses 2-27 for the rest of the letter, but also contrasts one of the major dichotomies in James, that is, *Vollkommenheit* (perfection) and *Verweltlichung* (worldliness/secularization). Johnson agrees, noting that the division between God/perfection and the world/double-mindedness is the primary angst that James addresses.[101] Within chapter 1 alone, τέλειος (complete or perfect) appears four times (twice in v. 4; v. 17; v. 25). Accompanying words that surround and support this idea of perfection are complete/mature/whole (v. 4), pure (v. 27), undefiled (v. 27), and spotless (v. 27). Tsuji recognizes that

> perfection for James is significant, as is apparent in the fact that the concept combines with other important words from the letter (*ergon* 1.4; 2.22; *sophia* 1.5, 17; *pistis* 2.22; *nomos* 1.25, 2.8, 10). One can find this theology of "perfection" from the individual paraeneses as well as from the basic treatises of James where he shows essential aspects of his theology: faith becomes 'perfect' in unity with works (2:14-26). . . . James is marked thus in all parts by the subject 'Christian perfection.'[102]

Although I would not consider the subject necessarily "*christliche*" or strictly theological, as does Tsuji, perfection clearly draws a boundary between opposing forces. This vocabulary definitively establishes the dichotomy that will persist throughout the letter. It is important to notice the characteristics of this binary. Purity and perfection are opposed to lack, doubleness, instability, and overabundance. The

100. Ibid.
101. Johnson, *Letter of James*, 83–87.
102. Tsuji, *Glaube zwischen Vollkommenheit und Verweltlichung*, 53.

rhetoric here is critical because it calls those in the Diaspora to a pure and perfect identity that is found with James (in Jerusalem), who is at the center of piety. By establishing a pure and undefiled identity based on the perfect law of liberty, James produces a nativist discourse that anticipates that of Aimé Césaire. James calls his diasporic readers to a piety that is unstained by the world (v. 27). The concentration on purity and perfection acts as an assault on the world's mixed and mingled amalgam of worthless piety. James strategically essentializes an identity of purity and perfection that confronts an essentialized identity of impurity. This is a classic nativist move that simultaneously reifies colonial binaries and inverts the dichotomy in preference for the marginalized.

James uses τέλειος twice in 1:2-4, which is the opening pericope for the introduction (vv. 2-27). Perfection, here, is the goal for "the twelve tribes in the diaspora." Enduring (ὑπομονή) the temptations (πειρασμοῖς) that exist in the Diaspora produces this kind of perfection and wholeness. In this opening pericope, perfection is contrasted with lack (λείπω), which has an abiding influence on the rest of the letter, as John H. Elliott recognizes: "This contrast between wholeness and incompleteness, further expanded upon in vv. 5-8, introduces a series of such contrasts spanning the letter from start to close, signaling both its structure and its basic thematic . . . and v. 12 restates the proposition concerning the endurance of trials leading to completeness and wholeness announced in vv. 2-4."[103] Perfection and its synonym, wholeness, are congruent with God's generosity in the next verse: "But if some of you lack [λείπω] wisdom, ask of God, who gives to all generously" (v. 5). The connection between perfection and God's generosity is made explicit later in verse 17: "Every good gift and perfect present [δώρημα τέλειον] from above descends from the father of lights, within whom there is no variation

103. Elliott, "Holiness-Wholeness," 72.

or shadowy turning." Here, James connects the concepts of perfection with God, who does not change. The language of "variation and shadowy turning" shows God's stability and immovability. In other words, perfection is stable; it does not shift or fluctuate, and it does not lack anything. Darian Lockett suggests that "[t]he entire group of terms conveying wholeness or perfection stand in opposition to terms relating imperfection or lack of wholeness. . . . In these contexts the author warns against double-mindedness and division as the opposite of wholeness/perfection."[104] Just before James reaches the thematic passage for the entire letter, he revisits "wholeness"/"perfection" in relation to ὁ νόμος, the cradle of James's nativist nostalgia: "But the one who looks into the perfect law of freedom [νόμον τέλειον τὸν τῆς ἐλευθερίας] and remains, is not a hearer of forgetfulness but a doer of works" (v. 25). Again, perfection is placed in an economy of oppositions. Verse 25 is full of important Jamesian terms with perfection characterizing James's authoritative text, that is, the Law understood through the Jesus tradition, which he uses throughout his letter as the foundation for his nativist call to action. If there is a home away from home for the twelve tribes of the Diaspora, it will be found in νόμον τέλειον τὸν τῆς ἐλευθερίας. The use and repetition of perfection with the most important concepts in the letter evidences the severity of perfection for his letter. This is why so many scholars conclude that perfection is the main theme in the Letter of James.[105]

Although perfection is used often in verses 2-25, it is not the only or primary theme in the introduction. It is, however, the drumbeat

104. Lockett, *Purity and Worldview*, 23.

105. Elliott, "Holiness-Wholeness," 71, agrees: "Within this rhetorical structure, the main theme of the letter is stated at the outset (1:3-4) and concerns the issue of completeness and wholeness and its implied opposite, division and fragmentation. This rhetorical analysis coincides with and confirms several studies which have independently identified the central theme of James as that concerning division and wholeness."

that leads to the thematic verses for the entire letter, that is, verses 26-27. The introduction culminates with the distinction between worthless piety (v. 26) and pure and undefiled piety (v. 27). This distinction between modes of pietistic behavior is set within the rhetoric of purity and pollution. Elliott makes this connection between perfection and purity clear although he prefers the terminology of wholeness and holiness. Within James 1:2-27, Elliott recognizes the terminological link between purity and perfection. In verse 21, James admonishes the Diaspora to put away "all filthiness and surplus of evil" (ῥυπαρίαν καὶ περισσείαν κακίας). Filthiness here literally means "physical dirt or filth" and comes within the semantic domains of purity rhetoric. Purity rhetoric, then, is set within the larger section of 1:19-25, where the major dichotomy is between those who forget who they are and become hearers of forgetfulness and those who look into the *perfect* law of freedom and become doers of works. In this passage, perfection and purity rhetoric are combined.[106] Luke Timothy Johnson agrees with Elliott and argues for a clear literary connection between "filthiness" and "purity" in verse 21 and verse 27.[107] As the Letter of James begins to expound on the themes in verses 2-27, the connections between purity and perfection are only strengthened:

> Later in the letter, further instances of division and wholeness are likewise discussed in terms of pollution and purity. An uncontrolled tongue is said to "stain" (*spilousa*, 3:6) the entire body (3:1-12). A divisive, devilish, earthly wisdom is contrasted to a "pure" (*hagne*) and peaceable wisdom from above (3:13-17). In 4:4-10 friendship with the world is declared to be enmity with God (4:4). To draw near to God requires resistance of the devil, cleansing (*katharisate*) one's hands, and "purifying" (*hagnisate*) one's heart (4:7-8). . . . Thus, for James, the

106. For Elliott's full analysis see "Holiness-Wholeness," 72–73.
107. Johnson, *Letter of James*, 201.

wholeness of the community and its members seems to be a function of its holiness and unvacillating commitment to its holy God.[108]

The conceptual connection between purity and perfection is supported further by the lexical connection between these terms. According to Patrick J. Hartin, the term τέλειος in James has its origins in the LXX.[109] In passages such as Exod. 12:5 the Hebrew term *tamim* (תמים) is translated in the LXX as τέλειος: "Your lamb shall be complete/perfect [תמים/τέλειον], a male yearling." Hartin argues that in the context of the "sacrificial worship of Israel . . . one can see the notion of perfection arising."[110] Perfection, according to Hartin, nearly becomes synonymous with purity. In his analysis of James 3:17–18, Hartin makes this connection complete: "In describing the qualities of a life led through the influence of wisdom, James places at the head the adjective 'pure' (ἁγνή). . . . [P]urity originally had a cultic connection and took on the meaning of something that is unblemished. . . . This is exactly what the adjective τέλειος has been used to indicate in other contexts."[111] Hartin's work provides additional connections between perfection and purity, but his analysis may overstate the relationship between these terms at the expense of making them synonymous. As closely related as these terms are in the Letter of James, their relationship deserves more nuance than Hartin provides, especially when these terms are considered to be the thematic lens through which one reads the entire text.

It is important not to conflate purity and perfection within the Letter of James. They are not synonymous terms, however interrelated they may be. Again, Darian Lockett's work is important

108. Elliott, "Holiness-Wholeness," 73.

109. Patrick J. Hartin, *A Spirituality of Perfection: Faith in Action in the Letter of James* (Collegeville, MN: Liturgical, 1999), 22–26.

110. Ibid., 23.

111. Ibid., 73.

in delineating the difference between these terms as well as highlighting their complementary usage. To date, Lockett's research represents the only book-length treatment of purity in the Letter of James. Lockett begins his work by creating a taxonomy of purity language within first-century Judeanness and then applies that taxonomy to James. In the process, he shows how purity and perfection relate within the letter. Following the work of Bauckham and Elliott, Lockett demonstrates how the "language of perfection is connected to the cultic language of purity and pollution."[112] Beyond the lexical connections, purity and pollution are used as conceptual modifiers for the major theme of wholeness and perfection. The connection between purity and perfection is important because, as Lockett observes, "whereas perfection has been identified as the major theme in the epistle, the purity language with which perfection is regularly articulated has not received the attention it deserves."[113] In fact, Lockett argues that one cannot "understand James's concern for perfection without first understanding James's concern for purity from the world."[114] This moves the argument regarding purity in James from the strictly metaphorical usage related to "individual morality or . . . corporate sectarianism" to regarding purity language as concrete or real. Lockett suggests that

> [f]undamentally the language of purity and pollution separates one sphere from another. It is boundary language distinguishing differences and encircling similarities. Purity language, in this way, functions like the lines of a map upon which the core values of an ancient society are charted. . . . Thus purity and pollution must be understood as significant labels functioning as building blocks of a textually created worldview.[115]

112. Lockett, *Purity and Worldview*, 23.
113. Ibid., 25.
114. Ibid.
115. Ibid., 107.

The worldview within the Letter of James, then, is constructed based on James's idea of purity and pollution that draws the lines between perfection and worldliness—a line that was becoming blurry within the Diaspora. In this way, purity functions in the Letter of James, according to Lockett's taxonomy, rhetorically rather than ritually or metaphorically. Rhetorically, purity language "highlights clear areas where readers are in 'danger' of either failing to construct a boundary line or crossing an existing one."[116] The line that James draws is a clear one; it is the line between God (ὁ θεός) and the world (ὁ κόσμος). God is pure and undefiled; the world is filthy and duplicitous. The Diaspora must choose: friendship with God or friendship with the world (4:4). Within this worldview, the world is a contaminating force that prohibits the Diaspora from becoming whole/perfect before God. Purity rhetoric creates and polices the boundaries around perfection.

The sociopolitical ramifications of the rhetorical use of purity and perfection are clear. The subaltern periphery in the Diaspora should reflect the center in Jerusalem and stay "unstained by the world" (v. 27). This is the goal of "pure and undefiled piety." According to Elliott's social-scientific conclusions,

> Cultures variously use purity and pollution schemes in order to organize everything in its proper place, to define and demarcate what is complete or incomplete, who is damaged or whole, sick or sound, what is allowable or forbidden, who belongs to the society and who does not, what preserves the society and what endangers it. Accordingly, to call a person or a social unit impure, unclean, or unholy is to identify and evaluate the object as out-of-order, damaged, incomplete. Correlatively, a pure, clean, or holy object is one judged to be whole, complete, integral.[117]

116. Lockett, *Purity and Worldview*, 139.
117. Elliott, "Holiness-Wholeness," 73.

This is precisely how purity rhetoric in the Letter of James functions. Lockett agrees, arguing that "[t]hese themes [purity and perfection] indicate a rejection of social standards most likely current in the dominant Greco-Roman culture. . . . At face value, it seems that through labeling ὁ κόσμος impure and casting it in opposition to God, the composition is counter-cultural or antagonistic toward the values of Greco-Roman culture."[118] The counter-cultural rhetoric of purity that James employs within the introduction to the letter is enlarged in the major sections that follow. The boundary between God/purity and world/pollution is immutable and permanent in what Fanon calls a perpetual "manicheism delirium" between "Good-Evil, Beauty-Ugliness, White-Black."[119] Within the counter-discourse of nativism, the cultural boundaries are maintained as a source of resistance. Fanon argues that "[r]ediscovering tradition, living it as a defense mechanism, as a symbol of *purity*, of salvation, the decultured individual leaves the impression that the mediation takes vengeance by substantializing itself. . . . The past, becoming henceforth a constellation of values, becomes identified with the Truth."[120] The purity rhetoric in James thus effectively separates the Diaspora from the world of pollution by rediscovering νόμον τέλειον τὸν τῆς ἐλευθερίας through the Jesus tradition.

Analysis of Major Sections of James

Once purity language is conceived as rhetorical rather than ritual or metaphorical, the social dimensions of the community are demarcated. The social dimension of purity rhetoric leads to political consequences when "the world" is equated with the Roman Empire.

118. Lockett, *Purity and Worldview*, 140.
119. Frantz Fanon, *Black Skin, White Masks*, trans. Charles Lam Markmann (New York: Grove, 1967 [French original, 1952]), 183.
120. Frantz Fanon, *Toward the African Revolution: Political Essays*, trans. Haakon Chevalier (New York: Grove, 1967 [French original, 1964]), 42–43 (emphasis mine).

Here, the similarities of purity rhetoric and nativist rhetoric "bear much fruit." In all nativist discourse, there are at least two fronts of opposition: colonial culture and cultural hybridity. Lockett makes the same observation with the way purity language functions in James: "The purity concern in James is to maintain a pure community (in its *internal constitution* and *external boundary*) in the midst of a polluting, antagonistic culture."[121] In James, this two-headed hydra ("internal constitution and external boundary") figures prominently, but at times it is difficult to determine who James is attacking because hybridity, for James, always colludes with empire. In other words, it is hard to differentiate between colonial culture and cultural hybridity, which is precisely the problem that James addresses. Johnson recognizes this vacillation between attacks on empire (outsider) and hybrid (insider), although he certainly does not use postcolonial terminology:

> James challenges insiders concerning the integrity of their lives as insiders. The moral dualism is turned expressly on those who profess 'the faith of Jesus Christ,' yet whose behavior is governed by the measure of 'the world.' . . . So emphatically does James use polemic against outsiders as a criticism of insiders, that it is difficult to be certain concerning the addressees of some passages and their social location.[122]

Structurally, James has a patterned fluctuation between attacking empire and hybridity. After the opening chapter, James immediately confronts empire (2:1-13, partiality toward the rich and the *real* royal law) and then hybridity in two segments (2:14-26, faith/works binary; 3:1-12, speech acts). After this two-part attack, James concentrates his attack on empire and hybridity with what constitutes the center of the letter (3:13-18, heavenly wisdom/worldly wisdom; 4:1-12, friendship with God/friendship with the world). After this

121. Lockett, *Purity and Worldview*, 40 (emphasis mine).
122. Johnson, *Letter of James*, 88.

refutation of "the world," James ends his letter revisiting his attacks on hybridity (4:13-17, critique of itinerant ministry) and empire (5:1-6, condemnation of the rich). James, then, is structured in a pattern of exhortations against empire (2:1-13; 3:13-18; 5:1-6) and hybridity (2:14-26; 3:1-12; 4:1-12; 4:13-17), which cumulatively emphasize James's nativist nature. The lines that James draws in these sections are lines of purity and pollution that distinguish the Diaspora from the polluted "world" in which they live. Strategically, James claims pure and undefiled identity—an essentialist identity—for himself and his audience while producing a filthy and double-minded identity—also an essentialist identity—for his dual enemies.

Rhetoric of Nativism

This kind of essentialism is a hallmark of nativist rhetoric. Césaire, in his famous interview with Haitian militant René Depestre, speaks to how these essentialist categories are created when answering Depestre's question about how the nativist concept of negritude was developed:

> [Negritude] was really a *resistance to the politics of assimilation*. Until that time, until my generation, the French and the English—but especially the French—had followed the politics of assimilation unrestrainedly. We didn't know what Africa was. Europeans despised everything about Africa, and in France people spoke of a civilized and a barbarian world. The barbarian world was Africa, and the civilized world was Europe. Therefore the best thing one could do with an African was to assimilate him: the ideal was to turn him into a Frenchman with black skin.[123]

The entire continents of Africa and Europe are essentialized as civilized and barbarian. This epistemological violence is turned on its head in nativist rhetoric, which is again exemplified by Césaire's characterization of European colonialism:

123. Césaire, *Discourse on Colonialism*, 88 (emphasis mine).

> Between colonizer and colonized there is room only for forced labor, intimidation, pressure, the police, taxation, theft, rape, compulsory crops, contempt, mistrust, arrogance, self-complacency, swinishness, brainless elites, degraded masses. No human contact, but relations of domination and submission which turn the colonizing man into a classroom monitor, an army sergeant, a prison guard, a slave driver, and the indigenous man into an instrument of production. My turn to state an equation: colonization = "thingification."[124]

Here, the European colonizer is the barbarian and all who are complicit with colonialism are "henceforth answerable for the violence of revolutionary action."[125] Césaire strategically uses the essentialized categories of colonialism as a way to resist colonial domination. This is resistance to both colonial culture and cultural hybridity, that is, native assimilation of colonial culture.

Nativism in James as Sectarian Center

It is at this strategic point that I part ways with Lockett. In an attempt to nuance James's argument regarding purity and pollution, Lockett does *not* regard the Letter of James as a sectarian document (although he fails to clearly define and/or nuance what he means by sectarianism). Lockett argues that James confronts an internal and external issue. The external issue relates to James's audience having "taken up the dominant cultural stance of deferring to the wealthy who may be in a position to offer material benefit, at the expense of the poor and socially marginal."[126] The internal issue relates to "slander or misuse of the tongue [which] is deemed a polluting influence. So, the audience is clearly not to assimilate with two *particular aspects* of Greco-Roman culture."[127] At these two fronts,

124. Ibid., 42.
125. Ibid., 55.
126. Lockett, *Purity and Worldview*, 159.
127. Ibid. (emphasis mine).

Lockett argues that James has a rigorist, antiassimilationist stance; therefore, he concludes that James only objects to "the dominant culture" at this level but never becomes "sectarian."[128] Lockett focuses on how James uses "dominant culture" within the writing style of the letter to show that James does not completely reject all of the cultural norms from the Greco-Roman world.

JanMohamed's analysis of native adaption/adoption of colonial language as a mode of resistance acts as a correction to Lockett's argument: "The Third World's literary dialogue with Western cultures is marked by two broad characteristics: its attempt to negate the prior European negation of colonized cultures and its adoption and creative modification of Western languages and artistic forms in conjunction with indigenous languages and forms."[129] From JanMohamed's assessment, I argue that James systematically uses the language of empire to engage a pure piety from the past in a way that reconstitutes an identity of otherness that opposes imperial assimilation. In Spivakian terms, James "catachresizes" colonial language. Ashcroft, Griffiths, and Tiffin call this the "process by which the colonized take and reinscribe something that exists traditionally as a feature of imperial culture."[130] Moore sees this reinscription at work in the Gospel of Mark in the way Mark catachresizes the term *basileia*.[131] James, in fact, uses multiple catachreses when he strategically appropriates and redeploys specific elements of imperial culture.[132] The way James adapts and adopts

128. Lockett, *Purity and Worldview*, 166.
129. JanMohamed, "Economy of Manichean Allegory," 84–85.
130. Ashcroft, Griffiths, and Tiffin, "Catachresis," in *Post-Colonial Studies: The Key Concepts*, 34.
131. Moore, *Empire and Apocalypse*, 37. As we shall see, James catachresizes the same term (*basileia*) in 2:1-13.
132. For examples of how Spivak uses the term catachresis, see Gayatri Chakravorty Spivak, *A Critique of Postcolonial Reason: Toward a History of the Vanishing Present* (Cambridge, MA and London: Harvard University Press, 1999), 14, 251–54. See also Morton, *Gayatri Chakravorty Spivak*, 34–35.

imperial language and culture shows less how James assimilated Roman imperialism, contra Lockett, and more how he used it for his own ends, which were strictly counter-imperial.

This, in fact, is a sectarian move away from dominant culture. For Lockett, James's only antagonism is "at the particular points of patron-client relationships with the 'rich' and inappropriate use of the tongue."[133] In other words, the Letter of James evidences a "high degree of acculturation [with Greco-Roman culture], while showing a low degree of accommodation."[134] While I agree with Lockett that "identifying opponents or enemies of James's audience is rather precarious,"[135] I find it enormously difficult to narrow James's entire argument to two issues and *not* see a broader sectarian argument in other passages in the letter that bifurcate the entire cosmos between God and "the world," that is, wisdom from above/earthly wisdom, friendship with God/friendship with the world, pure and undefiled piety/worthless piety, and so on. In each of those binaries, James is not simply making a rhetorical argument against patronage and slander. Throughout the Letter, James uses the rhetoric of purity and perfection to create two worlds that are diametrically opposed to each other, and the force of the rhetoric calls the audience to choose between the two. As Fanon states: "[T]he plunge into the chasm of the past is the condition and the source of freedom."[136] Fanon's remarks conjure νόμον τέλειον τὸν τῆς ἐλευθερίας. In the process of making this argument, James uses the language and style of the very culture he condemns. Fanon is instructive again: "A man who has a language consequently possesses the world expressed and implied by that language. What we are getting at becomes plain: Mastery of language affords remarkable power."[137] Later, Fanon adds,

133. Lockett, *Purity and Worldview*, 174.
134. Ibid., 169.
135. Ibid., 159.
136. Fanon, *Toward the African Revolution*, 43.

"To speak a language is to take on a world, a culture."[138] Adopting or accommodating the language of empire, in this case, does not necessarily provide Lockett with the proof he needs to argue that James is obviously not sectarian. James's use of Greek is not entirely different than reading Aimé Césaire's surrealist poetry completely composed in literary French. In fact, all three of the patriarchs of the Negritude movement, which was strictly antiassimilationist, wrote and spoke in French (Césaire, Senghor, and Damas). James's skillful use of Greek language and style is Lockett's main reasoning for arguing that James is not a sectarian voice. In the end, Lockett understands the rhetoric of purity and perfection in the Letter of James as "value boundaries" rather than "sectarian separation."[139] Lockett concludes, "The boundary between James's audience and the world is much more complex than an all-out rejection of the world in sectarian fashion."[140] His summary seems almost inexplicable in light of James 4:4, "Adulteresses! Do you not know that friendship with the world is enmity with God? Therefore, if someone wants to be a friend of the world, that one is constituted as an enemy of God." In this crescendo of invective, the rhetoric of purity, "cleanse your hands . . . purify your hearts" (4:8) does more than warn the Diaspora of showing partiality to the wealthy and speaking with integrity. This is a nativist rejection of imperial culture and cultural hybridity that calls the Diaspora to a home within νὸμον τέλειον τὸν τῆς ἐλευθερίας. The sheer force of the rhetoric demands total separation.

137. Fanon, *Black Skin, White Masks*, 18.
138. Ibid., 38.
139. Lockett, *Purity and Worldview*, 183.
140. Ibid.

Conclusion

Historically and politically situating James in first-century Palestine as a Jewish document that creates a pure center of piety places James in direct opposition to the Roman Empire and hybridity. Reading James politically has real significance due to the fact that Josephus narrates James's death by the hand of a factious rival of some sort. This only emphasizes James's Judeanness, especially when one accepts Josephus's word that this caused a major disturbance in Jerusalem. In other words, James's stance against Rome placed him at odds with others within Judeanness. This fact also calls into question the relation between James and Paul, as we shall see. Reading James as a nativist reaction to Rome provides a new way to evaluate how this letter functions antagonistically against Pauline thought.

An edited version of a portion of this chapter ("The Diaspora Identity" section) is published as K. Jason Coker, "Calling on the Diaspora: Nativism and Diaspora Identity in the Letter of James," in *The T. & T. Clark Handbook for Social Identity and the New Testament*, ed. J. Brian Tucker and Coleman A. Baker (London: Bloomsbury, 2014).

PART II

Confronting Colonialism and Hating Hybridity

4

Identifying the Imperial Presence

As James constructs a center based on purity and perfection, he systematically has two distinct adversaries: the Roman Empire and those who assimilate imperial sociopolitical practices. The Roman Empire stands for the absolute other in relation to the kingdom (James 2:5) to which James gives his utter allegiance and implores his readers/hearers to give theirs. James's argument against the Roman Empire finds its strongest vocalization in his condemnation of the wealthy (James 2:1-13; 5:1-6) and his condemnation of earthly wisdom (James 3:13-18). In both cases, James constructs a binary between the wealthy and the poor, and wisdom from above and earthly wisdom. If James's pure and undefiled piety manifests itself in care for the orphan and widow and is unstained by the world (1:27), then the Roman social system of patronage and economic system of landownership represent the world's opposition to his conception of purity. These two rival empires compete for the allegiance of James's audience; therefore, those in the "diaspora" who receive James's letter are either with him or against him. The recipients of the letter are forced to accept the imperatives of James or acquiesce to the values of Roman imperialism. Those who reject James's propositions and assimilate the sociopolitical values of Rome are characterized by James as double-minded (4:8), adulteresses and friends of the world (4:4). Their actions (2:14-26), speech (3:1-12), mind (4:1-12), and plans (4:13-17) are fully corrupted by "the world." This stringent dualism typifies nativist rhetoric. James's arguments fluctuate between anti-imperialism and antihybridity throughout his letter, which gives the letter an overall structure:

A. Anti-imperial argument regarding wealth (2:1-13)
  B. Antihybridity argument regarding faith/action (2:14-26)
    C. Antihybridity argument regarding speech/action (3:1-12)
      D. Anti-imperial argument regarding wisdom (3:13-18)
    C′. Antihybridity argument regarding friendship (4:1-12)
  B′. Antihybridity argument regarding travel itineraries (4:13-17)
A′. Anti-imperial argument regarding wealth (5:1-6)

This structure emphasizes the dual opponents in James's rhetoric. His drive toward purity put him at odds with the overarching sociopolitical structure of his day and only accentuated his frustration with those who assimilated that culture. What follows is an analysis of James's dual argument.

In his exhortations against empire, James concentrates on two aspects of Roman ideation: wealth and wisdom. James 2:1-13 and 5:1-6 deal explicitly with wealth and poverty. In both cases, James is clear that the poor are to be valued due to God's preference for them (2:5) and the wealthy are utterly outside the boundaries of the empire (βασιλεία), which is promised to the poor. James opens the body of his letter by confronting favoritism (προσωπολεμψία) within the community (συναγωγή) based on wealth. The final section of the body of the letter (5:1-6) closes with what may be the harshest critique of the wealthy in the entire New Testament besides Revelation 18.[1] In the language of prophetic literature (e.g., Jer. 5:5-6; Mal. 3:5), James condemns the wealthy and calls them to "weep" and "wail for the miseries that are coming upon" them (5:1). James 2:1-13 and 5:1-6 frame the entire letter with the indictment of the wealthy. It is clear from this *inclusio* that "the wealthy" are the main antagonists in the letter and are the recipients of James's harshest critiques. Patrick J. Hartin agrees, arguing that "[t]his topic of rich and poor is referred to again at the end of the body of the epistle (pericope N 5.1-6) thereby ensuring that the entire body of the epistle forms an inclusio within this consideration of rich and poor."[2] These "wealthy" are also the ones responsible for the "earthly wisdom" (σοφία ἐπίγειος) found in the center of the letter (3:13-18), which is in direct opposition to "wisdom that comes down from above" (σοφία ἄνωθεν κατακαυχᾶσθε). Hartin sees the entire pericope of 2:1-13 as wisdom exposition of sorts that "argues in true wisdom fashion that showing partiality is not reconcilable with faith in Jesus Christ as the Lord of glory. In this context Jesus as the Lord of glory is the source of the wisdom which enables a person to act as a true Christian, for whom showing partiality in dealings with the rich and poor would be totally contradictory."[3] Although Hartin's use of "Christian" may be premature, he makes a strong connection between James 2:1-13 and 3:13-18 relating to wisdom. The wisdom James espouses in 3:13-18 is characterized by purity (ἁγνή) that coincides with his conception of pure piety in 1:26-27. The center of the letter, then, consists of pure wisdom that comes from pure piety and is set against earthy, unspiritual, and demonic wisdom that comes

1. See Pedrito U. Maynard-Reid, *Poverty and Wealth in James* (Maryknoll, NY: Orbis, 1987), 97.
2. Patrick J. Hartin, *James and the Q Sayings of Jesus* (Sheffield: Sheffield Academic Press, 1991), 89.
3. Ibid., 90.

from the world. That "earthly wisdom" is characterized by "bitter jealousy" (ζῆλον πικρὸν), "selfish ambition" (ἐριθείαν), "boasting" (κατακαυχάομαι), "lying" (ψεύδομαι), "disorder" (ἀκαταστασία), and "all evil deeds" (πᾶν φαῦλον πρᾶγμα) indicates that James has in mind the same opponents as in 2:1-13 and 5:1-6. It is the wisdom of the "wealthy" world that James criticizes in 3:13-18. These three sections make up James's anti-imperial discourse as we shall see below.

The type of terminology that James employs to combat enemies in these passages reflects nativist resistance. In constructing the ultimate other, James positions himself as pure, peaceful, gentle, reasonable, full of mercy, impartial, and sincere (3:17). The fact that purity is the first of these characteristics connects the center of the letter to the theme of the letter (1:26-27) and pervades James's entire discourse. Purity stands against impurity; good stands against evil (4:7). This form of binary rhetoric is not unique to James or his ancient milieu. Significantly for our analysis, it also fueled the kinds of modern decolonizing movements exemplified in the writings of Frantz Fanon. In his depiction of colonizers and colonized as two different "species" of humanity, Fanon maintains that "decolonization is the meeting of two forces, opposed to each other by their very nature, which in fact owe their originality to that sort of substantification which results from and is nourished by the situation in the colonies."[4] He adds later, "The colonial world is a world cut in two."[5] Similar binary rhetoric is enforced throughout the Letter of James. There is no third option for James. Either there is pure piety (1:26-27), divine partiality for the poor (2:1-13), and wisdom from above; or there is no piety, partiality for the wealthy, and earthly wisdom. James's colonial world is also a "world cut in two." Fanon explains

4. Frantz Fanon, *The Wretched of the Earth* (New York: Grove, 1963), 36.
5. Ibid., 38.

this divided world in the language of early Christian heresiology, as we have seen, by adopting and adapting the term "Manicheism." The colonizer describes the colonized as absolutely other and develops a body of knowledge that defines the "native" or colonized.[6] Roman adoption of "barbarian" as a way to hegemonically describe non-Roman existence created the cultural boundary between Roman and Other.[7] The use of this kind of rhetoric by the colonizer "paints the native as a sort of quintessence of evil."[8] The nativist move is to accept these essentialized categories and invert the binary by championing nativist values and morals. This is precisely the move that James makes by affirming God's preference for the poor in direct contradiction to common social preference for the wealthy, which amounts to the incompatibility between wisdom from above and earthly wisdom.[9] In this divided world,

> The settler's work is to make even the dreams of liberty impossible for the native. The native's work is to imagine all possible methods for destroying the settler. On the logical plane, the Manicheism of the settler produces a Manicheism of the native. To the theory of the "absolute evil of the native" the theory of the "absolute evil of the settler" replies.[10]

The values of empire, then, become a mockery of values: "The violence with which the supremacy of white values is affirmed and the aggressiveness which has permeated the victory of these values over the ways of life and of thought of the native mean that, in revenge, the native laughs in mockery when Western values are

6. Fanon's emphasis here sows the seeds of Edward Said's work *Orientalism* (New York: Vintage, 1978).
7. See Iain M. Ferris, *Enemies of Rome: Barbarians through Roman Eyes* (Thrupp, Stroud, Gloucestershire, UK: Sutton, 2000), for examples.
8. Fanon, *Wretched of the Earth*, 41.
9. Greco-Roman patron/client and honor/shame cultural norms.
10. Fanon, *Wretched of the Earth*, 93. See also my previous reference in chapter 3 to Fanon's Manicheism, *Black Skin, White Masks*, trans. Charles Lam Markmann (New York: Grove, 1967 [French original, 1952]), 183.

mentioned in front of him."[11] Analogously, James claims a divided world and endorses his nativist position with imperatival force.

Wealth and Poverty within Imperialism (James 2:1-13): Alternative Empire

James opens the body of his letter (2:1–13) with a warning against showing partiality to the wealthy. The pericope is divided into two sections (vv. 1-7 and vv. 8-13) connected by the conjunction μέντοι that creates an emphatic position between the first two conditional sentences of the second section (vv. 8-9).[12] There is also a shift in the class of conditional sentences that happens in verse 8, which indicates a rhetorical shift. After the introductory sentence in verse 1, James uses a third class conditional sentence (v. 2) that controls the rest of the passage until verse 8,[13] where a series of three (vv. 8, 9, and 11) first class conditional sentences are employed that subtly change the topic of the pericope.[14] Verses 1-7 deal specifically with what kind of partiality is acceptable in the kingdom, while verses 8-13 highlight the laws of the kingdom that support that thesis.

James 2:1-7: Imperial Partiality

In the opening address of chapter 2, James identifies his addressees as the "brothers" (ἀδελφοί) and this construction is commonly accompanied by the possessive pronoun "my" (μου).[15] How this

11. Fanon, *Wretched of the Earth*, 43.
12. Luke Timothy Johnson, *The Letter of James: A New Translation with Introduction and Commentary*, Anchor Bible, 37A (New York: Doubleday, 1995), 230, sees this construction between μέντοι in verse 8 and δὲ in verse 9 as indicating a heightened opposition rather than translating as an adversative conjunction. In this case, the translation would be "If you really (μέντοι) perfected. . . . But (δὲ) if you show favoritism."
13. This is a classical third class conditional sentence with ἐὰν as the conjunction followed by the protasis in the subjunctive mood (εἰσέλθῃ) and the apodosis in any mood and tense—in this case aorist, passive, indicative: διεκρίθητε (v. 4).
14. Verses 8, 9, and 11b all use the conjunction *ei* followed by present, indicative protases, which indicates first class conditional sentences.

familial construction relates to the Diaspora is important in order to understand the relationship between James and his addressees. There is a certain tension between the distance created by using the term διασπορά and the closeness created by using the familial term ἀδελφοί. In other words, is ἀδελφοί a technical term that does not necessarily connote closeness, or does James move from the general διασπορά to specific ἀδελφοί? Already, James has used ἀδελφοί throughout his introductory chapter (vv. 2, 9, 16, and 19) and couples it with "beloved" in most cases (see ἀγαπητοί in vv. 16 and 19). The use of "beloved brothers" creates an inside language that places the addressees in a favorable position with James. Within the pericope of 2:1-13, James uses this familial vocabulary twice (vv. 1 and 5). In this case, James is pulling the marginal διασπορά into his cultural center thereby creating an indispensable connection. James is not at the center of pious life by himself. With the use of this familial love language, or fictive kinship, the addressees are among the family of James in spite of their diasporic existence. This familial unity is similar to Fanon's conception of the unity needed for decolonization: "Decolonization unifies that people by the radical decision to remove from it its heterogeneity, and by unifying it on a national, sometimes a racial, basis."[16] Family language, or fictive kinship, functions as this type of unifying effort; however, the addressees' capacity to follow James's teaching will determine if they will be able to stay within this familial setting. The familial love language also tempers the force of the imperatives used throughout the letter, which comes immediately to the fore in 2:1: μη . . . ἔχετε.

The first imperative in 2:1 indicates that favoritism was not acceptable in Jesus' faith. The use of the genitive form for τοῦ κυρίου

15. I prefer to keep the gender-specific language throughout in order not to ignore the androcentrism within the Letter of James.

16. Fanon, *Wretched of the Earth*, 46.

ἡμῶν Ἰησοῦ Χριστοῦ τῆς δόξης has various translations, but the most critical aspect of this genitive construction is whether it should be understood as objective or subjective in relation to τὴν πίστιν. In other words, does this phrase mean "the faith *of* our Lord, Jesus Christ" (subjective) or "the faith *in* our Lord, Jesus Christ" (objective)? The fact that this is one of only two references to Jesus in the entire letter, coupled with the fact that this is the first sentence of the body of the letter, indicates that what is communicated here is of primary importance. From the context, James seems to be using Jesus' faith as an example for his addressees. In this case, the subjective genitive would be the preferred translation since James is not referencing "the brothers'" faith but Jesus'.[17] In other words, there is no evidence that Jesus showed favoritism to the wealthy; therefore, the ἀδελφοί should not show favoritism to the wealthy. That James uses the Jesus tradition to denounce favoritism, and later, the wealthy (5:1-6), evokes *the faith of* Jesus as antielite, antiaristocratic, and anti-imperial. Richard Horsley's politicized conception of Jesus fits this view quite well: "Once we 'take the Gospel whole,' it is clear not only that Jesus spearheaded a program of renewal of the people. He also pronounced God's judgment on the people's rulers, on the Romans themselves as well as on their Jerusalem rulers, the face that the Roman imperial order presented to the people of Palestine."[18] Most scholars agree that James accesses the Jesus tradition, but they widely disagree about how much James *specifically* references the tradition. Patrick J. Hartin argues that there are at least twenty-six references to the Jesus tradition in the 108 verses that make up the Letter of James, while

17. Johnson, *Letter of James*, 220, convincingly shows that "faith" in James is always directed toward God, even the faith "of Jesus." Also, the constant "use of Jesus' sayings throughout the composition suggests a meaning like 'the faith of Jesus in God as reflected in his teaching,' or perhaps 'the faith that is from Jesus Christ,' in the sense 'declared by Jesus.'"

18. Richard A. Horsley, *Jesus and Empire: The Kingdom of God and the New World Disorder* (Minneapolis: Fortress Press, 2002), 79.

John S. Kloppenborg believes that "James is drawing on Q itself."[19] The "Gospel whole" to which Horsley refers, in fact, includes both Q and Mark:

> Although God's condemnation of the rulers may not seem as prominent in the Q sequence of speeches as in Mark's Gospel, the particular speeches that pronounce the judgment or exclusion of the rulers explicitly link that judgment with the coming/presence of the kingdom of God. The kingdom of God is the overarching theme that encompasses Jesus' prophetic condemnation of oppressive rulers as well as his prophetic renewal of Israel.[20]

Since James uses "empire" (βασιλικὸν) terminology as the alternative empire to Rome in 2:8, it is clear that the Jesus tradition James uses, and the faith of Jesus that James holds as a model for the ἀδελφοί, is none other than an anti-imperial faith and anti-imperial Jesus as we shall see below.[21] This specific reference to Jesus—the only specific reference to Jesus in the body of the letter—immediately precedes James's critique of favoring the wealthy over the poor. According to James's rationale in 2:1-7, the faith of Jesus would favor the poor over the wealthy ("Has God not chosen the poor [πτωχοὺς] . . ." [2:5]), which conjures Q 6:20: "Blessed are [[«you»]] poor [οἱ πτωχοί], for God's reign [ἡ βασιλεία τοῦ θεο] is for you."[22] The faith of Jesus, then, literally *works* for the poor rather than the rich, and functions as a model for how the ἀδελφοί faith is supposed to work, which foreshadows James's faith/works argument (2:14-26) that immediately follows this pericope: "If a brother or

19. Hartin, *James and the Q Sayings*, 140–98; John S. Kloppenborg, *Q, the Earliest Gospel: An Introduction to the Original Stories and Sayings of Jesus* (Louisville and London: Westminster John Knox, 2008), 114.
20. Horsley, *Jesus and Empire*, 78.
21. An expanded argument for James's conception of the "empire of God" being diametrically opposed to "the world," that is, the Roman Empire, is found later in chapter 5, the first section, where I analyze James's opposition between God and the world in terms of friendship.
22. Kloppenborg, Q, 125. Peter H. Davids, *The Epistle of James: A Commentary on the Greek Text* (Grand Rapids: Eerdmans, 1982), 47, makes a direct parallel between James 2:5 and Q.

sister is naked and lacks daily food, and one of you should say to them, 'Depart in peace, stay warm and be filled,' but do not give them bodily necessities, what use is that? So, indeed, faith, if it has no works, is dead by itself." Modeling the faith of Jesus, places the ἀδελφοί in opposition to the wealthy elite, who oppress them, drag them to court, and blaspheme the name by which the ἀδελφοί are called (2:6-7). Throughout the letter, when James draws on the Jesus tradition, it is always in utter opposition to Roman imperialism.

It is clear from the context that favoritism *to the wealthy* is the controlling issue in 2:1 and not favoritism *in general*. The illustration used in verses 2-5 emphasizes the indignity of showing favoritism to a "man wearing a gold ring and splendid clothing" rather than a "poor person in shabby clothing." Favoritism to the wealthy is then placed in absolute contrast to 2:5, where James calls to "the beloved brothers" with another imperative, and insists that God favors "the poor in the world" with the rhetorical question: "Listen, my beloved brothers, has God not chosen the poor in the world to be rich in faith and heirs of the kingdom which he promised to those who love him?" (2:5). The "beloved brothers" are called to choose the poor just as God has; therefore, favoritism is actually given toward the poor in "the kingdom" to which they are heirs. In this way, James condemns his "brothers" at the beginning of verse 6—"But you dishonor the poor"—because they have shown favoritism to the wealthy. Verses 6 and 7 end with three rhetorical questions that condemn the wealthy: "Don't the wealthy oppress you and don't they drag you into court? Don't they blaspheme the good name by which you are called?" The implied answer is an emphatic, "Yes!"[23] The wealthy do not deserve favoritism since their actions directly hurt James's addressees.

23. The use of οὐχ in verse 6 and οὐκ in verse 7 coupled with indicative verbs in both constructions demand a positive response: "Do the wealthy not oppress you? Do they not blaspheme?" The answer is emphatic: "Yes, they do!"

In the opening passage of the letter's body, James delcares that the poor are chosen by God and demand a place of honor among the assembly. He also emphasizes the fact that the wealthy do not deserve favoritism; rather, they are the ones who oppress, drag into court, and blaspheme. In other words, the poor are prized in James's kingdom rather than the wealthy.

There are two questions that need to be addressed before the second section of this pericope is analyzed. First, who are the poor (πτωχοί) and the wealthy (πλούσιοι) that James references in 2:1-7? Second, what does James mean by the world (κόσμος) and kingdom (βασιλείας)? Scholars disagree on whether James references an actual *social* event in 2:2-4 or whether he creates a *rhetorical* situation. Whether real or rhetorical, these verses highlight a socially acceptable way of understanding wealth and poverty in the Greco-Roman world based on patron-client relationships. Steven J. Friesen understands 2:1-7 as a critique of this "dominant social system" that tried "to distance fellow synagogue members from this status system based on wealth. . . . Normal social interaction that showed honor to someone simply because he or she was rich was wrong."[24] The patron-client system provides a possible social situation that is recounted in 2:1-7. According to this social system, it was a matter of honor for the wealthier members of society to act as patrons to the poorer or lower-standing members of society. In a zero-sum economy where resources were limited, access to the resources of the patron made life possible for the client.[25] The πτωχοί in James are so impoverished they are utterly outside this social system, without any access to patron resources. The poor, then, are people who

24. Steven J. Friesen, "Injustice or God's Will? Early Christian Explanations of Poverty," in *Wealth and Poverty in Early Church and Society*, ed. Susan R. Holman (Grand Rapids: Baker Academic, 2008), 24.

25. See David Hutchinson Edgar, *Has God Not Chosen the Poor? The Social Setting of the Epistle of James* (Sheffield: Sheffield Academic Press, 2001), 118–19.

actually lived in poverty rather than a "pietistic poor" or those who gave up their possessions for an ascetic lifestyle. Scholars such as David Hutchinson Edgar understand "the poor" as a spiritual office rather than impoverished people. Although Edgar's social analysis of James is helpful in many areas, there is no reason to connect the πτωχοί here with any form of "radical itinerant followers of Jesus."[26] Contrary to Edgar's thesis, Maynard-Reid insists that the πτωχοί are the actual economic poor. In his social-scientific study of James, Maynard-Reid finds nothing "in the illustration [2:2-4] to indicate that James is dealing with poverty in a pietistic sense."[27] The double accusative that is used in 2:5 to describe "the poor in the world" who are "rich in faith" supports Maynard-Reid's proposition. In this sentence, τοὺς πτωχοὺς functions as the direct object of the verb while the second accusative πλουσίους complements the first (πτωχοὺς) by predicating something about it; therefore, it acts as a predicate adjective, which necessitates a verbal construction using "to be." Literally, the poor are rich. There are two dative constructions that modify both of these accusative nouns that change this simple reversal: The poor in the world (τῷ κοσμῳ) are rich in faith (ἐν πίστει). Maynard-Reid interprets the dative case of τῷ κοσμῳ as "a local dative of place—it is the economic poor who are spatially in the world."[28] The dative construction ἐν πίστει, then, would be taken as a dative of reference. In this case, 2:5 would translate as "Listen, my beloved brothers, has God not chosen the poor who live in this world to be rich in reference to faith?" The poor in James 2:1-7, then, are the economic poor that constituted the majority of the population of the Greco-Roman world.[29]

26. See ibid., 107–14.
27. Maynard-Reid, *Poverty and Wealth*, 58–59.
28. Ibid., 62.
29. See Friesen, "Injustice or God's Will?," for an analysis of the economic inequality in the early Roman Empire. In his poverty scale percentages, 90 percent of the population that lived in the

The wealthy (οἱ πλούσιοι) in James 2:1-7 would then be the ruling elite. As I shall argue below, in James's Judean context, and in any Mediterranean context in the first century, the ruling elite would either be Roman governors or local elites that were complicit with Roman imperialism. In either case, οἱ πλούσιοι would be intimately connected to the Roman Empire. Ingeborg A. K. Kvammen understands the wealthy person wearing gold rings and good clothes in verse 2 as a Roman from the equestrian order.[30] This is significant because her work is the only book-length study on James and postcolonialism, so her optic for reading James emphasizes every aspect of empire. Although her analysis is entirely focused on James 2:1-13, her study stands alone as the single book-length postcolonial analysis on any section of James. In this interpretive process, Kvammen pays close attention to "markers of social affiliation" and "visible signs of social status," as these relate to "Roman etiquette."[31] The gold rings and good clothes of the wealthy person in James 2:1-13 are social symbols that represent the equestrian order in Roman society. This would have placed these rich among the highest-ranking people in the Roman imperial order. Gold rings, in particular, specifically marked the equestrian rank. Both Pliny the Elder and Suetonius make specific reference to the gold ring of the equestrian rank. In fact, Pliny the Elder speaks of over 400 people who were convicted in the judicial system for fraudulently obtaining a gold ring of equestrian rank.[32] When the equestrian order was incorporated, the gold ring was determined to be their status marker

early Roman Empire lived at or below "near subsistence." He argues that, according to James, "if the synagogue operates according to the normal standards of social status by showing honor to the wealthy and disrespect or neglect to the poor, then they are contradicting the faith of their Lord Jesus Christ," 18–21, 24.

30. See Ingeborg A. K. Kvammen, "Imperial Presence in the Assembly: An Interpretation of Jas 2:1-13 with a Postcolonial Optic" (Ph.D. diss., School of Mission and Theology, 2008), 65–67.
31. Kvammen, "Imperial Presence in the Assembly," 68.
32. See Pliny the Elder, *N.H.* 291.

by law, so "[a] rule was therefore imposed that no one should have the right to wear a ring unless he himself as well as his father and grandfather, was free-born, had capital assets amounting to 400,000 sesterces, and, under Julian law relating to the theatre, possessed a seat in the first fourteen rows."[33] These rings, according to Pliny the Elder, "clearly introduced a third order between plebeians and the Senate; the title of 'knight' [equestrian]."[34] Suetonius confirms Pliny's remarks when describing a misunderstanding between Julius Caesar and his troops. Caesar pointed to the finger on his left hand and "declared that he would gladly reward those who championed his honour with the very ring on his finger," but some soldiers who were standing far away, and could see Caesar better than they could hear him, thought the gesture was a promise of equestrian order, which would give them "the right to wear a gold ring and the 400,000 sesterces that went with it."[35] In both cases, the importance and legal demands of the gold ring intimately connect it with equestrian rank.

Kvammen questions whether the social positioning of the wealthy "can be understood as partiality (προσωπολημψία)" in James 2:1-13.[36] Gerd Theissen answers Kvammen's question in the affirmative: "Now James knows, according to ancient tradition, the entrance of rich people into the community makes them 'patrons' of the community, and makes the communities clients of these patrons. Such patrons are nothing other than wealthy householders. James vehemently protested against their influence, saying that nobody should be favored or opposed. The beggar in rags must be as well accepted in the community as the wealthy."[37] Although Theissen

33. Pliny the Elder, *N.H.*, trans. John F. Healy (London: Penguin Books, 1991), 290.
34. Pliny the Elder, *N.H.*, 289.
35. Suetonius, *The Twelve Caesars*, trans. Robert Graves (London: Penguin Books, 2007), 16.
36. Kvammen, "Imperial Presence in the Assembly," 68.
37. Gerd Theissen, "Éthique et communauté dans l'épître de Jacques: réflexions sur son Sitz im Leben," *ETR* 77, no. 2 (2002): 166–67.

nowhere equates the wealthy patron in 2:1-13 with an equestrian, he certainly understands James's critique of partiality as a critique of the whole patronage system—the precise move Kvammen makes. Under Augustus's imperial reforms, the equestrian order was given official status and the capacity to hold offices throughout the empire. In order to be categorized as an equestrian, one had to be wealthy. According to Keith Hopkins, "The senators and equestrians each wore distinctive dress, and between them filled the most important and honorific governmental posts. It seems especially significant that other orders depended upon a minimum property holding and election. In the aristocracy these requirements were reinforced by the competitive demands of ostentatious expenditure. The major source of income was land."[38] It is important to note that the equestrian order were wealthy, wore distinctive dress, and their primary income came from landownership. All three of these characteristics are specifically condemned in 2:1-13 and 5:1-6. Garments and accessories were not simply for decoration; they were specifically symbolic of one's rank in Roman society. Only Roman citizens could wear togas and tunics, whereas gold rings specifically marked the equestrian order.[39] There were various types of togas that represented the different ranks. For example, the *toga candida* was a bleached white wool outer garment that symbolically represented someone who was a political candidate and could only be worn by those in the senatorial or equestrian ranks.[40] The tunic, worn under the toga, also represented social difference among the elite ranks. The senatorial tunic had a broad purple stripe as is evidenced in Suetonius's

38. Keith Hopkins, "Elite Mobility in the Roman Empire," *Past and Present* 32 (1965): 12.

39. See Kvammen, "Imperial Presence in the Assembly," 80. For an extended analysis of Roman clothing, see Jonathan Edmondson and Allison Keith's edited volume *Roman Dress and the Fabrics of Roman Culture* (Toronto, Buffalo, and London: University of Toronto Press, 2008). These essays brilliantly demonstrate how clothing functioned as social control, gender boundaries, and identity markers in the late Republic and early Empire.

40. See Kvammen, "Imperial Presence in the Assembly," 81–82.

recollection of Vespasian's senatorial candidacy: "For years he postponed his candidature for the broad purple stripe of senatorial rank."[41] Likewise, clothing was also representative of the abject poor. Those without an outer garment had the lowest social rank. Kvammen concludes that "[a] member of the equestrian order would be recognised by his gold ring and his tunic with an *angustus clavus*. He could also wear a *toga candida*, if he was a candidate for political office. Poor persons on the other hand would be recognised by their lack of garments or by their unclean garments. Hence, clothing mattered because through garments rank, status and wealth were on display."[42] In addition to garments and jewelry, seating privileges were also reserved for those with a high status. Again, Suetonius offers an example of these seating privileges when describing some of Augustus's reforms:

> If insufficient candidates of senatorial rank presented themselves for election as tribunes of the people, Augustus nominated *equites* to fill the vacancies, but allowed them, when their term of office had expired, either to remain members of the equestrian order or to become senators, whichever they preferred. Since many *equites* had lost so much money during the civil wars that they no longer possessed the property qualifications of their rank, and therefore refrained from taking their seats in the fourteen rows reserved for their order, he announced that anyone who had once been an *eques* or was the son of an *eques* was not liable to punishment under the law governing theatres.[43]

Although Suetonius specifically references seats at the theater, Pliny the Elder shows that these seating privileges extended to the circus as well when Nero "added seats for the knights [equestrians]."[44] Kvammen argues that these seating privileges in public were

41. Suetonius, *The Twelve Caesars*, trans. Robert Graves (London: Penguin Books, 2007), 97.
42. Kvammen, "Imperial Presence in the Assembly," 83.
43. Suetonius, *The Twelve Caesars*, 65–66.
44. Pliny the Elder, *N.H.*, trans. John F. Healy (London: Penguin Books, 1991), 111. Suetonius, *The Twelve Caesars*, trans. Robert Graves (London: Penguin Books, 2007), 212, references Nero's

extended to the private sector as well in the form of banquet seats: "It is probable that a Roman senator or equestrian would be given an honourable seat wherever he came, whereas slaves, women, freedmen and poor likewise would be given a less honourable seat. This was Roman etiquette. Anything else would have been an insult. Thus again we see that seating at official, semi-official and even private occasions represented a display of honour, shame, rank, status and wealth."[45]

This partiality to the wealthy in Roman etiquette stands in stark relief to the "faith of Jesus" to which James calls the ἀδελφοί. James 2:2-5 reads as an illicit anti-imperial critique of the Roman patronage system:

> If a person with a gold ring wearing bright clothing should come into your synagogue, and a poor person in dirty clothing should also enter, and you favor the one wearing bright clothing and say, "You sit here in a good place," and to the poor you say, "You stand there or sit under my footstool," have you not made distinctions among yourselves and become judges with evil reasoning? Listen, my beloved brothers, has God not chosen the poor in the world to be rich in faith and heirs of the empire/kingdom that is promised to those who love him?

By systematically and emphatically choosing the poor as inheritors of the kingdom, James reaches into the Jesus tradition to show the utter reversal motif of the wealthy and poor. Without quoting Jesus, James clearly shows that "the last shall be first" and the "poor shall inherit the kingdom." The sociopolitical implications of "the faith of Jesus" for the ἀδελφοί would be tantamount to revolt. If Jesus was crucified as a Roman antagonist, then his brother, James, seems to be following in his brother's footsteps. As an opening to the body of the letter, James wastes no time getting to his point, that is, the Jesus tradition calls the

addition of equestrian seats as well: "He reserved seats for the *equites* at the Circus, and actually raced four-camel chariots!"

45. Kvammen, "Imperial Presence in the Assembly," 84.

ἀδελφοί to an anti-imperial faith that completely overturns the social system of patronage that was a hallmark of the Roman Empire. In this way, the Jesus tradition, for James, functions as the complete opposite of the Roman Empire.

As a counter-discourse to imperial "etiquette," to use Kvammen's term, James resembles more modern forms of anti-imperial discourse. Referencing the Jesus tradition is a way to remind the ἀδελφοί of the historic movement to which they belong. There are many similarities between James's nostalgic references and nativist independence movements in modernity. Paul Gilroy captures the "essence" of this essentialism: "At present, they remain locked symbiotically in an antagonistic relationship marked out by the symbolism of colours which adds to the conspicuous cultural power of their central Manichean dynamic—black and white. These colours support a special rhetoric that has grown to be associated with a language of nationality and national belonging as well as the languages of 'race' and ethnic identity."[46] James enforces a similar rhetorical binary throughout his letter that differentiates the diaspora/ἀδελφοί from the world/πλούσιοι. In this way, James produces a discourse that Gilroy problematizes—in fact, refutes—with his concept of the black Atlantic world. This discourse of "ethnic absolutism" functions as nativist rhetoric in the letter of James, and is in full relief in the opening pericope of the body of the letter, that is, the faith of Jesus and the empire of God versus the world and the Roman Empire.[47]

While Kvammen's analysis is helpful in connecting the rhetoric of James 2:1-13 with Roman imperialism proper, Richard Horsley

46. Paul Gilroy, *The Black Atlantic: Modernity and Double Consciousness* (Cambridge, MA: Harvard University Press, 1993), 1–2.

47. Gilroy constantly refutes the concept of "ethnic absolutism" because it essentializes identity in ways that prohibit solidarity. He critiques movements such as negritude for too narrowly defining identity. His concept of the "Black Atlantic" is an attempt to create an identity of shared experience rather than any precolonial African culture, which is why he is so opposed to nativism. See Gilroy, *The Black Atlantic*, 3.

reminds us that "[t]he face that Roman imperial rule presented in Palestine was that of its client rulers, the Herodian 'tetrarch' Antipas in Galilee and in Judea the high priests based in the Temple in Jerusalem."[48] This is all the more important considering Josephus's account of James's death at the hand of the high priest Ananus. James's critique of the patronage system, while an anti-imperial critique, would certainly include the wealthy elite in Palestine. Horsley's analysis of the "representation of Jesus in Q and Mark suggests some significant generalizations about the historical Jesus' opposition to the Temple and high priesthood."[49] This is the tradition that James adopts and uses in his nativist rhetoric against empire. In this way, Horsley is correct when he concludes that "Mark and Q offer us results of how Jesus' speech and action affected and took on significance for his followers in a particular historical situation as they referenced Israelite tradition."[50] James is not merely one of these followers, he is the inheritor of the movement; therefore, the ruling elite in Palestine would be understood as the embodiment of Roman imperial values and etiquette. They are quintessentially the Roman κόσμος.

The connection between οἱ πλούσιοι and Roman imperialism has serious implications for the referent of κόσμος in James. James uses the term κόσμος five times in his letter (1:27; 2:5; 3:6; and twice in 4:4). In every instance, κόσμος represents the ultimate "other" for James. In 1:27—the theme verse for the letter—James says that "pure and undefiled piety before God who is also father is to care for the orphaned and widow in their distress and to keep oneself unstained by the world" (ἄσπιλον ἑαυτὸν τηρεῖν ἀπὸ τοῦ κόσμου). This is the first time James employs κόσμος, and it stands in a

48. Horsley, *Jesus and Empire*, 86.
49. Ibid., 97.
50. Ibid., 98.

"climactic position in opposition to the measure of God."[51] In 3:6 where James emphatically exhorts his listeners/hearers to control their tongues, he exclaims that the tongue is a metaphorical "world of evil/injustice" (ὁ κόσμος τῆς ἀδικίας). Finally, in 4:4, where James uses κόσμος twice, he specifically contrasts "friendship with the world" (ἡ φιλία τοῦ κόσμου) and "friendship with God." Ultimately, being a friend of ὁ κόσμος is the same as being an enemy of God. Just as ὁ κόσμος is situated as the antithesis of God, so are the wealthy the antithesis of the poor. In this equation, the wealthy are the ones who control the world; therefore, οἱ πλούσιοι synecdochically represent the κόσμος.[52] The wealthy have the world, but the poor have the kingdom. Friesen is certainly correct when he makes the observation that "the rhetoric of this section [2:1-7] asserts that there are two alternatives: the system of the world and the system of God's kingdom."[53] According to verses 6b-7, it is the wealthy who control the world. They have the capacity to "oppress" (καταδυναστεύω)[54] and "drag" people "into court" (ἕλκω . . . εἰς κριτήρια) and they even "blaspheme the good name that is invoked" (βλασφημοῦσιν τὸ καλὸν ὄνομα τὸ ἐπικληθὲν) over James's addressees. The use of the intensive pronoun (αὐτοὶ) in verses 6-7 only accentuates James's force when he speaks of the wealthy. It is their κόσμος that stands in direct contradiction to God's βασιλεία.

Warren Carter's analysis of the way New Testament authors negotiated empire is instructive here. Carter argues that there were

51. Johnson, *Letter of James*, 213.

52. Even Martin Dibelius, *James: A Commentary on the Epistle of James*, trans. Michael A. Williams, Hermeneia (Philadelphia: Fortress Press, 1976), 138, understands the world as the antithesis of faith.

53. Friesen, "Injustice or God's Will?," 25. See also Edgar, *Has God Not Chosen the Poor?*, 112–13.

54. This term is adopted by James from the LXX where it is specifically used in reference to the socially oppressed. It is used in Amos 8:4 and Ezek. 18:12, 22:29 referring specifically to πτωχοί. Edgar, *Has God Not Chosen the Poor?*, 122, and Maynard-Reid, *Poverty and Wealth*, 63, make this observation.

"numerous options" for New Testament writers to evaluate Roman culture and politics. He points out five distinctive, yet overlapping, ways in which various writers in the New Testament related to Rome: 1) "empire is of the devil," 2) "Rome's world is under judgment," 3) God is transforming the world, 4) God is establishing an alternative world, and 5) followers are called to accommodate the world.[55] Differentiating between certain New Testament authors in their attempt to interpret pervading Roman culture helps account for the various competing voices in the New Testament. Rather than focus primarily on the "theology" of these writers, Carter shows how their piety and politics were inseparable. Carter's categories, however, are problematic because a single author can negotiate empire differently in a single work. For instance, Carter points out the fact that Romans 13 calls its readers to wholeheartedly accommodate the Roman authorities: "Let every person be subject to the governing authorities; for there is no authority except from God, and those authorities that exist have been instituted by God" (Rom. 13:1). It is clear that this fits within Carter's last category. Problematically, and Carter acknowledges this, in the previous chapter, Paul exhorts the Romans: "Do not be conformed to this world, but be transformed by the renewing of your minds" (Rom. 12:2). Carter, nevertheless, refers to James 2:1-7 as an example of the "alternative communities" model: "James counters the culturally imitative practice of favoring the wealthy at the expense of the poor by encouraging the opposite practice. God's favor elevates the poor (James 2:1-7)."[56] In this way, ὁ κόσμος is a functional synonym for empire in James. Yet James, like Paul, transgresses Carter's provisional categories. James's characterization of wisdom from

55. See Warren Carter, *The Roman Empire and the New Testament* (Nashville: Abingdon, 2006), 14–26.
56. Ibid., 22.

below as earthly (ἐπίγειος) and demonic (δαιμονιώδης) (3:15), and his demanding the readership to resist the devil (ἀντίστητε δὲ τῷ διαβόλῳ) (4:7), shows that he would easily fit into Carter's first category, that is, "the empire is of the devil."[57] Likewise, James's condemnation of the wealthy elite in 2:1-13 and 5:1-6 would certainly put his letter under the rubric "Rome's world is under judgment."[58] "Judgment will be merciless to anyone who has shown no mercy" (James 2:13). James, then, straddles at least three of Carter's categories, but all three of these categories are rigorously anti-imperial. Carter's work, however, is helpful in differentiating between different imperial negotiations within the New Testament. He concludes, "Followers of Jesus employed various strategies—survival, accommodation, protest, dissent, imitation—in negotiating Rome's world."[59] What Carter fails to notice, or fails to acknowledge, is that some of these various forms of cultural negotiation are mutually exclusive. James's condemnation of the Roman world, then, stands in stark contrast to any hybridized accomodationist model. Both may be anti-imperial, but both are antithetical to each other as well. I will pay closer attention to these competing modes of anti-imperial discourse in chapters 5 and 6. At the moment, it is enough to understand James's use of ὁ κόσμος as synonymous with the Roman Empire/world. In this way, James makes a case against the Roman world analogous to Rev. 11:15: "The empire of this world has become the empire of our Lord and of his Messiah." James's rhetoric "counters Rome's propaganda claim that it is the 'eternal city' with an 'empire without end.'"[60]

James identifies the imperial presence as οἱ πλούσιοι who govern the κόσμος, and it is clear that "the rich are outside the sphere of

57. Ibid., 16.
58. Ibid., 18.
59. Ibid., 26.
60. Ibid., 18.

salvation and faith."[61] This is classic nativist rhetoric. It is clear from this analysis that James's critique of the patronage system functions as anti-imperial discourse. James confronts Roman etiquette with the Jesus tradition that systematically overturns Roman conceptions of partiality. The way in which James uses the Jesus tradition as anti-imperial discourse reifies colonial boundaries of self and other, but inverts the binary: "Has God not chosen the poor?" This type of anti-imperial discourse fits well within the category of nativism. Understanding James's rhetoric as nativist specifies what kind of anti-imperial discourse James employs. In other words, there were various forms of Roman resistance throughout the empire during the first century. In fact, there were various forms of Roman resistance within Palestine in the first century. Josephus speaks of the Fourth Philosophy, the Zealots, and the sicarii as synonymous forms of anti-Roman resistance. Horsley's conception of Jesus as an anti-imperial figure who was crucified as a rebel, not to mention Crossan's analogous Jesus, adds another layer of anti-Roman sentiment within Palestine that is specifically related to the Jesus movement. The concentration on purity and perfection mentioned in the previous chapter, the focused critique of the patronage system here, and the nostalgic use of the Jesus tradition as a source of authority all position James as nativist resistance to empire, which has a particular form that is dissimilar, and even opposed, to other modes of resistance such as hybridity, for instance. Gilroy provides an excellent example of how these two modes of resistance are mutually exclusive as he critiques nativism: "Regardless of their affiliation to the right, left, or centre, groups have fallen back on the idea of cultural nationalism, on the overintegrated concepts of culture which present immutable, ethnic differences as an absolute break in the histories and experiences

61. Maynard-Reid, *Poverty and Wealth*, 63.

of 'black' and 'white' people."[62] What Gilroy critiques as "ethnic absolutism" is exemplary of nativist reasoning—the type of reasoning that James uses throughout the letter to draw an immutable line between the αδελφοί and κόσμος. Gilroy argues that these nativist claims "are associated with the idea of national belonging or the aspiration to nationality and other more local but equivalent forms of cultural kinship."[63] With the use of fictive kinship throughout the Letter of James, it is clear that the rhetoric of resistance James uses is kin to Gilroy's "local but equivalent forms of cultural kinship." Gilroy's preference for the "black Atlantic" as a transcultural and international option disparages nativist movements as too narrow in scope. Gilroy evidences the tremendous gap between modes of resistance. Clearly, he refuses simple nativism and prefers a more nuanced, hybridized discourse: "But that narrowness of vision which is content with the merely national has also been challenged from within that black community by thinkers who were prepared to renounce the easy claims of African-American exceptionalism in favour of a global, coalitional politics in which anti-imperialism and anti-racism might be seen to interact if not to fuse."[64] Gilroy is important for this analysis of James in order to not only position James's rhetoric as nativist discourse, but to also evidence of the massive difference between nativism as a particular form of imperial resistance and other, more hybridized forms of resistance, such as Pauline hybridity, to which we shall return below.

James 2:8-13: Imperial Law

As James subtly changes the subject from kingdom partiality (2:1-7) to kingdom law in verses 8-13, he continues his anti-imperial

62. Gilroy, *Black Atlantic*, 2.
63. Ibid., 3.
64. Ibid., 4.

engagement. In contrast to the wealthy who oppress and those who favor these wealthy oppressors, James concentrates on those who "perfect the kingdom law" (νόμον τελεῖτε βασιλικὸν). Here, James is appropriating and retooling βασιλεία and its cognates and turning them back against the empire in similar fashion to Spivak's idea of catachresis.[65] This section defines the law of the kingdom that contradicts the social system described in verses 2-4 and predicts that the law of the kingdom will triumph over that same system (2:13) without mercy.

James begins this second section with a reminder of his overall theme of purity and perfection with the use of the verb τελέω. Fulfilling, completing, or perfecting the law of the kingdom (νόμον βασιλικὸν) is exactly what James wants from his audience. In order to heighten the contrast between perfectly following the law of the kingdom and showing favoritism, James uses μέντοι (v. 8) in opposition to δὲ in verse 9. In the protasis of verse 8, James insists, "If you truly (μέντοι) complete the law of the kingdom." The previous section (vv. 1-7), however, makes it clear that this has not been the case. The protasis in verse 9, then, is accentuated by the use of the conjunctions μέντοι . . . δὲ: "*But* if you discriminate."[66] According to verses 2-4, this has been precisely the problem. These two first class conditional sentences rhetorically function as completely competing systems. The law of the kingdom (v. 8) is diametrically opposed to the system of discrimination (v. 9). This divide is only accentuated by what follows each controlling verb (τελεῖτε in v. 8 and προσωπολημπτεῖτε in v. 9). The kingdom law in verse 8 is clarified: "according to the Scripture, 'Love your neighbor as yourself.'" The

65. Both Neil Elliott, *The Arrogance of the Nations: Reading Romans in the Shadow of Empire*, Paul in Critical Contexts (Minneapolis: Fortress Press, 2008) and Warren Carter, *John and Empire: Initial Explorations* (New York and London: T. & T. Clark, 2008), in particular, see this move in other writers from the same period within the Jesus movement.

66. See Hartin, *James*, 121.

quote from Lev. 19:18c is directly from the LXX. James resorts to Leviticus 19 repeatedly throughout the letter;[67] yet, this quote also evidences the Jesus tradition (rich young ruler [Matt. 19:16-22; Mark 10:17-22; Luke 18:18-23] and the great commandment [Matt. 22:34-40; Mark 12:28-34; Luke 10.25-28; Rom. 13:8-10; Gal. 5:13-15]). In one short reference, James conjures the grounds of his authority by simultaneously referencing Leviticus and Jesus. The combination of the law and Jesus tradition added to the verb τελέω (fulfill, complete, perfect) creates a rhetorical overload.[68] In other words, who could resist this rhetoric? The apodosis of verse 8, then, may be the most understated two-word phrase in the Letter of James: "you do well" (καλῶς ποιεῖτε). Although short, it forcefully reminds the addressees of verse 3, where the finely dressed person is told to sit in a place of honor: "You sit here with honor" (Σὺ κάθου ὧδε καλῶς). The force of verse 8 is heightened by its antithesis and mirror image in verse 9. The protasis of verse 9 is only three words: "But if you discriminate" (εἰ δὲ προσωπολημπτεῖτε), with an extended apodosis that negatively reflects the protasis of verse 8: "you commit sin which results in you being condemned by the law as a

67. See Luke Timothy Johnson, *Brother of Jesus, Friend of God: Studies in the Letter of James* (Grand Rapids: Eerdmans, 2004). Probable references to Leviticus 19 occur at least in the following verses from James: James 4:11 = Lev. 19:16; James 5:4 = Lev. 19:13; James 5:9 = Lev. 19:18b; James 5:12 = Lev. 19:12; and James 5:20 = Lev. 19:17b.

68. It is clear from the context that James has the "entire" law in mind rather than the single "love command" from Lev. 19:18, contra Ralph P. Martin, *James*, WBC, 48 (Nashville: Thomas Nelson, 1988), 67; Sophie Laws, *The Epistle of James*, Harper's New Testament Commentary (San Francisco: Harper & Row, 1980), 108–9; and Edgar, *Has God Not Chosen the Poor?*, 126. Many commentators agree: Johnson, *Letter of James*, 230; Hartin, *James*, 121, 135; Davids, *Epistle of James*, 114; Dibelius, *James*, 144, for several reasons. First, if James wanted to refer to the kingdom law as a single command, he would have used ἐντολή rather than νόμος (see especially Hartin, *James*, 135). Second, considering the Jesus tradition, it is clear from the Synoptic Gospels that Jesus used Lev. 19:18 as the summation of the entire law (Matt. 22:34-40; Mark 12:28-34; Luke 10.25-28). Third, since James used the verb τελέω, which means to complete, fulfill, or perfect, this also seems to indicate his referent is the complete law rather than the single "love command." Finally, James references the whole law (ὅλον τὸν νόμον) in the next verse (v. 10) and the Decalogue in (v. 11), which indicates that the kingdom law is larger than the "love command."

lawbreaker." Verse 9 may also allude to Lev. 19:15, which accentuates the parallelism.[69] The symmetry and substance of these verses make a strong argument about the utter inconsistency between kingdom law and the social system of patronage. To complete kingdom law was to deny the patronal system, and to participate in the patronal system was to deny kingdom law.[70]

At this point, it is necessary to give an adequate, however provisional, definition of patronage in order to fully comprehend James's critique of it. Dionysius of Halicarnassus gives a famous and classical definition of patronage from the first century BCE when describing Romulus's founding of Rome. Although his definition is set within mythological speculation, it clearly shows the ideology of patronage that was common currency during Dionysius's lifetime—an ideology that extended through the early Roman Empire. Dionysius's definition deserves to be quoted at length:

> He [Romulus] placed the plebeians as a trust in the hands of the patricians, by allowing every plebeian to choose for his patron any patrician whom he himself wished. . . . Romulus not only recommended the relationship by a handsome designation, calling his protection of the poor and lowly a "patronage," but he also assigned friendly offices to both parties, thus making the connexion between them a bond of kindness befitting fellow citizens. The regulations which he then instituted concerning patronage and which long continued in use among the Romans were as follows: It was the duty of the patricians to explain to their clients the laws, of which they were ignorant; to take the same care of them when absent as present, doing everything for them that fathers do for their sons with regard both to money and to the

69. "Do not have [ποιήσετε] injustice [ἄδικον] in judgment [κρίσει]. Do not show partiality to the poor [πτωχοῦ] and do not show favoritism to the powerful [δυνάστου], rather judge your neighbor with justice [δικαιοσύνῃ]" Lev. 19:15 LXX.

70. Maynard-Reid, *Poverty and Wealth*, 66, agrees: "It is impossible to conduct oneself in the manner represented in the illustration [vv. 2-4] and claim to be fulfilling the law. This claim, however, seems to have been made by those who were catering exclusively to the rich. It is possible that they were using this 'law' as an excuse for honoring the rich—that is, by attending to the rich they were showing love to their neighbor."

> contracts that related to money; to bring suit on behalf of their clients when they were wronged in connexion with contracts, and to defend them against any who brought charges against them; and, to put the matter briefly, to secure for them both in private and in public affairs all that tranquility of which they particularly stood in need. It was the duty of the clients to assist their patrons in providing dowries for their daughters upon their marriage if the fathers had not sufficient means; to pay their ransom to the enemy if any of them or of their children were taken prisoner; to discharge out of their own purses their patrons' losses in private suits and the pecuniary fines which they were condemned to pay to the State, making these contributions to them not as loans but as thank-offerings; and to share with their patrons the costs incurred in their magistracies and dignities and other public expenditures, in the same manner as if they were their relations. For both patrons and clients alike it was impious and unlawful to accuse each other in law-suits or to bear witness or to give their votes against each other or to be found in the number of each other's enemies; and whoever was convicted of doing any of these things was guilty of treason by virtue of the law sanctioned by Romulus, and might lawfully be put to death by any man who so wished as a victim devoted to the Jupiter of the infernal regions.[71]

According to Dionysius's classical definition, patronage describes the social relationship of reciprocity between patrons and clients within the broad context of Roman social relations. Within this social structure, the social hierarchy is clear and justified. If followed correctly, "Romulus" has provided a social relationship that would bring stability to society. It is clear that Dionysius describes an ideal type of patronage, that is, the way it is *supposed* to work without any reference to how patronage functioned in reality. According to Richard P. Saller, there are "three vital elements" that characterize patronage: "First, it involves the reciprocal exchange of goods and services. Secondly, to distinguish it from a commercial transaction in the marketplace, the relationship must be a personal one of some

71. Dionysius of Halicarnassus, *Roman Antiquities* II.9.2–10.3 (trans. E. Cary, LCL).

duration. Thirdly, it must be asymmetrical, in the sense that the two parties are of unequal status and offer different kinds of goods and services in the exchange—a quality which sets patronage off from friendship between equals."[72] Patronage, then, was an integral part of Roman public life that extended throughout the empire. There was a remarkable difference, however, between the "patronal language and ideology" that "permeated Roman society" and the reality of the patronage system.[73] In the "living out" of the patronage system, Saller argues that "Roman officials were not restrained by concepts of the impropriety of all favoritism, and they were relatively free to indulge in the natural human propensity to use their official positions to aid family and friends."[74] Saller echoes ancient critiques of the abuse of the patronage system. In some cases, the clients were rebuked for being flatterers rather than friends, and patrons are demonized as exploitive and narcissistic in their lust for honors. In what sounds like an apologia for the patronage system, Seneca surmises that "[m]en must be taught to be willing to give, willing to receive, willing to return; and to place before themselves the high aim, not merely of equaling, but even of surpassing those to whom they are indebted … the one class must be taught to look for no return, the other to feel deeper gratitude."[75] Here, there is a subtle critique of the patrons who need to learn how to give "willingly" and of the clients who need to learn how to receive "gratefully." Later, Seneca is more explicit in his critique of abusing the patronage system: "[H]e who gives acts like a god, he who demands repayment acts like a money-lender. Why

72. Richard P. Saller, *Personal Patronage under the Early Empire* (Cambridge: Cambridge University Press, 1982), 1. In chapter 5, I devote considerable attention to the concept of friendship, especially how James specifically sets "friendship with God" as diametrically opposed to "friendship with the world."
73. See Saller, *Personal Patronage*, 37.
74. Ibid.
75. Seneca, *On Benefits*, trans. Aubrey Stewart (London: George Bell & Sons, 1905), 1.4.3.

then, by trying to protect the rights of the former class, should we reduce them to the level of the basest of mankind?"[76]

Alicia Batten uses these passages from Seneca to argue that Seneca does not have the patronage system in mind in his remarks; rather, Seneca deals specifically with benefaction. Batten persuasively argues that there was a fundamental difference between patronage and benefaction, which is the issue in the Letter of James. Batten understands benefaction as a system where the giver/benefactor gives freely without any desire for reciprocity. Patronage, on the other hand, demands honor and services in return, and is usually manipulated by patrons at the expense of the clients. In relation to James, Batten understands James's "attack upon patronage" in terms of "God's beneficence in contrast to the human in chapter 2. The description of God in Jas 1:5–8 conforms more to the ideal selfless and generous benefactor who provides for the community than to a patron who delights in the honors served up by clients."[77] Although Batten's argument is appealing, it fails to convince due to the fact that Seneca, one of her main sources for benefaction, is remorseful about the failure of benefaction rather than its success. In other words, Seneca's critique of benefaction is similar to Batten's critique of patronage. In the end, both benefaction and patronage function analogously rather than synonymously. Clearly, I agree with Batten that James is criticizing the patronage system, but not due to James's preference for benefaction.

Alan B. Wheatley's analysis of patronage in early Christianity charts New Testament writers' response to patronage and is helpful in determining James's position. Wheatley argues that within the Jesus tradition, Jesus functions as a broker for God in a divine patronage

76. Seneca, *On Benefits*, trans. Aubrey Stewart (London: George Bell & Sons, 1905), 3.15.4.
77. Alicia Batten, "God in the Letter of James: Patron or Benefactor?" in *The Social World of the New Testament*, ed. Jerome H. Neyrey and Eric C. Stewart (Peabody, MA: Hendrickson, 2008), 57.

scheme. The patronage system, however, is turned on its head, where the clients are honored rather than the patrons.[78] In other words, Jesus accepted the patronage system, but transformed it: "It is clear that in this complex of teaching, Jesus identified and rejected a pattern of accepted religious patronage, while he pointed to a radical alternative."[79] James follows this alternative patronage, according to Wheatley, and "was attempting to deal with an evasion of the redirection that Jesus had indicated."[80] James's warnings against the patronage system, then, function as a warning "against a class who represent the antithesis of the values of their [the brothers' and sisters'] God. . . . Thus, the values here mentioned cannot be accepted in the church, and those who belong to this class should not be welcomed because of their wealth. It must be noted that the terms of this passage express a distinct echo of Jesus' Sermon (Matt. 6:19-34)."[81] It is important that Wheatley sees a connection between James's critique of the patronage system and the Jesus tradition. The values of favoritism explicit within the system of patronage are diametrically opposed to the values of the kingdom of God. James inverts the patron/client binary using the authority of the Jesus tradition and boldly proclaims an altogether different social structure where the "brother who is lowly boast in being raised up, and the rich in being brought low" (1:9-10).

Verses 10-11 only intensify this rhetoric with more elaborate literary style. James continues his emphatic and rhetorical use of conditional sentences and scriptural references; yet, he adds alliteration, rhyme, and word order to enhance his argument. The substance of this style is vital, that is, every command in "the whole

78. See Alan B. Wheatley, *Patronage in Early Christianity: Its Use and Transformation from Jesus to Paul of Samosata* (Eugene, OR: Pickwick, 2011), 13–19.
79. Wheatley, *Patronage in Early Christianity*, 16.
80. Ibid., 26.
81. Ibid., 28.

law" is equally important. To break one (ἐν ἑνί) command is to break all of them (γέγονεν πάντων ἔνοχος). In other words, to violate the law of the kingdom by discriminating against the poor and favoring the wealthy is a complete abomination to the entire law of the kingdom.

By beginning verse 10 with the indefinite relative pronoun ὅστις, James creates an alliterative rhythm with ὅλον that then rhymes with what follows, that is, τὸν νόμον.[82] James keeps the subjunctive verb (τηρήσῃ) until the end of the comparative clause, then begins the second clause with another subjunctive verb (πταίσῃ) that continues the rhythm of the sentence. Having the two verbs beside each other also functions as a paranomasia between "keeping" and "stumbling," which is the contrast that governs this entire section. Using the verb πταίω, which is from the same semantic domain as πτωχός, also creates an interesting connection between "the poor" in 2:1-7 and the ones who stumble in 2:8-13. In 2:1-7, the πτωχόι are the ones chosen by God; yet in 2:8-13, the ones who have shown partiality to the wealthy are those who πταίσῃ. This literarily functions as a divine reversal. The protasis finally ends with another rhythmic flourish (δὲ ἐν ἑνί). The assonance in the protasis of verse 10 is unparalleled in James. This rhetorical force makes his argument even more emphatic. The apodosis in verse 10 concludes James's point that if one law is broken, then ὅστις . . . γέγονεν πάντων ἔνοχος ("That very one . . . has become guilty of them all"). The argument made here prefigures James's antihybrid pericope on faith/works in 2:14-26. In other words, the works that James has in mind in 2:14-26 are clearly works related to the law of the kingdom, but this does not and cannot exclude any single commandment or section of

82. Since James focuses here on the nature and/or essence of the one who is "keeping" and "stumbling," the indefinite relative pronoun (ὅστις) should be translated as a qualitative rather than generic relative pronoun. Instead of "whoever," the context demands a more emphatic translation, i.e., "the very one who."

commandments in the law, as he makes clear by using a scriptural illustration in verse 11.[83] Here, James and Matthew's "Christian-Jewish" community shows striking points of convergence around issues of Torah.[84] What Anthony J. Saldarini affirms for the author of the Gospel of Matthew, I affirm for James, that is, he falls authentically within the broad boundaries of Judeanness and fully upholds Torah. As such, James, like Matthew, interprets Torah through the teachings of Jesus. Likewise, "The outlook and practice which Matthew promotes in his gospel is thoroughly Jewish and based on the Bible as understood through the teachings and actions of Jesus."[85] Simply put, Saldarini argues that Matthew "maintains the boundaries and practices of Judaism, interpreted a different way (15:1-20; 5:17-19)."[86] Of course, the "different way" is through the

83. Johnson, *Letter of James*, 235–36, argues that verse 10 has Lev. 19:18 in mind rather than the whole law. Later, he asserts that James *specifically* refers to "moral" law; therefore, circumcision and other rituals are not a part of James's argument. With James's concentration on "law" in 2:8-13 and his specific insistence on "the whole law" in verses 10-11 in particular, it is hard to imagine that James does *not* have "works of the law" in his purview when he changes topics in 2:14-26. It is also hard to envision a Judean purview that dissected the law into "moral" and "ritual" parts. It is clear that James takes it for granted that "the whole law" encompasses both ritual and moral aspects. That he does not specify between the two indicates that he understands one to implicate the other. Although Hartin understands "the law" in the passage as Torah, he agrees with Johnson regarding the moral/ritual divide. Hartin, *James*, 111–12, accentuates this apparent contradiction between emphasizing *both* the entire Torah *and* a division between moral and ritual law by arguing in one place that "without doubt the Torah is the main way in which God's people are constituted as a nation separate from the nations and peoples around them," yet "the aspect of Torah to which James gives attention is God's moral law for God's people rather than the ritual or ceremonial law." It is hard to imagine, given James's argument regarding "the whole law," that James would accept Johnson's or Hartin's interpretation. There is absolutely no evidence from the Letter of James that supports a moral/ritual division within the law. In fact, the evidence from James argues otherwise. In an attempt to lessen the contradiction between James and Paul regarding the law, Johnson and Hartin resort to this moral/ritual division. By creating this division, they effectively *make* James and Paul "speak" about different issues. More will be said about this issue in chapter 5. See Gal. 3:10-14 and 5:3 to see how Paul constructs an argument regarding the law. Here, Paul makes a similar point about keeping "the whole law"; however, it is an impossible proposition for him.

84. See Anthony J. Saldarini, *Matthew's Christian-Jewish Community* (Chicago and London: University of Chicago Press, 1982).

85. Saldarini, *Matthew's Christian-Jewish Community*, 7.

86. Ibid., 74.

Jesus tradition. Saldarini's interpretation of Matt. 5:19 ("If someone should break one of these lesser commandments and teach such things to people, that one will be called least in the kingdom of heaven; but if someone should do and teach such things, that one will be called great in the kingdom of heaven") shows that James 2:10 is not an isolated phenomenon. In fact, Matthew may be the inheritor of the Jesus tradition that James uses in his letter. The way in which James engages the Decalogue in the following verses is extremely close to Jesus' "Sermon on the Mount" in Matthew 5–7. What Saldarini suggests in relation to Matthew, therefore, may also be suggested in relation to James, namely that Matthew "seems to be one of a diminishing number of Christian Jews who accept the whole Jewish law and way of life (understood according to the teaching of Jesus) as authoritative."[87]

James quotes the Decalogue in verse 11 in order to provide an illustration for his point in verse 10. The way in which James quotes the Decalogue is important. The word order he uses (μὴ μοιχεύσῃς ... μὴ φονεύσῃς) seems to indicate Deut. 5:17-18 is in view rather than Exod. 20:13 and 15, but the way James uses the negation μὴ rather than οὐ and his choice of grammar may indicate a different tradition. In the Synoptic tradition, Jesus references these same passages from the Decalogue in Matt. 5:21, 27; 19:16-22; Mark 10:17-22; and Luke 18:18-23. In both the Markan and Matthean passages, the word order follows that which is found in the Masoretic Text rather than the LXX. Luke, however, matches James in word order, negation, and grammar (the aorist subjunctive μοιχεύσῃς rather than the present indicative μοιχεύεις).[88] In other words, the way James "quotes" the Decalogue may implicate the Jesus tradition as well as the Decalogue. If this is the case, then James is repeating

87. Ibid., 8.

88. See also Rom. 13:9.

the interpretive move he made in verse 8 when he beckoned both the Jesus traditions and scriptural traditions. By folding Jesus into the Torah, James refuses to drive a wedge between them. Jesus, then, is the nativist that James follows and calls those in the Diaspora to follow. James is intent on maintaining a "nativist" Jesus as an emblem of Judean difference, which functions as a call to resist the Roman imperial order. This nativist stance, however, was only one way among others to resist empire.[89]

What makes these two commandments important is that they come from the same source, that is, God, "the one who said." This drives home the point that James is making about the whole law of the kingdom. Every command comes from God; therefore, every command is equally important. James finishes his argument about the law of the kingdom with a final first class conditional sentence that shifts the verbs from third person to second person to make a stronger point: "If *you* do not commit adultery but kill, *you* have become a breaker of the law."[90] For the second time within the span of three sentences James uses the word παραβάτης (lawbreaker, transgressor).[91] Outside of James, the word only appears in Gal. 2:18 and Rom. 2:25, 27 within the New Testament. In both Pauline passages, the relevance of the law is at issue. What is striking is how similar the vocabulary is between these passages;[92] yet, the differences

89. Pauline hybridity is another example of anti-imperial discourse; although it is a competing mode of discourse that is totally incongruent with nativism. This will be the focus of chapters 5 and 6.

90. See Matt. 5:17-30. Here in the Sermon on the Mount, Jesus speaks about "completing the law," then begins a series of exhortations regarding specific laws. The first section of these exhortations has to do with "killing" and the second section has to do with "committing adultery." James uses this language in accusatory fashion later in his letter: μοιχαλίδες (adulteresses) in 4:4 and ἐφουεύσατε (you all killed) in 5:6.

91. See Deut. 27:26 and 1QS 8:16-17.

92. The following words occur in each of the passages in Romans, Galatians, and James: εἰ (Rom. 2:17; 3:5, 7; Gal. 2:17, 18, 21; James 2:8, 9, and 11), νόμος (Rom. 2:17, 18, 20, 23 [x 2], 25 [x 2], 26, 27; Gal. 2:16 [x 3], 19 [x 2], 21; James 2:8, 9, 10, 11, and 12), παραβάτης (Rom. 2:25, 27; Gal. 2:18; James 2:9 and 11), ἐὰν (Rom. 2:25 [x 2]; Gal. 3:16; and James 2:2), and ἁμαρτία (Rom. 3:7; Gal. 2:15, 17; and James 2:9). The following words agree only in Romans and James:

between James and Paul are remarkable.[93] In both Pauline passages, Paul champions the importance of faith rather than the law. This issue will certainly occupy James 2:14-26, but James is content with only setting up that argument in verses 10-11 by employing vocabulary and content that contradicts certain Pauline arguments exemplified in texts like Gal. 2:15-21 and Rom. 2:17—3:8. The focus of verse 11 primarily concerns establishing the foundations of the law of the kingdom, but already there is a transition moving from an anti-imperial strategy to an antihybridity strategy.

After grounding his argument regarding the law of the kingdom in scriptural traditions/Jesus traditions and showing how the law of the kingdom is contrary to the social system of "the world," James transitions from this anti-imperial pericope to an antihybridity pericope with verses 12-13, which is happening subtly in verses 10-11. These verses bring 2:1-13 to a close and begin to introduce the addressees to the next section of material, 2:14-3:12. The two imperatives (λαλεῖτε, ποιεῖτε), each accompanied by the demonstrative pronoun οὕτως, create an emphatic conclusion.[94] "Talk like this" refers to the argument that James has just completed, but also looks forward to James's pericope regarding the tongue (3:1-12). "Act like this" also refers to the previous argument, but directly relates to the following pericope on faith and action (2:14-26). In both cases, the imperatives and demonstrative pronouns

κατακαυχάομαι/καυχάομαι (Rom. 2:17, 23; and James 2:13), μοιχείω (Rom. 2:22 and James 2:11 [x 2]), βλασφημέω (Rom. 2:24; 3:8; and James 2:7), various forms of κρίνω (Rom. 2:27; 3:6, 7; James 2:4 [x 2], 12, and 13 [x 2]), and τελέω (Rom. 2:27 and James 2:8).

93. Johnson, *Letter of James*, 232, admits that "Paul's statement as well as James's points to a widespread conviction that since the commandments all came from God, all required obedience." Hartin, *James*, 122, agrees: "James's understanding reflects a universal belief within Judaism that since the Law and the commandments came from God and were an expression of God's will they must all be obeyed." In spite of these statements, both Johnson and Hartin do not think James has "the whole law" in mind; rather, they profess that James is only referring to "moral" law and not "ritual" law. Neither gives an example of this moral/ritual division in any ancient texts.

94. See the emphatic use of οὕτως in James 1:26-27 and 2:1-7.

point backward and forward. In the context of verse 12, however, these words and actions have immediate relevance related to the law of freedom (ἐλευθερίας). The addressees are "about to be judged" (μέλλοντες κρίνεσθαι) by this very same law.[95] There is no reason to translate the genitive construction διὰ νόμου as a genitive of means as do Johnson and Hartin: God judges "on the basis of" or "by means of" the law.[96] Already in verse 9, the law is personified as an entity with enough agency to convict; therefore, a genitive of agency is a better translation here. It is the personified law of the kingdom with a heightened sense of liberation that will judge individuals seemingly based on words and actions.[97] For the imperial elite, this would be their judgment revisiting them. In other words, the law embodied here (in Jesus?) returns the unjust actions of the wealthy when they dragged the αδελφοί to court, oppressed them, and blasphemed the name. Here, we have the absolute condemnation of the wealthy in 5:1-6 prefigured. This judgment, according to verse 13, is merciless (ἀνέλεος) to the one who does not do (τῷ μὴ ποιήσαντι) mercy. "To the one who does not have/do mercy" is a clear reference to the imperative in verse 12 ("Act like this") and the entire pericope that follows (2:14-26). This construction also negatively echoes the beatitude in Matt. 5:7, "Happy are the merciful, for they will have mercy." In other words, as James brings this pericope to a close, he again references the Jesus tradition. The last three words of this section, however, strategically bridge what has been said to what will be said. It is clear from the reference to the Jesus tradition that ἔλεος is indicative of the kingdom, but so is judgment, which makes the final clause κατακαυχᾶται ἔλεος κρίσεως somewhat difficult. Most commentators translate it as "mercy triumphs over judgment." This

95. Both Johnson, *Letter of James*, 233, and Hartin, *James*, 123, read μέλλοτες eschatologically; however, it may only have a proleptic sense, which is revisited in 5:1-6.

96. See again Johnson, *Letter of James*, 233; Hartin, *James*, 123.

97. See Hartin, *James*, 111–15.

makes sense only if the κρίσεως here refers back to the bad judgments being made by the addressees in verse 4.[98] What is more important than this awkward construction is the fact that κατακαυχᾶομαι is another term that is used only by James and Paul in the New Testament.[99] When James critiques the travel itineraries of business people in his antihybridity pericope in 4:13-17, he will use the root of this term (καυχᾶται and καύχησις) as well as other vocabulary that is also found in both of these passages in James (κρίνω, νόμος, ποιησής, πλησίον). In other words, this is the rhetoric James uses when he confronts colonial hybridity, which is the nature of his next two sections 2:14-3:12. What cannot be missed in this transition, however, is the ultimate triumph (κατακαυχᾶομαι) of the law of the kingdom through judgment over those who oppose it or do not follow it with integrity. The prefix κατα intensifies the verb and makes it more aggressive, hence "to boast *over* or *against*." Ending this pericope with the verb "to exult over" or "boast against" emphasizes James's aggression toward the social system that he criticizes throughout 2:1-13. This anti-imperial rhetoric anticipates the total condemnation of the wealthy in 5:1-6.

Wealth and Poverty within Imperialism: Economics and the Condemnation of the Wealthy in James 5:1-6

The agrarian society of Roman Palestine in the first century CE was defined by an extractive or tributary economy whereby the aristocracy owned large swaths of land and controlled almost all the economic production from these estates.[100] The peasants, artisans, and

98. Due to the awkward construction, there are several textual variants that attempt to clarify the grammar.

99. See James 2:13, 3:14, and Rom. 11:18. See also chapter 6, the second section, for an extended discussion of this terminology.

100. See K. C. Hanson and Douglas E. Oakman, *Palestine in the Time of Jesus: Social Structures and Social Conflicts* (Minneapolis: Fortress Press, 2008), 105, 181–82.

slaves that labored on these farms were exploited by the aristocracy in the ever-increasing mode of production that enabled the aristocracy's exorbitant lifestyle. According to K. C. Hanson and Douglas E. Oakman, in this environment, the "elites need to control and remove any agricultural surpluses (leaving peasants at a survival level) in order to live their valued leisure lives."[101] The elite leisure came at the expense of the laborers. As the aristocracy grew wealthier, the economic gap between them and their laborers also grew. For the subsistence laborer, "the margin of surplus production was narrow and was largely siphoned off by the imperial authorities and city-based landlords in taxes and rent."[102] This growing system of economic oppression characterized Roman Palestine and led to the Judean revolt in 66 CE. Josephus recounts how the *sicarii* burned down the public archives in Jerusalem in order to destroy all accounting of debts so that they would "win over a host of grateful debtors and to cause a rising of the poor against the rich, sure of impunity."[103] Debt forgiveness, then, was "frequently encountered as a revolutionary slogan of the disenfranchised, usually accompanied by a demand for the redistribution of land."[104] Both Josephus and Tacitus provide examples of the aristocracy attempting to lower tax and debt burdens in an attempt to hedge off revolt.[105]

101. Hanson and Oakman, *Palestine in the Time of Jesus*, 105. This economic arrangement was only exacerbated by the issue of absentee landowners as mentioned by Josephus, *Life* 422, 425. See also David A. Fiensy, "Ancient Economy and the New Testament," in *Understanding the Social World of the New Testament*, ed. Dietmar Neufeld and Richard E. DeMaris (London and New York: Routledge, 2010), 196; John E. Stambaugh and David L. Balch, *The New Testament in Its Social Environment* (Philadelphia: Westminster, 1986), 91. The parable of the wicked tenants evidences the issue of absentee landlords within the Jesus tradition (Mark 12:1-12; Matt. 21:33-45; Luke 20:9-19).
102. Peter Garnsey and Richard Saller, *The Roman Empire: Economy, Society and Culture* (Berkeley and Los Angeles: University of California Press, 1987), 51–52. See also Hanson and Oakman, *Palestine in the Time of Jesus*, 104.
103. Josephus, *J.W.* 2.427 (trans. Thackery, LCL).
104. Douglas E. Oakman, "Jesus and Agrarian Palestine: The Factor of Debt," in *The Social World of the New Testament: Insights and Models*, ed. Jerome H. Neyrey and Eric C. Stewart (Peabody, MA: Hendrickson, 2008), 66. See also Fiensy, "Ancient Economy," 204.

This kind of consolidation of landownership and the widening gap between the impoverished and wealthy were not unique to Roman Palestine. According to Pliny the Elder, the elite in other areas of the Roman Empire were also expanding and consuming smaller farms and lands since "the wealth of the elite was based on land" in the Roman economy.[106] Pliny states this fact with remorse: "And truth to tell, large estates have ruined Italy and indeed are now also ruining the provinces."[107] Landownership was the primary institution that guarded personal and private wealth as Pliny indicates: "Cato tells us that to praise a man by saying he is a good farmer and cultivator of the soil is the highest accolade. This is the origin of the word for 'wealthy', *locuples*, which means 'full of room', that is, land."[108] Although there was considerable wealth to be made in mercantilism, it was considered risky and unwise among most aristocratic families, who relied on traditional and more stable forms of securing wealth like landownership. Merchants represented "new" money and the "get rich quick" ambition of this rising class, which is satirized in Roman literature through characters such as Trimalchio.[109] From the eastern Mediterranean to the western borders of the empire, landownership was the primary way to secure wealth in the Roman Empire. Each macro farm was structured on traditional household

105. Josephus, *J.W.* 2.85-86; Tacitus, *Annals* 2.42. See Oakman, "Jesus and Agrarian Palestine, 71, for an extended discussion of debt and revolution.

106. Stambaugh and Balch, *New Testament*, 65.

107. Pliny the Elder, *N.H.*, trans. John F. Healy (London: Penguin Books, 1991), 18.35.

108. Pliny the Elder, *N.H.*, 18.11. See also Stambaugh and Balch, *New Testament*, 74; Hanson and Oakman, *Palestine in the Time of Jesus*, 104; Fiensy, "Ancient Economy," 195; Garnsey and Saller, *Roman Empire*, 64.

109. According to Garnsey and Saller, *Roman Empire*, 45, this devaluation of the merchant class was a result of the landed aristocracy's defensive response to the potential growth in this economic sector. They argue that "[t]reaties on agriculture and morality defend landowning as the safest occupation (the least likely therefore to impoverish the aristocracy and weaken its position) and as the most honourable (the most conducive to the lifestyle appropriate for the senator), and manifest hostility in differing degrees to trade as a source of income." See Petronius, *Satyricon* 76, for the full satire of the merchant class through the character Trimalchio.

codes of the Greco-Roman world that supposedly produced social stability and supported Augustus's *Pax Romana*. In other words, these large estates were the Roman Empire in microcosm, that is, they were part of "Caesar's estate." Hanson and Oakman show that

> [e]lite families controlled the mainly agricultural economy as well as the interurban commercial networks of the Roman Empire. Caesar and his "family" (agents, political kin) had an interest in everything; Caesar's estate was overseen in Palestine at the time of Jesus by prefects (Roman "governors"). Local elites like the Herods or Judean high priests controlled land and organized agricultural production by means of large estates. They kept liens on the labor power of peasants and artisans in towns through debt mechanisms.[110]

Any threat to the Roman Empire in microcosm could be a threat to the Roman Empire writ large; therefore, these threats were systematically and brutally extinguished by the Roman military. Richard A. Horsley describes the *sicarii* tactics mentioned by Josephus as an example of how some groups revolted against such immense power as that exemplified by the Roman military:

> Because nonviolent protests were merely met with further violent repression by Roman troops, the Sicarii must have felt that their only recourse was some sort of counterviolence. Being a small group of intellectuals, moreover, they had no power base among the people from which they could have built a wider movement. Also, like certain twentieth-century anticolonial movements (e.g., the Mau Mau in Kenya or EOKA in Cyprus), they targeted privileged power-holders of their own society who were collaborating in imperial rule, rather than the alien rulers themselves. Insofar as Roman imperial rule in Judea worked through the high-priestly rulers in the Jerusalem Temple, moreover, the Sicarii may have thought they were also striking symbolic blows against empire.[111]

110. Hanson and Oakman, *Palestine in the Time of Jesus*, 96.
111. Horsley, *Jesus and Empire*, 43.

In such a socioeconomic environment, James's absolute condemnation of the wealthy is the clearest anti-imperial rhetoric in the letter. In James 5:1-6, James antagonizes the Roman Empire with his "pure" and unequivocal damning of the rich and wealthy, that is, the aristocracy of the Roman Empire.

Introduction to James 5:1-6

James 5:1-6 brings the body of the letter to a close in dramatic fashion. This pericope creates an inclusio with James 2:1-13, which brackets the entire body of the letter with vitriolic rhetoric against the wealthy. The intensity of the condemnation of the wealthy in 5:1-6 is matched in the New Testament only by Luke and Revelation 18, where the fall of "Babylon the great" (v. 1) symbolically represents the Roman Empire.[112] There is no option for repentance for the wealthy as James brings the body of his letter to a close. What the wealthy have and have *not* done with their wealth condemns them utterly and "cries out against them" (5:4). The lack of imperatives here shows that James is not commanding the wealthy in order for them to change their ways, pay their laborers, and stop living extravagantly. Contrarily, every imperative used earlier in 2:1-13 calls the addressees to change: "Do not *have* distinctions, my brothers" (2:1), "*Listen*, beloved brothers" (2:5), and "*Speak* like this and *act* like this" (2:12). In two of the three sentences where James uses imperatives in 2:1-13, he uses ἀδελφοί. This illustrates that when James used imperatives in 2:1-13, it was an attempt to compel the ἀδελφοί to stop favoring the wealthy. In 5:1-6, where James employs direct speech to the wealthy, there is no such call for change. There is an unequivocal difference between the ἀδελφοί and the πλούσιοι. In fact, the two imperatives that are used in 5:1 only call for the wealthy

112. See Maynard-Reid, *Poverty and Wealth*, 97.

to listen (ἄγε) and weep (κλαύσατε). It is clear that οἱ πλούσιοι are not a part of James's audience due to the aggressiveness of his language.[113] Within this short pericope, James uses ὑμῶν eight times, ὑμῖν twice, and seven second-person plural verbs that accentuate the distance between James and οἱ πλούσιοι. The way in which James uses the perfect tense also highlights his stance toward οἱ πλούσιοι. Since the wealthy's wealth, clothes, and money are the very issues that James condemns in verses 2-3, using the perfect tense to describe the current state of these items as rotted, moth-eaten, and rusted must be understood as a rhetorical device. In this case, translating these verbs as intensive perfects stresses the results of their past action in the present, which necessitates translating the perfect tense as present tense. Instead of simple perfects, "Your wealth *has rotted* and your clothes *have become* moth-eaten, and your gold and silver *have rusted*," the use of intensive perfects heightens the sense of condemnation: "Your wealth *rots* and your clothes *are* moth-eaten, and your gold and silver *rust*."[114] In verse 4, James uses an iterative perfect to describe how "the cries of the harvesters" have reached "the ears of the Lord of War." With this nuance, it is best to translate "have reached" (εἰσεληλύθασιν) as "have repeatedly reached," which emphasizes the repetition of the cries. These intensive and iterative perfects exacerbate the level of condemnation that the wealthy receive. Judgment and condemnation are inevitable for the wealthy as Maynard-Reid explains: "These fulminations then were not a call to repentance. Rather they were probably intended more as a comfort and consolation to the oppressed who could be solaced by the fact that ultimate judgment would be meted out upon their oppressors."[115]

113. See Theissen, "Éthique et communauté," 169–73.

114. Dibelius, *James*, 236, interprets these perfect-tense verbs prophetically as indicative of a future disaster. Martin, *James*, 45, disagrees and argues that the disaster has started to happen and there is more on the way; therefore, he translates ἐν ἐσχάταις ἡμέραις as "in the last days" rather than "for the last days."

Denunciation of the Wealthy: Landownership in 5:1-6

The wealthy in 5:1-6 are characterized with much more detail than in 2:1-13. In 2:2-3, the wealthy person wears gold rings and fine clothing, which may be the referent in 5:2-3 where the wealthy are told that their clothes are moth-eaten and their gold and silver rust. In 2:6-7, the wealthy oppress, drag into court, and blaspheme the good name. Beyond this, James only chastens his addressees (ἀδελφοί) for showing favoritism to these wealthy oppressors, who symbolize the system of the world. James 5:1-6 gives more specificity regarding these wealthy oppressors and prophetically pronounces their complete destruction. This marks a move from condemning a system, like the patronage system, to condemning people. In this case, it is not only an evil system; it is an evil system governed by evil people—total corruption.

The wealthy in 5:1-6 have wealth, fine clothing, and money (v. 2-3); they hoard their wealth (v. 3); they own land and have laborers who work for them (v. 4); they live luxuriously and self-indulgently (v. 5); and finally, they condemn and kill (v. 6). Landowners seem to be the particular target of James's prophetic denunciations here. As stated earlier, the agrarian economy of first-century Roman Palestine was profitable for a very small percentage of people and most of those were large landowners. For the masses of people who subsisted on farming, whether it was small personally owned farms or the larger landholdings of the landowners, life was incredibly difficult.[116] The relationship between small farmers and large landowners was tenuous as Maynard-Reid notes: "The difficulties encountered by the smaller holder vis-à-vis the large landowner were not limited to the manipulations of the big proprietor in the marketplace. The

115. Maynard-Reid, *Poverty and Wealth*, 81–82.
116. See Oakman, "Jesus and Agrarian Palestine."

giving of loans, the pressure exercised in the collection of loans, and the very real threat of expropriation on account of nonpayment of loans were a great source of tension."[117] This economic situation also extended to the Diaspora. According to Maynard-Reid, "Empire-wide there was an increasing concentration of rural wealth in the hands of just a few."[118] On a macro level, Philip A. Harland argues that "the economy of Palestine should not be understood in isolation; despite regional peculiarities that may be identified, this region was part of the larger economic world of the Roman Empire, and social-economic conditions in the region have their counterparts elsewhere in many respects."[119] The denunciation of the wealthy in James 5:1-6, then, includes the landowners in Palestine, but is not confined to them. As his diasporic audience heard James's denunciation of the wealthy, they could apply his rhetoric to their own situations in the Diaspora. For instance, on the Italian peninsula, landowners "tried to consolidate [their] holdings into a single enormous economic entity for greater efficiency."[120] This consolidation process is evidenced in a number of ancient sources in Palestine and abroad. In both cases,

117. Maynard-Reid, *Poverty and Wealth*, 89.

118. Ibid., 86.

119. Philip A. Harland, "The Economy of First-Century Palestine: State of the Scholarly Discussion," *Handbook of Early Christianity: Social Science Approaches*, ed. Anthony J. Blasi, Jean Duhaime, and Paul-André Turcotte (Lanham, MD: Altamira, 2001), 514–15.

120. Ramsay MacMullen, *Roman Social Relations: 50 B.C. to A.D. 284* (New Haven: Yale University Press, 1974), 6, goes into more detail, showing that "Cicero, Horace, Seneca, and many other writers censure this ruthless drive toward consolidation so often that one suspects a cliché (*De leg. Agr.* 3.4.14; Plin., *Ep.* 3.19; Petron., *Sat.* 48.3, 77.3; Hor., *Serm* 2.6.8f.; Sen., *Ep* 90.39; *De benef* 7.10). It is, however, a phenomenon not peculiar to Italy. The great estates of pasturage in Greece have been noted above, and Pliny the Elder reports that in his day 'six landlords owned half of Africa' (Plin., *N.H.* 18.35). Empire-wide, the unmistakable effects of this drive are visible in the increasing concentration of rural wealth into fewer hands, a gradual development that needs more study but is unquestioned fact. The details of its procedures can be seen at work in many specific cases. More than buyer and seller on a free market were involved, but rather a variety of cruel pressures exerted by the strong against the weak, the arrogant rich, 'the powerful,' against the adjoining farm, villagers, or the 'poor' (Plin., *Parad. Stoic* 6.46; Dio Chrysos. *Or* 46.7; Sen., *Ep* 90.39), sometimes by crooked litigation, sometimes by armed force (Sen. *De brev. vit.* 3.1; *Dig.* 47.11.9)." Josephus also offers several examples of land consolidation in *Ant.* (17.11.2, 17.13.5, 18.1.1) and *J.W.* (2.117, 2.214–17).

absentee landowners flocked to the cities and lived on the revenue generated from their rural farms. Urban environments, then, profited greatly from the rural areas, which created economic disparity and sociopolitical tension. Ramsay MacMullen summarizes this tension: "The two worlds regard each other as, on the one side, clumsy, brutish, ignorant, uncivilized; on the other side, as baffling, extortionate, arrogant."[121] MacMullen's analysis sounds eerily similar to Aimé Césaire's assessment of colonialism that we reviewed in chapter 2. Césaire's nativist critique of colonialism and MacMullen's analysis of the Roman economy contextualize James's condemnation of the wealthy in 5:1-6. Under such conditions, "For the native, life can only spring up again out of the rotting corpse of the settler."[122] Or, to use James's words, the rust of the aristocracy's money "will eat" their "flesh like fire" (5:3) "on the day of slaughter" (5:5). The social, political, and economic critique within James's denunciation of the wealthy reflects the agrarian economy that produced the Letter, but it also reflects a strong tradition that James inherits.

Traditions behind 5:1-6

As James begins the end, he prophetically calls the wealthy landowners to listen in the same way he called on the itinerant merchants in 4:13: ἄγε νῦν. After he has their attention, he demands that they weep using the same imperative that was used in 4:8-9 when denouncing ἁμαρτωλοί and δίψυχοι. As soon as the wealthy are commanded to weep, James begins to use the language of his pietistic tradition found in the prophets. The anarthrous participle ὀλολύζοντες modifies the wealthy as those who are supposed to wail. Although this is a *hapax legomenon* in the New Testament, the term is used multiple times as an imperative in Isa. 13:6, 14:31, 15:2-3,

121. MacMullen, *Roman Social Relations*, 15.

122. Fanon, *Wretched of the Earth*, 93.

23:1, 14, 24:11, and 52:5. In many of these cases, the prophetic call to mourn out loud is due to the devastation of the Day of the Lord when justice will be meted out by God on all those who have done wrong. Earlier in Isaiah, the prophet speaks against the leaders because they have plundered the poor (LXX πτωχοῦ): "The Lord enters into judgment with the elders and princes of His people: It is you who have devoured the vineyard; the plunder of the poor is in your house. What do you mean by crushing my people, by grinding the face of the poor? says the Lord God of hosts" (3:14-15). God's judgment on the leaders for "grinding the face of the poor" and "plundering the poor" clearly identifies this as James's ideological background. Borrowing "this onomatopoetic word [*ololuzontes*] vividly describes the howls of rage and pain of the damned, as it did in the Isaiah denunciation."[123] Isaiah 5:8 also describes the issue of consolidating land that is undoubtedly part of James's condemnation of the wealthy landowners: "Woe to you who join house to house, who add field to field, until there is room for no one but you, and you are left to live alone in the midst of the land!" It is clear from the content and vocabulary of the prophetic tradition that James is drawing on this tradition to condemn the wealthy landowners of his own time.

As James continues his denunciation, he calls on the Day of the Lord in 5:2-3 as a way to add to his invective. The wealthy have hoarded their wealth, garments, and money for "the last days" and their deterioration "will eat" their "flesh like fire" (5:3). Ralph P. Martin argues that the imminence of the end forces one to translate "in the last days" as if the end has already begun; "thus, with such an ominous event on the horizon, the misuse of wealth is taking place as a prelude to the coming of the Lord."[124] This interpretation

123. Maynard-Reid, *Poverty and Wealth*, 82.
124. Martin, *James*, 178.

strengthens the argument for translating the perfect verbs in these verses as intensive perfects as mentioned above. The destruction of the wealthy has already started to happen because their hoards of wealth, clothes, and money have already started to rot. This disdain for empire is reflected in Fanon's denigration of Europe's wealth that came by virtue of imperialism: "For in a very concrete way Europe has stuffed herself inordinately with the gold and raw materials of the colonial countries: Latin America, China, and Africa."[125] The reference to gold and clothing reminds the recipients of the situation in 2:2 where the wealthy were favored over the poor. Here, the wealthy are flatly condemned by the temporality of their possessions—a temporality that certainly is part of the Jesus tradition from which James borrows and to which he contributes: "Do not store up [θησαυρίζετε] for yourselves treasures on earth, where moth [σὴς] and rust [βρῶσις] consume and where thieves break in and steal" (Matt. 6:19).

Gold and silver were the currency of the aristocrats in antiquity. In the provinces, like Roman Palestine, the masses would have handled local bronze coinage. The gold coins of imperial Rome were aurei, and the silver coins—mentioned often in the New Testament—were denarii. According to Hanson and Oakman, "Gold and silver were employed regularly as media for storing 'value' by those who had precious metals to hoard."[126] They go on to argue that "[o]nly elites had large sums at their disposal and real monetary functionality."[127] In this socioeconomic situation, the aristocratic landowners hoarded massive wealth while the masses begged for "daily bread" and "forgiveness from debt" (see Matt. 6:11-12).[128] Adding insult to injury, money changers would inflate the exchange rate between

125. Fanon, *Wretched of the Earth*, 102.
126. Hanson and Oakman, *Palestine in the Time of Jesus*, 114.
127. Ibid., 116.

bronze and silver coinage to benefit themselves and the wealthy. John E. Stambaugh and David L. Balch's analysis of coinage in Roman Palestine shows that money changers in the East would inflate the price of one denarius as much as fifty percent, which was detrimental for those who primarily used bronze currency.[129] In this economic system that destroyed the poor and continually favored the wealthy, James echoes the prophet Zephaniah: "Neither their silver nor their gold will be able to save them on the day of the Lord's wrath; in the fire of his passion the whole earth shall be consumed; for a full and terrible end he will make of all the inhabitants of the earth" (1:18).

In 5:4, James identifies the condemned wealthy as landowners who systematically oppress and defraud their laborers. Using the literal "Jacob" rather than "James," Friesen argues that "[h]ere Jacob criticizes a fundamental feature of the Roman system of inequality: wealthy landowners exploiting the laborers who worked their fields."[130] Again, James uses a common motif from Torah and the prophets to critique the economic oppression levied against laborers. Here, at the heart of his pericope against the wealthy, James returns to Leviticus 19, which is the tradition he used when he opened the body of his letter in 2:1-13. Revisiting the terminology and ideation from Lev. 19:13 brings the anti-imperial argument to a close while clearly identifying the imperial other.[131] Leviticus 19:13 is important to quote in order to show how rooted James's argument is in this tradition: "You shall not *defraud* your neighbor; you shall not steal; and you shall not keep for yourself the *wages* of a *laborer* until morning" (emphasis mine).[132] It is clear that "Jacob relocates this

128. For the "Lord's Prayer" as revolutionary, see Oakman, "Jesus and Agrarian Palestine," 75–80; John Dominic Crossan, *The Greatest Prayer: Rediscovering the Revolutionary Message of the Lord's Prayer* (New York: HarperCollins, 2010).
129. Stambaugh and Balch, *New Testament*, 79.
130. Friesen, "Injustice or God's Will?," 25.
131. See Johnson, *Brother of Jesus*, 132.

ancient [prophetic] critique to the contemporary oppression of the urban poor by the local aristocracies of the Roman Empire."[133] Gerd Theissen agrees with Friesen and makes the argument that James's critique of the aristocratic landowners is an "indirect criticism" that is focused on "those who have political power," that is, the Roman imperial elite.[134] In this sense, the wealthy are equated with the world and its wisdom (James 3:13-18). The wages of the laborers that have been withheld by these Roman imperialists and the cries of the harvesters have continued to reach the ears of the Lord of war (κυρίου Σαβαὼθ). While these Roman imperialists may have the capacity to live in luxury, live in self-indulgence, fatten their hearts, and condemn and kill (5:5-6), their end is near.[135] Theissen understands verse 6 literally, which compels him to see Roman officials as the target for this hidden transcript: "But we talk of court cases (as already in 2:6ff) that end in death sentences. In the Roman Empire, the death sentences were pronounced by officials of the Empire, then by the imperial elite."[136] The string of aorist active indicative verbs in 5:5-6 rhetorically create a powerful case against the aristocratic landowners as murdering thieves; however, their greed is happening "on the day of slaughter" and their exorbitant lifestyle will only be experienced "on the earth" (ἐπὶ τῆς γῆς) as opposed to the competing kingdom of heaven. At every turn in 5:1-6, the wealthy, who represent Roman imperialists, are utterly condemned without any recourse for repentance. The Lord of war opposes these representatives of the world and the day of the great reversal is at hand. The violence envisioned by James's nativist rhetoric is best summed up by Fanon:

132. Other passages that evidence the depth of the tradition that James uses include Deut. 24:14-15, Job 31:38-40, Jer. 22:13, Mal. 3:5, Tob. 4:14, and Sir. 34:22-26.

133. Friesen, "Injustice or God's Will?," 26.

134. Theissen, "Éthique et communauté," 170.

135. See Martin, *James*, 180.

136. Theissen, "Éthique et communauté," 171.

"[D]ecolonization is always a violent phenomenon. . . . For if the last shall be first, this will only come to pass after a murderous and decisive struggle between the two protagonists."[137] In light of the cruel practices exercised by landowners inside and outside Palestine, James 5:1-6 is an anti-imperial assault that persuades the Diaspora to succinctly separate from the wealthy who controlled the Roman world.

Wisdom Two Ways

In what constitutes James's central argument against Roman imperialism, James 3:13-18 concentrates on two types of wisdom.[138] Wisdom from above is characterized as pure, peaceable, gentle, reasonable, full of mercy and good fruit, impartial and sincere (v. 17). The antithesis to wisdom from above is wisdom that is earthly, unspiritual, and demonic; full of jealousy, selfish ambition, disorder, and all kinds of wickedness (vv. 14-16).[139] This earthly wisdom is connected to James's critique of the patronage system (2:1-13) and his condemnation of the wealthy (5:1-6). Just as James 2:1-13 and 5:1-6 draw a clear distinction between the forces of good/poor and evil/wealthy, 3:13-18 sets these ideologies apart based on wisdom. Wisdom from above governs those who live under kingdom law (2:1-13) while earthly wisdom governs the "world." The Manicheism manifested in this section is indicative of nativist rhetoric that claims essentialist notions of identity and uses them against imperial

137. Fanon, *Wretched of the Earth*, 35, 37.

138. See Hartin, *James and the Q Sayings*, 97, who calls 3:13-18, coupled with 4:1-10, the "very heart and centre of the body of the epistle."

139. Hartin, *James and the Q Sayings*, 104, argues that there is only one "real" wisdom within the 3:13-18 pericope. There are those who are wise and those who are not wise: "James does not operate with a dualistic concept of wisdom. His aim is to emphasize that there is only one wisdom and it comes from above and is incompatible with a lifestyle that is characterized by jealousy, bitterness and party spirits." Hartin's argument would be stronger if the text did not actually describe a wisdom that was "earthly, unspiritual, and demonic" (3:15). In light of the text itself, James seems to be constructing a bifurcated world between rivaling wisdoms.

dominance.[140] What Jacques Chevrier said about African literature rings true for James's argument: "Born out of the realities of colonialism, and defined in reaction against those realities, African literature could hardly have had anything other than a polemical relationship with power, whatever form it takes, whether colonial, neo-colonial or post-colonial."[141] Seth Schwartz's comment is even closer to the source: "It is intuitively obvious that the ancient Jews (assuming that they behaved like a recognizably human group) were profoundly affected by the imperial powers under which they were constrained to live."[142] James, indicative of at least one Judean reaction to empire, creates a polemic in 3:13-18 by constructing an argument about wisdom that is nuanced by echoes from the Jesus tradition.[143] The wisdom of the world constitutes the cultural assumptions of the Roman Empire found in systems like patronage and landownership. These systems gave exorbitant favor to the wealthy and kept the poor in poverty. James rebukes this earthly wisdom with wisdom from above—a wisdom that springs from the Jesus tradition and utterly contradicts worldly wisdom. Here, wisdom from above equals the kingdom law that James explains in 2:1-13.[144]

140. Manicheism as defined in postcolonial terms rather than early Christian terms. See my previous discussion of this term above.

141. Jacques Chevrier, "Des formes variées du discours rebelle," *Notre Librairie* 148 (July–September 2002): 64.

142. Seth Schwartz, *Imperialism and Jewish Society, 200 bce to 640 CE* (Princeton and Oxford: Princeton University Press, 2004), 16.

143. Kloppenborg, Q, 116, shows that James reflects rhetorical sophistication by the way he paraphrases the Jesus tradition. Rather than quoting Jesus or a source verbatim, James paraphrases these traditions to suit his argument and/or audience: "The virtue of paraphrase was to recast a traditional saying in a form that was *apt* to the intended audience." In this way, James reflects common Greek rhetorical strategy found in writers such as Hermogenes and Aphthonius.

144. Hartin, *James and the Q Sayings*, 81, argues for a close connection between 3:13-18 and 2:1-13 based on the theme of wisdom. These two passages, along with the introductory pericope that alludes to them (1:2-8), are the "[t]hree main pericopae in James (1.2-8; 2.1-13; 3.13-18) [that] give attention to the nature of wisdom."

The dramatic contrast between "wisdom two ways" constitutes 3:13-18 as a thematic pericope distinct from what precedes and follows it. James tames the hybrid tongue in 3:1-12 and disparages the *dypsuchos* dichotomy in 4:1-12. Sandwiched between these two extended passages that warn against cultural hybridity, James critiques imperial wisdom and clarifies wisdom from above. Albert Memmi calls this process "a recovery of self and of autonomous dignity."[145] By rejecting imperial wisdom, James offers a different identity that reaches back into the past to authenticate a pure and unstained piety that is untouched by imperialism. Within James's rhetoric, there is no possibility to bridge the gap between "earthly" wisdom and wisdom from above. It is an absolute rejection. Again, Memmi: "Considered *en bloc* as *them, they* or *those,* different from every point of view, homogeneous in a radical heterogeneity, the colonized reacts by rejecting all the colonizers *en bloc.*"[146] Rejecting imperial wisdom and asserting traditional wisdom happens simultaneously and revives a "historic" self and community identity. To that end, James "re-explains the forgotten messages and adapts them to present-day needs."[147] These "forgotten messages" in the Letter of James are evidenced in the way James uses the Jesus tradition to shore up authentic, anti-imperial identity. The nativist rhetoric, then, is used "to rebuild his people, whatever their authentic nature; to reform their unity, communicate with it and to feel that they belong."[148] In this way, wisdom from above in 3:13-18 functions in a similar fashion as 2:1-13 and 5:1-6. All three pericopae utterly deny and reject imperial ideology and practice: "Before and during the revolt, the colonized always considers the colonizer as a model

145. Albert Memmi, *The Colonizer and the Colonized*, trans. Howard Greenfeld (Boston: Beacon, 1965 [French original, 1957]), 128.
146. Ibid., 130 (emphasis original).
147. Ibid., 132–33.
148. Ibid., 135.

or as an antithesis."[149] It is clear from James's rhetoric that Roman imperialism is the antithesis.

In order to support this thesis, however, I need to accomplish at least three things: (1) I need to connect James 3:13-18 with 2:1-13 and 5:1-6 in order to show that these three passages all function as refutations of empire; (2) I need to connect the heavenly wisdom of this passage with the Jesus tradition that James uses throughout this short letter; and (3) I need to connect earthly wisdom with the Roman Empire. In this exegetical process, I will use postcolonial literature and theory as a dialogue partner since so much of James relates to empire.

As I have noted above, the overall structure of James connects 3:13-18 with 2:1-13 and 5:1-6. Most scholars agree that James 1 functions as a table of contents that foreshadows all that follows, and many argue that James 5:7-20 functions as a closing to the letter. This introduction and conclusion leave James 2:1-5:6 as the body of the letter. According to this structure, the first and last pericopes of the body of James are 2:1-13 and 5:1-6. Both 2:1-13 and 5:1-6 deal with issues of wealth and poverty, however, on different levels. James 2:1-13 is a refutation against common patronage systems that rebukes those who would favor the wealthy. James uses the authority of the Jesus tradition, that is, the law of the kingdom, to make the case against patronage. James 5:1-6 culminates with an absolute refutation of wealthy landowners and their business practices. The material that separates 3:13-18 from these two passages at the beginning and end of the body of James interrupts the anti-imperial emphasis to concentrate on devaluing cultural hybridity. James 2:14-26 and 3:1-12 concentrate on criticizing those from within James's purview who would collude with empire. People who would emphasize faith rather than works and speak with forked tongues occupy these two

149. Ibid., 140.

sections. Immediately following the "wisdom two ways" passage, James returns to this critique of cultural hybridity arguing against the double-minded in 4:1-12 and business-savvy itinerant ministers in 4:13-17. Structurally, this places James 3:13-18 at the center of the body of the letter. It is at this center where James draws a complete distinction between the wisdom that guides him, that is, the wisdom of the law of the kingdom, and the wisdom that governs the world, that is, the social and economic systems of oppression.

The structural connection between these three passages evidences the thematic connection. Thematically, the beginning and ending of the body of James deals with culturally assumed systems of association between the wealthy and the poor. These culturally assumed social and economic systems constitute the wisdom of the Roman world. This is the earthly, unspiritual, and demonic wisdom that James references in 3:13-18. It is bitter jealousy (ζῆλον πικρὸν) and selfish ambition (ἐριθείαν) that fuel the patronage system, which James zealously condemns in 2:1-13. These two characteristics are important enough to mention twice in verse 14 and verse 16. In verse 14 these two vices are found in the heart, which is a term also used in 4:8, 5:5, and 5:8. There is a close connection with 4:8 where James implores the double-minded to "purify their hearts" and with 5:5 where James condemns the wealthy for "fattening their hearts for the day of slaughter." In both cases, the δίψυχοι and the πλούσιοι are driven by earthly wisdom. All three passages have empire as their primary focus of critique. All focus on an ancient way of life that is more ethical than the imperial values that constitute current socioeconomic relations. This turn toward a historic wisdom that comes from above and a kingdom law that governs rightly culminates with an utter rejection of those who embody the worldly system, that is, the wealthy. This nativist turn toward a precolonial past is best evidenced by Fanon when he remarks

> that this passionate search for a national culture which existed before the colonial era finds its legitimate reason in the anxiety shared by native intellectuals to shrink away from that Western culture in which they all risk being swamped. Because they realize they are in danger of losing their lives and thus becoming lost to their people, these men, hotheaded and with anger in their hearts, relentlessly determine to renew contact once more with the oldest and most pre-colonial springs of life of their people.[150]

In 2:1-13, James reaches back to the law of the kingdom. In 3:13-18, James reaches back to wisdom that comes from God. In 5:1-6, James reaches back to a prophetic declaration of doom for those who represent empire. James thus connects these three passages as the main anti-imperial passages within the letter.

The primary way that 3:13-18 critiques empire is with the Jesus tradition. This is true for both 2:1-13 and 5:1-6. Again, this is a tool of nativism. For James, the Jesus tradition is the way to access the ancient wisdom of Israel so that the "wisdom from above" is precisely the wisdom that comes from the Jesus tradition. James 3:13-18 begins with a rhetorical question that beckons Deut. 4:6 (LXX): "You will keep and do [φυλάξεσθε καὶ ποιήσετε] [them] because this is your wisdom and understanding [σοφία καὶ σύνεσις] before all the nations, who, when they hear all these regulations, will say, 'Behold, this great nation is a wise and understanding [σοφὸς καὶ ἐπιστήμων] people.'" James's question, "Who is wise and understanding [σοφὸς καὶ ἐπιστήμων] among you?" pulls the Diaspora back to Deuteronomy 4, where God is making Israel into a nation based on the statutes and commandments of Moses. There is no coincidence here that James is beckoning the Diaspora back to a time before Roman imperialism, where God constituted Israel as a sovereign people. Keeping and doing the commandments

150. Fanon, *Wretched of the Earth*, 209–10.

constituted wisdom and understanding then, and continues to constitute wisdom and understanding under Roman rule. The twofold expression "wisdom and understanding" also permeates Sirach (10:25; 21:15) and Daniel (5:11), both dating to an intense period of anti-imperial sentiment among Judeans during the Seleucid Period. For James, not unlike Deuteronomy, wisdom and understanding are evidenced by what one does, or to use a more accurate translation, by works. Lest one think that James is clearly referring back to ancient Scripture, one must not overlook a peculiar passage from the Jesus tradition. In Matt. 11:19 and Luke 7:35, there is an obscure short explanatory sentence that follows Jesus' statement about being called a "glutton and drunkard." Within the obscure sentence there is a textual variant in the Matthean version. To explain why Jesus would be called a glutton and drunkard, Matthew reasons, "Wisdom is justified by her deeds" (καὶ ἐδικαιώθη ἡ σοφία ἀπὸ τῶν ἔργων αὐτῆς). The textual variant has "Wisdom is justified by her children [τέκνων]." Luke 7:35 only differs from the variation in Matthew by adding "Wisdom is justified by *all* her children." Matthew's wisdom and works clearly echo or are echoed in James 3:13, where the terminology is the same. In a similar hermeneutical pattern as that found in 2:1–13, James uses the Jesus tradition to access ancient Scripture as a way to resist imperial wisdom.

The term "heart" (καρδία) is used repeatedly throughout the Hebrew Bible and the New Testament. It should be noted that James, who uses a wide variety of vocabulary, returns to this term often in his letter. As has been discussed briefly above, James uses καρδία here in 3:14 as well as in 1:26, 4:8, 5:5, and 5:8. In every case but 5:8 (strengthen your hearts), it is used negatively: "deceive their hearts" (1:26), "bitter jealousy and selfish ambition in your hearts" (3:14), "purify your hearts, you double-minded" (4:8), and "fatten your hearts for the day of slaughter" (5:5). The way James uses this term is reminiscent of the prophetic literature of the LXX. James 5:5 evokes Isaiah 6:10: "Fatten the heart of this people." In Isa. 29:13, where Israel is punished by God, James's negative use of heart may be seen: "The Lord said, 'These people draw near me with their lips honoring me, but their hearts are far from me." Again, however, instead of making a direct connection between James and ancient Scripture, the Jesus tradition mediates James's hermeneutic. In Matt. 15:8, these same words are put on Jesus' lips: "This people honors me with their lips, but their hearts are far from me." Matthew and Luke use "heart" more than any of the other writers of the New Testament.[151] In a passage that is shared by both Matthew and Luke, the Gospel writers have Jesus using this term in the most influential sermons in their Gospels: "For where your treasure [θησαυρός] is, there will be your heart [καρδία]" (Matt. 6:21/Luke 12:34). This connection between heart and treasure in the Jesus tradition also illumines 2:1-13 and 5:1-6. Later in Matt. 11:29, Matthew has Jesus tell his disciples, "Take my yoke upon you, and learn from me; for I am gentle [πραΰς] and humble in heart [ταπεινὸς τῇ καρδίᾳ]." The word for gentle there is identical to James 3:13: "gentleness that comes from wisdom," and ταπεινὸς is used in James 1:9. I do not want to overstate this point about the way James uses the word καρδία, but it is clear that this term connects James 3:14 to the Jesus tradition.

James 3:18 also echoes the Jesus tradition: "And a harvest of righteousness is sown in peace by those who do peace." Although there are important terminological connections between James 3:18 and the Jesus tradition with regard to "fruit/harvest" (καρπὸς), "righteousness" (δικαιοσύνης), "is sown" (σπείρεται), and "peace" (εἰρήνην), oddly the word in this passage that bears the most fruit is

151. Matthew uses καρδία/καρδίας/καρδίαν thirteen times, while Luke uses these terms thirty-two times between the Gospel and Acts.

the participle ποιοῦσιν. The most striking occurrence of ποιοῦσιν in the Jesus tradition is found in Matthew and Luke. Matthew 5:46—6:2 uses this word in repetitive fashion along with a list of thematic vocabulary that is found throughout the Letter of James:

> For if you love those who love you, what good is that? Don't tax collectors *do* [ποιοῦσιν] the same thing? And if you greet your brothers and sisters [ἀδελφοὺς] only, what are you *doing* [ποιεῖτε] excessively? Don't the Gentiles *do* [ποιοῦσιν] the same thing? Therefore, be perfect [τέλειοι] like your heavenly Father is perfect [τέλειός]. Beware doing [ποιεῖν] your righteousness in front of people to be seen by them; otherwise you have no wages [μισθὸν] from your Father in heaven. So whenever you give alms do not sound a trumpet before you, as the *hypocrites* [ὑποκριταὶ] *do* [ποιοῦσιν] in the synagogues and in the streets so that they might be glorified by people. Truly I tell you, they have received their wages [μισθὸν].

This passage from Matthew uses ποιοῦσιν in the same way as James but represents the actions of antagonists rather than protagonists. The term for hypocrites in Matt. 6:2 (ὑποκριταὶ) also echoes its opposite in James 3:17 that immediately precedes this passage (ἀνυπόκριτος). These close terminological connections link James 3:13-18 with the Jesus tradition.[152] James employs the tradition to refute imperial claims to authentic identity and action. Since the Jesus tradition offers James the authority he needs to reject imperialism, Jesus becomes James's anti-imperial agent or vice versa. The wisdom that comes from above is from God as 1:5 indicates, but it is mediated through the Jesus tradition. If wisdom from above comes from God through the Jesus tradition, then earthly wisdom from the world comes from the devil through the Roman Empire.

152. Many scholars make the specific connection between James 3:18 and Matt. 5:9 regarding the terms "those who do peace" (τοῖς ποιοῦσιν εἰρήνην) in James and "peacemakers" (οἱ εἰηνοποιοί) in Matthew. In fact, Hartin, *James and the Q Sayings*, 155, makes the compelling argument that there are "[o]nly two texts in the New Testament [that] speak of making peace, namely Mt 5.9 and Jas 3.18."

According to James 3:13-18, the world is driven by a logic or wisdom that runs counter to the logic/wisdom from above. Earthly, unspiritual, and demonic wisdom is none other than the cultural assumptions and economic systems of the Roman Empire. The wisdom from above creates a "resistance to the politics of assimilation" that had pervaded Palestine in the first century.[153] This wisdom that does not come down from above (v. 15) is full of jealousy, selfish ambition, disorder, and all kinds of evil deeds (v. 16). This kind of irredeemable wisdom is embodied by the wealthy in 5:3-4, who "have laid up treasure for the last days. Behold, the wages [μισθὸς] of the laborers who mowed your fields, which you kept back by fraud, cry out, and the cries of the harvesters have reached the ears of the Lord of hosts." Although the vocabulary is different, there is a remarkable congruent binary between 5:4, where James describes wealthy landowners, and 3:18, where he describes the peacemakers: "And a harvest of righteousness is sowed in peace by those who make peace." Wisdom from above is exemplified by these peacemakers. Wisdom from below is exemplified by these wealthy landowners. According to Fiensy's analysis of the ancient economy of the Lower Galilee during the first third of the first century, he shows that the economic "system, however, was against the peasant agriculturalist. It was hard just to survive, let alone to thrive or get ahead in that kind of economic world."[154] Fiensy goes on to declare that the economy was better during the first third than in the middle of the century. In other words, by the time the Letter of James was written, the economic situation in the Lower Galilee had worsened. Fiensy recollects what James predicts: "It may well have been better for the average farmer in Lower Galilee than the rest of Palestine during the time of Jesus

153. Aimé Césaire, *Discourse on Colonialism*, trans. Joan Pinkham (New York: Monthly Review Press, 1976 [French original, 1955]), 88.
154. Fiensy, "Ancient Economy," 204.

and Antipas. But Galilee's day was coming."[155] One wonders if Fiensy had James 5 in mind: "You have laid up treasures for the last days . . . you have fattened your hearts in a day of slaughter" (5:3, 5). The wisdom of these economic practices that arguably produced the Jewish Revolt four years after the death of James was directly generated by Roman provincial administrations and their client kings in Palestine (see Josephus's *J.W.* 2.427). According to Richard A. Horsley,

> [E]conomic hardship would have quickly resulted in social disintegration as well. Under pressure, families that had extended loans to other families would themselves have come to need repayment in order to survive. But the debtors would have been unable to repay. Ordinary *jealousies and backbiting* in the village community would have escalated into more serious conflicts. Families that had fallen heavily into debt would have been vulnerable to their creditors, who were most likely the Herodian elite, taking control of the production process, perhaps even taking their land outright.[156]

This economic system of *bitter jealousy and selfish ambition* that is full of disorder, wickedness, and all kinds of evil deeds seems to be the focus of James's earthly, unspiritual, and demonic wisdom. The connection between wisdom from below with the Roman Empire is only accentuated when James's critique of the patronage system in 2:1-13 and his condemnation of the wealthy in 5:1-6 are referenced. The accumulation of evidence identifies the Roman Empire as the source of the demonic wisdom that permeates society and functions as an opponent that James adamantly resists with nativist rhetoric.

James's nativist rhetoric of "wisdom two ways" reinforces, yet overturns, a binary of utter opposites in 3:13-18. James rescues a past through the Jesus tradition that gives the letter authority over

155. Ibid., 205.
156. Horsley, *Jesus and Empire*, 61 (emphasis mine).

Roman imperialism. From this authentic, pure, and perfect identity, something analogous to what Stuart Hall calls an "act of imaginative rediscovery," comes an alternative to the oppressive regime of imperialism.[157] In this way, the Letter of James functions as a "narrative of decolonization" as it calls on the disavowal of demonic wisdom.[158] In support of this anti-imperial strategy of nativism, Benita Parry argues that "[t]his of course means affirming the power of the reverse-discourses by arguing that anti-colonialist writings did challenge, subvert and undermine the ruling ideologies, and nowhere more so than in overthrowing the hierarchy of colonizer/colonized, the speech and stance of the colonized refusing a position of subjugation and dispensing with the terms of the colonizer's definitions."[159] The wisdom that James espouses calls the wealthy imperialists to "weep and wail for the miseries that are coming to" (5:1) them, and yet, reminds his diasporic audience that "a harvest of righteousness is sown in peace for those who make peace" (3:18). This is, indeed, wisdom two ways.

157. Stuart Hall, "Cultural Identity and Diaspora," in *Identity: Community, Culture, Difference*, ed. Jonathan Rutherford (London: Lawrence & Wishart, 1990), 223–24.
158. See Benita Parry, *Postcolonial Studies: A Materialist Critique* (London and New York: Routledge, 2004), 40.
159. Ibid.

5

Identifying the Mimetic Monster, Part 1

Now that the imperial presence in the Letter of James has been exposed, we will turn to the passages within the letter that discipline the mimetic monster, that is, hybrid identity. Roman imperialism was certainly an object of scorn for James, but those from his own movement who would befriend the sociopolitical world of Rome posed the greatest threat to his "authentic" identity. Hybridized identity that could morph depending on the circumstance represented the infiltration of Roman imperialism into the static identity of purity and perfection that James promotes. James confronts this infiltration in four passages in his short letter: 2:14-26 (Actions as Evidence), 3:1-12 (Talk as Walk), 4:1-12 (Duality as Difference), and 4:13-17 (Road to Conflict). In each section, James challenges notions of hybridity that are exemplified in certain Pauline writings. At this point, it is important to analyze Paul's complex negotiations of empire.

A Postcolonial Paul

Although her work on Paul is not specifically postcolonial, Caroline Johnson Hodge highlights an aspect of Paul's identity relevant to postcolonial concerns that hitherto has been largely unexplored. In contrast to James's static identity, Hodge portrays Paul's identity negotiation as fluctuating between fluidity and fixity. Paul has multiple identities that are hierarchically structured and used strategically depending on his (or his audience's) circumstance. In the end, however, Paul's identity as one who is "in Christ" trumps all of his other nested identities as Hodge argues: "Paul would place his status as being 'in Christ' above being 'of the tribe of Benjamin' or 'blameless in the Law,' even as these are all a part of his Judeanness. . . . Like Paul, these baptized gentiles have added another facet to their own complex, multiple identities. Paul urges them to put their 'in-Christness' first, as he has done, above all other components of their identity."[1] In this instance, Paul's calling to be the apostle to the gentiles "necessitates some reprioritizing of the other facets of his Judean identity."[2] Elsewhere Hodge emphatically makes her case that Paul always understands his nested identities within the realm of Judeanness, and his writings, specifically Galatians and Romans, capture him in the process of "mythmaking" that retells "the story of Israel to make a place for the gentiles."[3] Here, she follows one version of the new perspective on Paul by understanding his letters to be addressed only to gentiles who were *in Christ*. Paul incorporates gentiles into the story of Israel through ethnic and kinship reasoning.[4]

1. Caroline Johnson Hodge, "Apostle to the Gentiles: Constructions of Paul's Identity," *Biblical Interpretation* 13, no. 3 (2005): 286.
2. Ibid., 277.
3. Caroline Johnson Hodge, *If Sons, Then Heirs: A Study of Kinship and Ethnicity in the Letter of Paul* (Oxford: Oxford University Press, 2007), 5.
4. Further on "ethnic reasoning," see Denise Kimber Buell, *Why This New Race? Ethnic Reasoning in Early Christianity* (New York: Columbia University Press, 2005).

Paul, then, is "a *Ioudaios* writing to those [gentiles] committed to the messiah of Israel about how they fit into God's larger plan."[5] Ethnically, gentiles are made into the seed of Abraham when they "are baptized into Christ."[6] In this way, their genealogy within Israel is fixed in procreative terms (Abraham) in spite of the fact that their gentile-ness becomes fluid within this system. *Ioudaioi*, on the other hand, continue to be faithful to God through the Law. Through this understanding, Hodge "suggests that individuals and groups might embody several ethnic or other identities, situationally emphasizing one while downplaying others. This interpretive framework helps us understand Paul's careful construction of Jews and gentiles, now descended from the same founding ancestor and belonging to the same God, but not collapsed into one group."[7] Paul's writings display a remarkable sense of identity entrepreneurship that reprioritizes both his identity as a teacher of gentiles and the identities of the gentiles-in-Christ to whom he writes. In the end, Hodge proposes that "Paul adjusts his own identity to accommodate gentiles, a decision rooted in pedagogical strategy and theological conviction."[8]

In postcolonial terms, Paul creates and justifies hybrid identities, and actively pushes the boundaries of his own hybridity, as Hodge rightly concludes:

> As I have shown, being in-Christ is not ethnically neutral; rather, it falls under the umbrella of Jewishness. Yet Paul does not imagine gentiles-in-Christ as Jews; in fact, he still calls them gentiles. Thinking in terms of multiple identities, we might imagine these gentiles as occupying a mixed or "hybrid" identity that is not completely "other" than what they were, but is certainly not identical to their previous status. Postcolonial theorists use the term "hybridity" to describe a complex process whereby

5. Hodge, *If Sons, Then Heirs*, 10.
6. Ibid., 16.
7. Ibid., 117.
8. Ibid., 121.

> the interaction of the colonized and colonizer inevitably influences the self-definition of each.[9]

In Bhabha's terms, these Christ-confessing gentiles, as Hodge understands them, might be said to occupy a Third Space: they are no longer simply gentiles nor are they now simply Judean, but they are both and neither at one and the same time. Hodge's quick gaze into postcolonial biblical criticism at the end of her analysis is not surprising, as Paul's hybridity has been noticed by others in this field. Jeremy Punt, for instance, understands Paul's hybridity in terms of postcolonial mimicry where Paul may "subtly challenge and subvert" colonial systems of oppression such as the patronage system. Punt asks, "[H]ow would the Pauline insistence on faithfulness (*pistis*) 'apart from works (*erga*)' have resonated when Roman patronage and the 'works' of benefactors determined people's lives and livelihood (as ultimately underwritten by the emperor as benefactor *par excellence* who readily claimed his 'works' [cf. Augustus and the *Res Gestae*])?"[10] In this case, Paul stands against empire in the way he uses empire against itself. As Punt suggests: "Through dissenting deference, Paul's mimicry of Empire created the impression that he internalized and replicated imperial culture while he actually used the ambivalence of the hegemonic discourse to his advantage."[11] In another place, Punt argues that Paul's anti-imperial rhetoric is more explicit concerning the theme of freedom in Paul's writings: "As much as the communal implications of 'freedom' threaten the established order and its power structure, and not merely posited a neutral alternative, Paul's freedom is not only a 'social' matter but quite pointedly has strong political

9. Ibid., 141.
10. Jeremy Punt, "Empire as material setting and heuristic grid for New Testament interpretation: Comments on the value of postcolonial criticism," *HTS Teologiese Studies/Theological Studies* 66, no. 1 (2010), http://www.hts.org.za/index.php/HTS/article/view/330, doi: 10.4102/hts.v66i1.330.
11. Punt, "Empire as material setting."

implications."[12] By co-opting imperial terminology, Paul used the master's tools as a way to "win" his audience. This form of mimicry as resistance is common in Bhabhan postcolonial theory. In this way, Paul is the mimetic monster that intervenes in the imperial-colonial encounter in an attempt to provide different ways of being—specifically, in Christ. "Paul undoubtedly insists on an apocalyptic rupture introduced by Christ, symbolized by the formulas *en Christō* and *en Iēsou*, and leading to a new world-order without the sociological oppositions so characteristic of his world."[13] Paul's (mis)use of freedom and other imperial terms functions as a form of Spivakian catachresis where Paul is replicating empire in an attempt to turn it against itself.[14] Paul's retooling of imperial terminology is noted by other Pauline scholars, who also read Paul in relation to empire.

This anti-imperial Paul is even less nuanced in Neil Elliott's *The Arrogance of Nations: Reading Romans in the Shadow of Empire*. Elliott sees Paul's letter to the Romans as a "shot across the bow of imperial propaganda."[15] The "sinful degeneration" in Rom. 1:18-32 is intended, according to Elliott, to lead Paul's hearers to "recognize definite allusions to none other than *the Caesars themselves*."[16] Paul's anti-imperial rhetoric in Romans, then, challenges the imperial house as the site of corruption and degeneration, but only does so implicitly as "hidden discourse." Romans, in this sense, does not represent

12. Jeremy Punt, "Towards a Postcolonial Reading of Freedom in Paul," in *Reading the Bible in the Global Village: Cape Town*, ed. Justin S. Ukpong (Atlanta: Society of Biblical Literature, 2002), 135–36.
13. Ibid., 142.
14. See Punt, "Towards a Postcolonial Reading," 139. Here, Punt specifically mentions "euangelion, sōtēr, pistis, dikaiosunē, and ekklēsia" as terms that Paul (mis)uses with political overtones. Paul's adaptation of these terms reassigns meaning and acts as political resistance. For Spivak's concept of catachresis, see above.
15. Neil Elliott, *The Arrogance of Nations: Reading Romans in the Shadow of Empire* (Minneapolis: Fortress Press, 2008), 72.
16. Ibid., 79 (emphasis original).

explicit anti-imperial discourse as much as it lays "claim on the allegiance of [Paul's] listeners with which the rival claims of empire inevitably interfered."[17] Paul, however, provides the Romans with what Elliott calls "an alternative offstage transcript," in which Jesus is exemplified as the *true* Son of God in contrast to Nero, who was an adopted son of the deified Claudius.[18] The opening lines of Paul's letter to the Romans emphasize, according to Elliott, "the reality of Jesus' messianic identity, as confirmed by sacred writing, royal lineage, and the power of God, and thus offer an implicit contrast with the ubiquitous, but in Paul's view unreal, claims of the imperial house."[19]

This anti-imperial Paul that Elliott portrays seems to be betrayed by the text of Romans itself—specifically Rom. 13:1-7, which begins, "Let every person be subject to the governing authorities; for there is no authority except from God, and those authorities that exist have been instituted by God." This passage is so incomprehensible to Elliott that he suggests "that aspects of Paul's language militate against hearing this passage as an unambiguous endorsement of Roman rule."[20] Elliott emphasizes Roman peace as Neronian imperial propaganda, and how ideologically Nero's policies made "the sword" unnecessary. Highlighting ancient sources that shower Nero with encomium, Elliott argues that Paul's use of "be subject" (ὑποτασσέσθω), "fear" (φόβος), and "sword" (μάχαιραν) all conspire against this Neronian imperial propaganda that suggests there was nothing to fear and there was no need to "be subjugated" when you were a friend of Rome. For Elliott, Paul's statement that

17. Ibid., 15.
18. Ibid., 70–71.
19. Ibid., 71.
20. Ibid., 155. This is exactly how James D. G. Dunn interprets this passage in his commentary on Romans. Cf. James D. G. Dunn, *Romans 9–16*, WBC, 38B (Dallas: Word, 1988), 757–74 (specifically 759, 769–71).

"the authority does not bear the sword in vain" (Rom. 13:4) counters imperial claims that Nero's Roman peace was so pervasive that he did not need a sword to govern. Elliott declares that "Paul cannot have declared that the authority 'does not bear the sword idly' without his audience hearing a pointed refutation of a central theme in Nero's propaganda."[21] In spite of his insistence, Elliott later retreats somewhat by conceding that "[i]t is impossible to read a single coherent posture in Rom 13:1-7."[22] It neither supports nor subverts Roman imperialism. Elliott summarizes his analysis of Rom. 13:1-7 by showing how Paul's argumentation is fraught with inconsistencies:

> We have seen contradictions on the surface of Romans that reveal tensions beneath the surface: for example, God is the one who subjects the world to futility, *yet* God's Spirit groans for deliverance from that bondage (8:18-25). God calls human beings to free and willing obedience, not to slavery, *yet* this obedience also requires submission to God (8:7; 10:3) and, improbably, subjection to the governing authorities (13:1). And we have seen that these tensions arise, not from an idiosyncratic incoherence on Paul's part, but from fundamentally irresolvable contradictions in the material and ideological conditions in which the letter was written and which the letter was an attempt to resolve.[23]

Elliott's work on Paul and empire reveals a deep-seated postcolonial ambivalence at work in the writings of Paul. Paul is difficult to locate specifically because of his ambivalence that is indicative of postcolonial hybridity. In his analysis of Pauline hybridity, Robert Seesengood shows that "[h]ybrids have no stable cultural identities; they are not completely subaltern, colonized identities conscripted into and influenced by the values, and in this case rhetoric, of the

21. Elliott, *The Arrogance of Nations*, 156.
22. Ibid.
23. Ibid., 156 (emphasis original).

colonizer."[24] Hybrid identity is "simultaneously compliant and subversive," so in Paul's context, "[t]here were no 'pure' Romans or Greeks or Jews."[25] In this sense, hybridity creates a liminal space/identity that problematizes simple binary notions of colonizer/colonized. This construction of liminal identity provides an area that can be manipulated in ways that resist imperial power via mimicry that performs a mockery. It is in this liminal space where Paul, according to Seesengood, mimics conventional athletic tropes "to create a new, communal, hybrid identity."[26] Offering himself as a model of the agonized athlete always training/running for the prize, Paul calls for his listeners' allegiance—even their citizenship (πολίτευμα in Phil. 3:20)—to his hybridized identity.

Joseph Marchal complicates this discussion on Paul as an anti-imperial hybrid by using a feminist, postcolonial bifocal lens to read Paul—specifically Paul's letter to the Philippians. He focuses on the intricacies of imperialism but also how imbedded patriarchy is in both imperial-colonial constructions and Paul's writings. His skillful reading against Paul shows Paul's participation in imperialism by uncritically using patriarchal norms to structure his gospel and worldview. In this case, Marchal resists reading Paul as a simple anti-imperial agent bent on decolonization. In Marchal's analysis, Paul participates in more of a neocolonial enterprise rather than disrupting imperial-colonial structures. He interprets Paul from the standpoint of one who mimics empire not merely to resist it but to co-opt its authority for his own purposes. He also highlights the weakness of postcolonial theory itself as a form of liberation and justice: "Aside from the hopefully now obvious shortcomings in terms of gender,

24. Robert Paul Seesengood, "Hybridity and the Rhetoric of Endurance: Reading Paul's Athletic Metaphors in a Context of Postcolonial Self-Construction," *Bible and Critical Theory* 1, no. 3 (2005): 1.
25. Ibid., 2.
26. Ibid., 9.

Bhabha's focus on the ambivalently hybrid 'mimic man' may not be nearly as seditious as originally hoped."[27] Marchal, focusing his bifocals but emphasizing feminism, wonders "what makes an imitation *different enough* from the coercive call that it troubles the dynamic."[28] In this sense, rather than mimicking/mocking empire as model (do as I do/mimic me), Paul mirrors this imperial move and applies it to his audience in Philippi in coercive mimeticism: "In this way, Paul's arguments coincide with and reinforce imperial power: the common strategy of divide-and-conquer."[29] Here, Marchal follows Rey Chow's critique of mimesis and understands Paul's form of mimicry as "internal policing of group boundaries" as "a way to attack or shame others as disloyal for not being properly 'authentic,' leading to lateral violence within or across ethnic groups rather than resistance."[30] Marchal is correct in seeing "lateral violence" within Pauline writings as Paul attacks his opponents; however, this does not preclude Paul from being an anti-imperial agent. In fact, this bolsters Paul's identity as a hybrid rather than some form of Pauline nativism, a concept to which Marchal alludes but never explicitly names. Paul's "anti-models," who "work out of envy, rivalry, and divisiveness ([Phil.] 1:15-17; cf. 2:3) and 'seek their own things' (2:21; cf. 2:4)" and whom Paul "labels a 'crooked and twisted generation' (2:15), dogs, evil-workers, and the mutilation (3:2), as well as enemies (3:18; cf. 1:28)," are better understood as meriting the nativist label than Paul's strategic assimilation.[31]

27. Joseph A. Marchal, *The Politics of Heaven: Women, Gender, and Empire in the Study of Paul* (Minneapolis: Fortress Press, 2008), 82.
28. Ibid., 81.
29. Ibid., 78.
30. Ibid., 76. Cf. Rey Chow, *The Protestant Ethnic and the Spirit of Capitalism* (New York: Columbia University Press, 2002), 95–127.
31. John M. G. Barclay, "Paul among Diaspora Jews: Anomaly or Apostate?," *Journal for the Study of the New Testament* 60 (1995): 89–120, argues persuasively that Paul's assimilation with the Greco-Roman world is precisely what caused him so much trouble among other diaspora Judeans. In this sense, Paul is both anomaly (highly assimilated to but not accommodating with

Paul's reception among modern scholars as either an anti-imperial agent or Roman replica adds strength to the argument that Paul is a hybrid. In fact, it is because of Paul's hybridity that there is so much difficulty in defining him. In many ways, John M. G. Barclay is surely correct: "The Apostle Paul defies categorization."[32] Paul is not anti-Roman in a nativist sense (contra Marchal) and Paul is not easily subordinate to Roman imperialism (contra Dunn's analysis of Rom. 13:1-7). It is clear, insofar as hybridity can be clear, that Paul's hybridity blurs the boundaries between simple acquiescence and subversion, as Seesengood adequately explains. In other words, hybridity entails ambivalence. Paul uses imperial ideology when necessary to argue against empire, but supports imperial claims at other times. Overall, Paul negotiates a hybrid Judeanness that resists—however subtly—both empire and notions of "pure" Judeanness. This process of hybrid identity negotiation is what seemingly created so many problems for Paul's many opponents. Paul emerges as an anti-imperial hybrid who negotiates his identity within the Roman Empire to wrestle away gentiles' allegiance from Rome to Christ, which contradicts notions of any "pure and undefiled piety" (James 1:27). He is self-identified as a Judean in many of his letters, but his identity *in Christ* is his primary means of self-expression specifically among gentiles. His audience is explicitly gentile, and in Galatians and Romans he writes in a way that incorporates gentiles into the story of Israel through the genealogy of Abraham by being baptized *in Christ*. It is also clear from his letters that Paul had opponents within the Jesus movement who did not agree with Paul's strategy of incorporating gentiles into the story of Israel. In Galatians, Paul explicitly refers to one group of opponents as "men from James"

Greco-Roman culture) and apostate (due to the way his identity negotiation was rejected by other Judeans—even Judeans who were "in Christ").

32. Barclay, "Paul among Diaspora Jews," 89.

(2:12), who, it seems, vehemently disagreed with him regarding his teaching related to the incorporation of gentiles into the covenant between God and Israel. Within the same letter, Paul describes his encounter with James in Jerusalem as one where Paul presented his "gospel" that he preached to the gentiles in order to make sure he "was not running, or had not run, in vain" (Gal. 2:2). According to Paul, he was exonerated of any wrongdoing by James himself. However, after (re)constructing what is, in effect, a postcolonial Paul who is hyper-hybrid in his anti-imperialism, it is hard to imagine a nativist James who would be so affirming of such an "entrepreneur of identity"—especially an entrepreneur who "no longer had a recognised authority relationship with the churches in Galatia."[33] It is to this conflict within the Letter of James between nativism and hybridity that I now turn.

Actions as Evidence (2:14-26)

The faith/works binary in James 2:14-26 received a tremendous amount of attention during and after the Reformation due to the anti-Pauline rhetoric that James employs. Although many modern scholars downplay the oppositional nature of James 2:14-26 vis-à-vis certain Pauline sensibilities, I will highlight these differences and argue that James is directly responding to Pauline notions of hybridized identity. The conflict between James and Paul, however,

33. N. H. Taylor, "Apostolic Identity and the Conflicts in Corinth and Galatia," in *Paul and His Opponents*, ed. Stanley E. Porter, Pauline Studies, 2 (Atlanta: Society of Biblical Literature, 2005), 104. Hans Dieter Betz, *Galatians: A Commentary on Paul's Letter to the Churches in Galatia*, Hermeneia (Philadelphia: Fortress Press, 1979), emphasizes the frustration that the Jerusalem leaders would have experienced with Paul, "Thus Paul did not go [to Jerusalem] as a humble petitioner, but as a tough negotiator who forced the Jerusalem authorities to make a decision which one can imagine they made only with great reluctance," 86. Paul's forcefulness, according to Betz, could cause readers to wonder about the trustworthiness of Paul's assessment of the Jerusalem leaders' affirmation of his preaching. See also J. Louis Martyn, *Galatians: A New Translation with Introduction and Commentary*, Anchor Bible, 33A (New York: Doubleday, 1998), 188–93.

has less to do with a faith/works binary than with the issue of identity. The faith/works binary simply functions as one site for James's and Paul's respective politics of identity. As I have shown, James takes a nativist position in contrast to a hybrid position—a hybrid position in which Paul is comfortably at home. The polemical nature of this "dialogue" between James and Paul is then set in the context of anti-imperial discourse. James takes a very conservative position and argues that identity should come from a pure piety that is set in opposition to oppressive cultural norms and has continuity with that which is old, that is, the piety of Abraham and Rahab. Paul, on the other hand, argues for an identity that is based on something new and, to use postcolonial terminology, hybrid. James's and Paul's arguments can then be seen as an argument between nativist resistance to colonial power, which is characterized by reproducing colonial representations as instruments of resistance, and hybrid resistance, which is characterized by blurring the boundaries of colonizer/colonized in order to renegotiate a new set of power relations within a liminal space.

Meeting(s) of James and Paul

The tenuous relationship between James and Paul is narrated in Galatians 2–3 and Acts 15. Both Gal. 2:1-10 and Acts 15:1-29 recount the events that happened at what scholars call the Jerusalem Council or the Apostolic Council.[34] In both accounts, Paul meets James and

34. Although Douglas R. De Lacy, "Paul in Jerusalem" *New Testament Studies* 20 (1973–1974): 82–86, argues that Paul's visit to Jerusalem in Gal. 2:1-10 is described in Acts 9; and Lloyd Gaston, *Paul and the Torah* (Vancouver: University of British Columbia Press, 1987), 108, is cautious of the connection between Gal. 2:1-10 and Acts 15:1-29, there is wide consensus that these two passages reflect the same event, however differently. For the consensus view, see John M. G. Barclay, "Mirror-Reading a Polemical Letter: Galatians as a Test Case," in *The Galatians Debate: Contemporary Issues in Rhetorical and Historical Interpretation*, ed. Mark D. Nanos (Peabody, MA: Hendrickson, 2002), 380; Betz, *Galatians*, 79–85; James D. G. Dunn, "The New Perspective on Paul: Whence, What and Whither?" in *The New Perspective on Paul*, rev. ed. (Grand Rapids: Eerdmans, 2005), 30, 38; Philip F. Esler, "Making and Breaking an

there is a discussion about how Gentiles are incorporated into the Jesus movement. The central issue is circumcision. Hans Conzelmann calls this "the great turning point, the transition from the primitive church to the 'contemporary' church. From this point on the apostles disappear, even in Jerusalem itself. In Jerusalem continuity is represented by James, in the Gentile Christian church by Paul."[35] Conzelmann divides the formation of the Jesus movement in two: James represents the traditional Judean formation and Paul represents the newer gentile formation. Luke Timothy Johnson, on the other hand, emphasizes the apparent unity that resulted from the meeting: "But we must observe now that the decision by James emphatically agrees with the perception of Peter, Paul, and Barnabas, that God was at work in the Gentile mission that the Church must respond obediently to God's initiative. The Pharisaic position is emphatically rejected. The equal status of the Gentiles in the messianic community is confirmed by the head of the Jerusalem community."[36] Johnson's analysis of Acts 15 seems to inform his later commentary on James. For Johnson, there is absolutely no indication of any dispute between James and Paul in Acts 15. According to Acts 15:6-7, however, the apostles and elders consider the matter of circumcision for the gentiles *at length*, which indicates that this was still an important issue during the time Acts was written. It is also worth noting that in both Acts 10:1-11:18 and Peter's speech in Acts 15:7-11, Luke presents Peter as the inaugurator of the mission to the

Agreement Mediterranean Style: A New Reading of Galatians 2:1-14," in *Galatians Debate*, 277; Joseph A. Fitzmyer, *The Acts of the Apostles: A New Translation with Introduction and Commentary,* Anchor Bible, 31 (New York: Doubleday, 1998), 538–41; Robert Jewett, "The Agitators and the Galatian Congregation" in *Galatians Debate*, 336, 341; Luke Timothy Johnson, *The Acts of the Apostles*, Sacra Pagina, 5 (Collegeville, MN: Liturgical, 1992), 270; and Martyn, *Galatians*, 111, 200.

35. Hans Conzelmann, *Acts of the Apostles: A Commentary on the Acts of the Apostles* (Philadelphia: Fortress Press, 1987), 115.

36. Johnson, *Acts*, 272.

gentiles—a presentation that conflicts sharply with Galatians 2. Luke is intent on presenting Peter as the original champion of the gentile mission because he wants to present that mission in turn as rooted in the activity of the apostles (the twelve, Luke's narrow conception of apostleship) and hence standing in smooth continuity with the legacy of Jesus. This aspect of Acts is important in order to draw a sharp distinction between Acts 15 and Galatians 2 in spite of the passages narrating the same episode.

Acts

After a speech from Peter (Acts 15:7-11) and a report from Barnabas and Paul (Acts 15:12), James finally speaks. His speech ends the debate and brings the meeting to a close with these words: "Therefore I have reached the decision that we should not trouble those Gentiles who are turning to God, but we should write to them to abstain only from things polluted by idols and from fornication and from whatever has been strangled and from blood" (Acts 15:19-20). Although James decrees that gentiles do not have to be circumcised, he does insist that they observe certain food laws prescribed in the Torah (see Lev. 17:8-18:30). These conditions also highlight a difference between the Lukan account of this meeting in Jerusalem and Paul's in Galatians, where Paul says that he was only told to "remember the poor" (Gal. 2:10). Barnabas and Paul are then sent to the Antioch church with a letter describing the results of the meeting. In the Acts story, written decades after James's death, James is portrayed as *the* authority figure at the Jerusalem Council and Paul is characterized as someone under James's authority. I mention the meeting in Acts only to show that the significance of the meeting still mattered decades after the event. This event mattered to Luke primarily as the myth of origins for gentile mission that was the dominant form of "mission" in his own day—and he seems intent on rooting that myth in the authority of

Jesus' elected apostles, as noted above. This myth of origin, however, also evidences the power differential between James in Jerusalem and Paul in the Diaspora—at least from the point of view of the author of Acts. Fitzmyer's warning about Acts 15, however, must be heeded:

> Its conflated character is widely admitted, even if agreement in analysis is not found. In this chapter one has to distinguish the historical background of what is recounted from the Lucan literary presentation of it and what seems to have been the Lucan telescoping of materials, and to reckon also with the relation of what is recounted here not only to other things to come in Acts, but also to Galatians 2.[37]

Galatians

Paul's own account of the Jerusalem Council in Galatians portrays a much more hostile and ambiguous encounter with James, and is our only first-person source for the encounter. Paul tries not to reveal his subservient position in relation to James, but seemingly slips in Gal. 2:2: "Then I laid before them (though only in a private meeting with the acknowledged leaders) the gospel that I proclaim among the Gentiles, in order to make sure that I was not running, or had not run, in vain." In other words, these leaders—James in particular—had the power to authorize or deny the legitimacy of Paul's message. Martyn muddies these waters by claiming that Paul's response to James and the other leaders is more ambiguous: "What is Paul's stance toward these men? Noting that he uses the expression [acknowledged leaders] four times in the present paragraph (in the NT it emerges only here), not always in what one would call the same tone of voice, we are prepared for some ambivalence."[38] Martyn argues that "Paul does see these persons in a special light," but is "equally firm that God's *eschatological* vocation is the only authorization to be

37. Fitzmyer, *Acts*, 552. Johnson, *Acts*, 270, also cautions any overhasty reading of Acts 15, recognizing it as "partial and tendentious."
38. Martyn, *Galatians*, 191–92.

acknowledged among human beings."[39] In other words, Paul writes this to show that "it is their responsibility to recognize God's gospel when it is laid before them."[40] Throughout Paul's narration Paul minimizes James's influence in determining the course of Paul's gentile mission. From the first verse in his letter to the Galatians, Paul emphasizes his divine commission to the gentiles—"Paul an apostle, sent neither by human commission nor from human authorities, but through Jesus Christ and God the Father, who raised him from the dead" (1:1)—as well as the divine origin of the gospel he received—"For I want you to know, brothers, that the gospel that was proclaimed by me is not from human origin; for I did not receive it from a human source, nor was I taught it, but I received it through a revelation of Jesus Christ" (1:11-12). In order to emphasize his divine commission, Paul states that he did not go to Jerusalem after he received the revelation in order to confer with leaders there. Only three years after his revelation did he go to Jerusalem and meet with Cephas (Peter) and "James the Lord's brother" (1:19). Paul, feeling the need to stress the importance of this meeting happening *three years* after his revelation, concludes: "In what I am writing to you, behold, before God, I do not lie!" (1:20). The emphatic "behold" (ἰδοὺ), coupled with his assertion that he is not lying, makes one wonder if the "divine" status of Paul's revelation was doubted by some in Galatia. Betz shows that this kind of oath "provides a kind of 'proof' to cover what is in doubt. But Paul's words are too concise to conclude from them precisely what was in doubt and why."[41] Betz alludes to the different version of this event in Acts as a place that supports "the doubts rather than Paul's assurances."[42]

39. Ibid., 192.
40. Ibid.
41. Betz, *Galatians*, 79.
42. Ibid.

After this window into Paul's doubters, Paul explains that his next visit to Jerusalem comes fourteen years later as a result of another divine revelation. During his second clandestine meeting with "acknowledged leaders" (δοκοῦσιν), Paul declared/submitted for consideration (ἀνεθέμην) to them his gospel that he proclaimed to the gentiles (2:1-2). The very nature of his gospel proclamation was the basis for this meeting. Was Paul's "gospel proclamation to the gentiles" legitimate or not? This question inevitably leads to others: What was Paul's "gospel proclamation to the gentiles" and why was it controversial? James D. G. Dunn answers these questions by pointing to the volatile sociopolitical landscape both in Palestine and Syria during the time Paul wrote Galatians. According to Dunn, "During the period in which the Antioch incident took place Jews had to be on their guard against what were or were seen to be repeated threats to their national and religious rights. . . . Against this background the hypothesis becomes rather compelling that the open table-fellowship practiced at Antioch was perceived by the Jerusalem church (and perhaps by other Jews) as such a threat. The mission of the men from James would then have been their reaction to that threat."[43] Paul's preaching, according to Dunn, threatened certain Judean identity within Antioch.

It is important to see how Paul narrates the rest of this encounter with the "acknowledged leaders" in Jerusalem. Paul had to defend his gospel before the acknowledged leaders against "false believers." In this instance, Paul describes his gospel as freedom in Christ Jesus and makes reference to his gentile companion not having to be circumcised. Paul adamantly refuses to concede to these "false believers" and then makes a disparaging parenthetical remark about the "acknowledged leaders," saying, "What they actually were makes

43. James D. G. Dunn, "The Incident at Antioch (Gal 2:11-18)," in *Galatians Debate*, 206.

no difference to me; God shows no partiality" (2:6). In this verse, Paul characterizes the Jerusalem authorities in a manner "analogous to the characterization of the opponents."[44] Through this rhetoric Paul attempts to show a clear independence from the Jerusalem leaders' capacity to judge his gospel proclamation, but Betz asks the questions that Paul's letter begs: "If Paul did not receive his gospel and commission from the Jerusalem authorities but from God himself (cf. 1:1, 12), he must come to terms with the question of what role these authorities should play for him. More specifically, why did he and Barnabas even go to Jerusalem? What really did happen at the conference? If this conference did not prove Paul's dependence on Jerusalem, what did the meeting prove?"[45] Paul leaves these questions dangling. By the end of the meeting, Paul says that the acknowledged leaders "saw" that he was "entrusted with the gospel for the uncircumcised [ἀκροβυστίας]" by God, and James, Cephas, and John—the acknowledged pillars—recognized this and extended the "right hand of fellowship." This handshake, according to Paul, sealed the deal. After authorizing Paul's message, Paul says that they only gave him one command, "remember the poor [πτωχῶν]" (Gal. 2:10). In Paul's own words, his position in relation to the gentiles prevailed.

This "prevailing," however, was short-lived, and is exactly why he was so angered by Peter in Antioch. Peter, in Paul's view, reneged on the agreement reached in Jerusalem when he refused to eat with Gentiles in Antioch after certain "men from James [τινας ἀπὸ Ἰακώβου]" visited him (2:11-14). These "men from James" and those like them—possibly the "circumcision faction" in 2:12—constituted at least one form of Paul's opposition in Galatia, and there is no reason to argue that these men were not expressly from James in Jerusalem.[46] Esler, interpreting the "losers of the Jerusalem meeting"

44. Betz, *Galatians*, 92.
45. Betz, *Galatians*, 92.

as the instigators that pressured James to change his mind, concludes "that the strict Jewish Christians, having lost the first round when Paul and Barnabas were in Jerusalem, found an effective way of restoring this slight to their honor by bringing to bear on James (and Peter as well) some kind of threat significant enough to have them renege on the agreement they had reached with Paul."[47]

This opposition, and reversal of position in Antioch, had enough persuasion/authority to sway gentiles-in-Christ in Galatia to subscribe to certain practices prescribed by the law. Circumcision was the main issue, but the observance of certain religious holidays may have also been an item (see Gal. 4:10). The Galatians' denial of Paul's gospel in turning to a proclamation that was closer to that made by "those from James" is what prompted Paul to write his letter. Three times in Gal. 2:16, Paul argues that one "is not justified by works of the law [οὐ δικαιοῦται ἄνθρωπος ἐξ ἔργων νόμου]" but rather by "the faith of Christ [διὰ πίστεως Ἰησοῦ Χριστοῦ]."[48] However dated, Dunn's analysis of "works of the Law" is important in clarifying the meaning behind Paul's prohibition. Dunn follows the monumental work of E. P. Sanders in translating "works of the law" as "covenantal nomism," which simply means adherence to the main pillars or badges of Judean identity (circumcision, food laws, the Sabbath)—an interpretation emblematic of first-phase "new perspective" scholarship in Paul. Specifically related to the Antioch event, Dunn argues: "For many Jews, then, the practice of the law,

46. See Betz, *Galatians*, 108; Esler, "Making and Breaking," 277.
47. Esler, "Making and Breaking," 277. Jewett, "Agitators," 334–47, makes a compelling argument that James and the leaders of the Jerusalem Jesus movement felt pressure to change their verdict from Zealot agitators who threatened reprisals. See also James D. G. Dunn, *The Theology of Paul's Letter to the Galatians* (Cambridge: Cambridge University Press, 1993), 64–100, but especially 72–75.
48. I follow Hodge, *If Sons, Then Heirs*, 81, and argue for a subjective genitive, contra Mark D. Nanos, *The Mystery of Romans: The Jewish Context of Paul's Letter* (Minneapolis: Fortress Press, 1996), 368.

the works of the law, which most clearly maintained covenant distinctiveness from other peoples in the practicalities of daily life were those which governed table-fellowship."[49] In a more recent analysis, Hodge follows Dunn's agreement, but stresses Paul's focus on "the faith of Christ:"

> Thus Galatians 2:16 continues the "ethnic reasoning" of the previous verses by further explaining the oppositional identities of Jews and gentiles. It is as though Paul says to his colleagues: as Jews, we share knowledge regarding how to address the gentile problem, through the faithfulness of Jesus Christ. Paul acknowledges that there are some features or behaviors of Jewish identity that are *flexible*: Jewish teachers can adapt to gentiles in some ways (such as forgoing the Law so as to eat with gentiles). Other aspects of Jewish identity—and specifically the identity of these teachers of gentiles—remain immutable (such as loyalty to the God of Israel and knowledge of the gentile problem). Gentiles are "sinners," in need of being made righteous, or being brought into a right relationship with God and being made moral. Jews, already God's people, know how to accomplish this. The problem is that Paul and *his fellow Jews disagree as to how this is to come about for gentiles*. Paul juxtaposes two possibilities, "on the basis of the works of the Law" and "through the faithfulness of Christ," arguing strongly for the latter.[50]

This disagreement with "his fellow Jews" regarding gentile incorporation into the Judean covenant is one of the deciding factors between James and Paul. Paul's flexibility/hybridity confronts James's immutability/nativism.

Indeed, Paul's agony expressed in his rhetoric shows that he wonders if he "ran in vain." Hodge argues that Paul shifts "the components of his identity to gain access to gentile communities. Paul has adjusted his own observances so that he can eat and live with gentiles without asking them to observe the Law."[51] Paul prioritizes

49. Dunn, *Theology of Paul's Letter*, 78. For a somewhat updated and certainly extended version of Dunn's assessment of "works of the law," see James D. G. Dunn, *The Theology of Paul the Apostle* (Grand Rapids: Eerdmans, 1998), 354–71.

50. Hodge, *If Sons, Then Heirs*, 59 (emphasis mine).

his identity as "teacher of the gentiles" in such a way that it takes precedence over other allegiances he has within his overall Judean identity. In this way, "Paul lives gentilishly"[52] as he negotiates his identity in a way that is both faithful to his identity as a Judean and to his identity as a teacher to gentiles. By adapting his multiple and complex identities, Paul accommodates a liminal space between "'living *ethnikōs*' and 'living *Ioudaikōs*' (Gal 2:14)."[53] This liminal space is indicative of the postcolonial notion of hybridity. Paul is embodying an identity that he wants gentile adherents to mimic—even Peter for that matter. Living gentilishly helps Paul negotiate the space between Judeanness and gentile-ness in a way that "wins" gentiles and incorporates them into the story of Israel. This movement of allegiance to in-Christness would have had political ramifications for gentiles. Through this hybridized identity negotiation, Paul is claiming gentiles for God, which would have an impact on how they understood themselves in the Roman Empire. In this way, Paul's hybridity is subtly anti-imperial and explicitly contrary to the claims of "those from James" as he calls the gentiles to devote themselves to Christ as Lord (τοῦ κυρίου Ἰησοῦ Χριστοῦ) and accept the freedom that comes from Christ: "For freedom Christ has set you free. Stand firm, therefore, and do not submit again to a yoke of slavery" (Gal. 5:1). Paul's hybridity may have made a space for him to incorporate gentiles into the story of Israel, but this is precisely where other Judeans took exception to Paul's gospel. Barclay accurately shows that Paul's "tactical abandonment of key Jewish practices in the course of his mission, and his particularly close associations with Gentile believers, made him dangerously assimilated in the eyes of many."[54]

51. Ibid., 122.
52. Ibid.
53. Ibid.
54. Barclay, "Paul among Diaspora Jews," 104.

Faith/Works Binary in Galatians, Romans, and James

In describing the events at Antioch that divided Paul and Peter, Paul declaratively proclaims, however unsystematically, his gospel for gentiles. Paul carefully attacks "those from James" and their rigorous position on the Law with the faith/works binary. Paul says, "We ourselves are Judeans ['Ιουδαῖοι] by birth and not gentile sinners; yet we know that a person is justified not by the works of the law [ἐξ ἔργων νόμου] but through [the] faith [διὰ πίστεως] of Jesus Christ, so that we might be justified by the faith of Christ, and not by doing the works of the law, because no one will be justified by the works of the law" (Gal. 2:15–16). To paraphrase Dunn here, Paul is arguing that one is not justified by the traditional identity markers of Judeanness embraced and extolled by Judean nativists. In verse 21, Paul reaches the pinnacle of his argument saying, "I do not nullify the grace of God; for if justification comes through the Law, then Christ died for nothing." After directly addressing the Galatians in 3:1 ("You foolish Galatians!"), Paul then turns to a figure in Israelite history that would function as his proof text: "Just as Abraham 'believed God, and it was reckoned to him as righteousness,' so, you see, those who believe are the descendants of Abraham. And the scripture, foreseeing that God would justify the gentiles by faith, declared the gospel beforehand to Abraham, saying, 'All the gentiles shall be blessed in you.' For this reason, those who believe are blessed with Abraham who believed" (Gal. 3:6–9, quoting Gen. 15:6). As stated above, Paul uses Abraham as a genealogical link for gentiles to be ethnically incorporated into Israel. By doing so, he hybridizes gentile identity, which converts gentiles to Judeanness, but not quite. The "not quite Judean" is due to the relationship between gentiles-in-Christ and the Law. After using Abraham as his proof text for including gentiles, Paul goes on to "free" his gentile audience from the Law and provide them with the reasons why God gave the Law to Judeans in the first place (3:19-29). The entire theme of faith/works, with Abraham as a proof text, functioned as 1) Paul's argument against his opponents in Galatia, those who required circumcision for gentiles-in-Christ (3:1-5), and whom he implicitly aligns with those whom he describes as "false believers" at the Jerusalem Council (Gal. 2:4) and those "from James" at Antioch (Gal. 2:12); and 2) Paul's argument for his assimilation of gentiles into the covenant with the God of Israel.

Although the purpose of Paul's letter to the Romans was different than Galatians, he uses the same faith/works argument. In Rom. 3:28, Paul says, "For we hold that a person is justified by faith apart from works prescribed by the Law [δικαιοῦσθαι πίστει ἄνθρωπον χωρὶς ἔργων νόμου]." In the following verses, Paul uses Abraham as his example of how believers are justified by faith and not by works: "For what does the scripture say? 'Abraham believed God, and it was reckoned to him as righteousness'" (Rom. 4:3). The faith/works binary with the use of Abraham as an example was central to Paul's gospel, as James D. G. Dunn rightly affirms:

> Here [Rom. 3:28] again, as in 3:20, the train of thought comes so close to that of Paul's argument in Galatians that the phrasing of the earlier letter is closely reproduced: Gal 2:16—εἰδότες ὅτι οὐ δικαιοῦται ἄνθρωπος ἐξ ἔργων νόμου ἐαν μὴ διὰ πίστεως. Since it was also Gal 2:16 which was paralleled in 3:20, and since Paul was hardly writing Romans with a copy of Galatians at hand, the obvious conclusion is that the theological assertions formulated in Gal 2:16 were a fundamental part of Paul's understanding of the gospel, and fundamental in these terms.[55]

Not only should the faith/works binary be understood as central to Paul's message, it should also be understood as his central argument against his opponents at the Jerusalem Council and in Galatia. It is

55. James D. G. Dunn, *Romans 1–8* (Dallas: Word, 1988), 187.

precisely the faith/works binary that provides Paul with a rationale for including gentiles. He understands this as the gospel that was revealed to him through Jesus Christ, and in response to it, Paul feels like he has the freedom to live "gentilishly." Considering how this was the nature of the problems Paul faced with other Judeans, either the Jerusalem authorities or those from James, when James uses the faith/works binary in James 2:14–26, then, one has to understand it in relation to and in tension with Paul's message of hybridity.

In light of this argument, the Letter of James represents a type of nativist rejection of hybridity, mimicry, and ambivalence as found in writings such as Galatians 2–3 and Romans 3–4. The hybridity that Paul espouses blurs the boundaries that James carefully constructs. James interprets Paul's negotiation of multiple and complex identities as assimilation and compromise. James criticizes Pauline sensibilities for not considering the severe and brutal effects of the empire on the native soul/soil (cf. James 1:9–11; 2:1–13; and 5:1–6). James writes in order to promote a pure native identity. In his commentary on Galatians, J. Louis Martyn characterizes Paul's opponents in this way:

> In addition to identifying themselves and their Law-observant Gentile converts as "descendants of Abraham," the Teachers [Paul's opponents in Galatia] speak of Jerusalem as their "mother," referring thereby to the Jerusalem church. We cannot say with great confidence that the Teachers have come to Galatia from Jerusalem, but there are grounds for thinking that they claim to be the true representatives of the Jerusalem church, and that, in making that claim, they are confident of the support of a powerful group in that church.[56]

What Martyn comes close to saying here regarding Paul's opponents as those from James, he later makes explicit: "We can be sure, however, that the total impact of the Antioch episode left Paul feeling

56. Martyn, *Galatians*, 126.

suspicious of James."[57] Betz also makes this connection between Paul's opponents and James, saying:

> The gospel which the opponents proclaimed was, in Paul's view, "another gospel." In some way, this gospel was associated with observance of the Jewish Torah and with the ritual of circumcision. The opponents had, in Paul's words, "confused" the churches. Paul also puts the opponents in a historical perspective. He names as their historical predecessors the dissenting faction at the Jerusalem conference, "the men from James," and the Cephas group at Antioch.[58]

It is clear from Galatians and these commentators that there existed a deep conflict between Paul and James. The polemical passage of James 2:14-26 criticizes Paul's notions of faith and works by turning them upside down.

James 2:14-26 is flanked by two passages that indicate James's insistence on Law observance (2:1-13) and his attempt to silence his opponents (3:1-12). In James 2:8-13, which introduces the faith/work binary, James refers to the Law as the imperial law (v. 8, νόμον βασιλικὸν) and the law of freedom (v. 12, νόμου ἐλευθερίας). What follows in James 2:14-26 can hardly refer to anything other than works of the Law.[59] In fact, James assumes these traditional identity

57. Ibid., 244.

58. Betz, *Galatians*, 7.

59. Other commentators do not account for James 2:8-13 as an introduction to 2:14-26. Because of this, they conflate James and Paul and argue that James and Paul are saying the same thing or that James and Paul are addressing different problems. Brevard S. Childs, *The New Testament as Canon: An Introduction* (Valley Forge, PA: Trinity Press International, 1994), 440, argues, "Thus, an apparently minor shift in vocabulary from Paul's 'apart from works of law' to 'apart from works' in James is actually of major significance, and reveals that an entirely different understanding of faith and works if operative. Paul is defending the sufficiency of faith in Christ's salvation against claims of the law, whereas James is calling for a true faith which is demonstrated by concomitant deeds of charity. James' polemical adversary emerges as a caricature of Pauline theology." In his commentary on James, Luke Timothy Johnson argues, "I underline the point: James' usage concerning 'works' is both unconnected to 'law' and is entirely consistent with the dominant NT usage concerning moral effort as an expression of convictions." *The Letter of James: A New Translation with Introduction and Commentary* (New York: Doubleday, 1995), 60.

badges with his conception of the Law and explicitly includes a strong emphasis on economic justice—a classic nativist position. The opening rhetorical questions in verse 14 not only champion *works*, but also seriously doubt the effectiveness of faith by itself: "Faith is not able to save you, is it?" James 2:14-26 ends with an emphatic, "so also, faith without works is dead." Following the faith/works binary polemic, he quickly censures any opposition with his negative concentration on speech acts. James effectively tells his audience and his opponents to bite their tongues (3:1-12).

In James 2:14-26, James attempts to "undo" and undermine the Pauline usage of the faith/works binary. It is from the textual evidence above that the faith/works binary was central to the gospel Paul preached. James, then, most likely heard Paul's faith/works binary during the Jerusalem Council as Paul explained the nature of his gospel to the gentiles. The reaction that we read in James 2:14-26 does not necessarily need to be a reaction to Galatians or Romans proper. It could be James's reaction to what he heard from Paul at the Jerusalem Council and which Paul continued to preach afterward. James uses Paul's faith/works binary as a means to undermine Paul's own argument. In verse 14, James begins his antihybrid polemic by asking two rhetorical questions, "What is the benefit, my brothers, if someone says he has faith [πίστιν] but does not have works [ἔργα]? Can faith save him?" The answer to the first question is "Faith without works is good for nothing" and the answer to the second is "No, such a faith cannot save you." In fact, the second sentence may be a declarative rather than an interrogative. In that case, James simply, but with authority, declares: "Faith is not able to save him!" Both answers deal with "faith alone" negatively. By opening with these two rhetorical questions, posed immediately following a passage concerning the Law, James directly attacks Paul's gospel. James argues that the workless faith that Paul promotes is worthless.

In the protasis of the first question, James indicates that the "someone" (τις) *only* "says" *he* has faith rather than actually having it. In other words, this "someone" does not have faith at all. The dichotomy between faith and works, for James, represents an inconsistency that does not fit in his politics of purity. Faith must be accompanied by works, or better completed/perfected by works (v. 22).

James and Paul in Scholarship

At this point, it is important to situate the anti-Pauline polemic in contemporary scholarship. Historically, scholars understood this polemic as a way to champion Pauline concepts of "faith alone," which served the Protestant Reformation efforts. The use of "faith alone" as a whipping board through the Reformation led Martin Luther to famously call the Letter of James an "epistle of weeds." Following the aftermath of the Reformation, biblical scholars interpreted Paul as a universalizing Hellenized Christian and James as a particularist Judaized ur-Christian. This divide held consensus until Pauline scholars began to reevaluate their perspective on Paul. The well-documented "New Perspective" on Paul concentrated on his Judeanness and opened up windows of understanding Paul as a Judean attempting to navigate a new Judean movement that recognized Jesus of Nazareth as the Messiah. By repositioning Paul as Judean, scholars attempted to get past centuries of anti-Semitic and anti-Jewish biblical scholarship. In the process, the relationship between James and Paul was also revised. Partly from the "New Perspective" and partly from theological bias, New Testament scholars began to "patch things up" between James and Paul. If Paul was a Law-observant Judean, why would James—another Law-observant Judean—disagree with him? This aspect of the "New Perspective" on Paul has dramatically shifted the scholarship on James 2:14-26. The most recent commentaries on the Letter of James adamantly deny any *theological*, much less any sociopolitical, unrest between James and Paul. As Margaret M. Mitchell accurately notices, these attempts to "rehabilitate" James from Paul's influence have become a "movement" in recent scholarship on James.[60] The most impassioned and popular argument against reading James 2:14-26 in particular as an anti-Pauline polemic—and this is the only passage on which the "rehabilitation movement" concentrates regarding an anti-Pauline polemic—is a concentration on terminology. The argument is simple: James and Paul use similar terms, that is, works (ἔργα), faith (πίστις), and justification/justice (δικαιόω/δικαιοσύνη), but define them differently. Luke Timothy Johnson: "They use the same words but in different ways. The direction of James' argument is different from the direction of Paul's."[61] Patrick J. Hartin: "James and Paul share a vocabulary that is similar, but at the same time acquires a unique meaning in each of their *theological* visions. . . . [T]here is in reality no opposition between James and Paul since they are merely stressing different aspects."[62] William F. Brosend, II: "*James and Paul simply do not mean the same thing when they write of 'works,' and interpreters who write as if they did distort the thought of both.*"[63] Richard Bauckham follows this argument but slightly nuances it by acknowledging "surface disagreements" between James and Paul, but these are certainly overwhelmed by the "deeper agreements" between the two.[64] The "terms"/"meaning" argument that all of these scholars espouse hinges on the difference between "moral" and "ritual" acts.

60. Margaret M. Mitchell, "The Letter of James as a Document of Paulinism?," in *Reading James with New Eyes: Methodological Reassessments of the Letter of James*, ed. Robert L. Webb and John S. Kloppenborg (London: T. & T. Clark, 2007), 75, n. 1.

61. Johnson, *Letter of James*, 250.

62. Patrick J. Hartin, *James*, Sacra Pagina, 14 (Collegeville, MN: Liturgical, 2003), 163 (emphasis mine).

63. William F. Brosend II, *James and Jude* (Cambridge: Cambridge University Press, 2004), 81 (emphasis original).

64. Richard Bauckham, *James* (London and New York: Routledge, 1999), 134.

According to this argument, when James refers to "works," he only deals with acts/deeds of morality and nowhere "speaks" of ritual, that is, circumcision, food taboos, idolatry, and so on. Likewise, when Paul refers to "works of the Law" in Galatians and Romans, he is only speaking of "ritual" acts rather than "moral" acts. Johnson makes this distinction between "moral" and "ritual" even in James's use of purity and perfection. Whenever James uses the rhetoric of purity and perfection, James "involves moral rather than ritual behavior."[65] However, James never makes this distinction, only these commentators! It is clear in 2:14-26 that James illustrates his point about works with charity by using "a brother or sister who is naked and has no food" (v. 16), but he also uses Abraham's sacrifice of Isaac as an illustration of works. None of these commentators deal with the "ritual" aspect of human sacrifice as a work of faith. It is true that James never mentions circumcision and food laws in his letter, but James insists in his previous pericope (2:1-13) that "whoever keeps the whole Law but fails in one point has become accountable for all of it" (v. 10). Possibly reflecting a Jesus tradition in this passage, James is more of a rigorist than libertarian when he specifically is dealing with the Law (see chapter 4). The division between "moral" and "ritual" deeds on which "rehabilitation" scholars so heavily depend in order to make their claims in the "term/meaning" argument may be a division projected onto the text. In other words, this may be their "voice" rather than James's. In fact, given James's rigorist/nativist insistence on purity and perfection, James may never specifically address "ritual" deeds simply because he *takes it for granted* that the "ritual" part of the Law should be followed as much as the "moral" part.

All of these scholars believe that James and Paul agree more than they disagree on most issues that are in their letters, and all of them

65. Johnson, *Letter of James*, 30.

attempt to recuperate "James's voice" without being influenced by Paul or Pauline scholarship. Mitchell is again instructive in her correction to this wave of research: "But as a move in historical research it merely begs the question by assuming, rather than proving, that there was no intersection between Paul and his letters and the author of James. In other words, in historical research, 'to read James on his own terms' *must include grappling with Paul if Paul was one of those terms*."[66] In effect, these scholars "read" Paul out of the argument before they begin their argument. When they discuss the possible interaction between James and Paul—rather than flatly denying any interaction whatsoever[67]—they do so flippantly: "In a canonical conversation between James and Paul there would be much nodding of heads and smiling agreement, as well as some knitting of brows and some exclamations of surprise."[68] This renders James and Paul so casual in their relations to each other that you would think they are two well-esteemed scholars or pastors discoursing politely in an ivory tower or a cathedral. The fact that tradition has both James and Paul being killed by imperial and elite forces is remarkably overlooked due to this scholarly preoccupation with *theology*. All of these commentators concentrate on the theological similarities and differences between James and Paul—nowadays focusing primarily on the similarities. Even when dealing with clear sociopolitical issues like poverty and patronage, they interpret James in theological terms. I argue that James is not theologizing works (ἔργα), but he is exercising a political term. What are the politics of this passage? Let us put Punt's question about Paul and politics—specifically related to works—to the Letter of James: How would James's insistence on

66. Mitchell, "The Letter of James," 75 (emphasis original).

67. Johnson begins his section on 2:14-26 by saying, "There is absolutely no reason to read this commentary section as particularly responsive to Paul." *Letter of James*, 249.

68. Bauckham, *James*, 140.

works "have resonated when Roman patronage and the 'works' of benefactors determined people's lives and livelihood (as ultimately underwritten by the emperor as benefactor *par excellence* who readily claimed his 'works' (cf. Augustus and the *Res Gestae*)?"[69] Here James and Paul seemingly are resisting empire in two contradictory ways. Paul responds ambivalently; James responds nativistically. It is precisely because of systems of patronage that you have brothers and sisters who are naked and lacking daily food. Where James is not attacking empire—2:1-13, 3:13-18, and 5:1-6—he is attacking monstrous mimesis (2:14-26; 3:1-12; 4:1-12; and 4:13-17). The first verse of James's argument in 2:14-26 functions to remind readers/listeners of Paul's mimetic message, and then James proceeds to turn it upside down.

The next two verses, 15-16, relate James's concern for the poor and his disdain for a faith that does not specifically address such poverty.[70] Throughout the letter, James concentrates on the relationship between the rich and the poor. James 1:9-11, 2:1-7, and 5:1-6 all address the rich as seriously flawed if not all together unredeemable. James 1:9-10 says, "Let the believer who is lowly boast in being raised up, and the rich in being brought low, because the rich will disappear like a flower in the field." As the previous chapter indicates, James is certainly no "friend" of the wealthy imperialists in 2:1-13, 3:13-18, and 5:1-6. These passages show tremendous disdain for the rich. It is important to notice that at the very beginning of James's faith/works binary, he references the poor again. At this point, the poor—rhetorically the naked and hungry—are brought into dialogue with those whose faith has no action. Does James consider Paul one of these rich people that do not take care of the poor? In Gal.

69. Jeremy Punt, "Empire as material setting and heuristic grid for New Testament Interpretation."
70. The conditional sentence using naked (γυμνί) and hunger is reminiscent of the Jesus tradition from Matt. 25:35-36, where clothing the naked (γυμνός) and feeding the hungry are conditions that are fulfilled in order to inherit the "Empire" (βασιλείαν) (Matt. 25:34).

2:10, Paul says that the only command that James, Peter, and John gave him was to "remember the poor." Many scholars see this as a command to take up an offering from all of his assemblies and bring it to the Jerusalem assembly. Indeed, in many of Paul's epistles he says that he is taking up a collection for the church in Jerusalem (Rom. 15:25-27; 1 Cor. 16:1-4; 2 Cor. 8:12-14; 9:6-12; and Gal. 2:9-10).[71] If Paul is indeed taking up an offering for the "poor among the saints in Jerusalem" (Rom. 15:26), one wonders if they ever received it based on James's comments here. Paul's collection activities may be the direct address of James 2:15-16, "If a brother or sister is naked and lacks daily food, and one of you says to them, 'Go in peace; keep warm and eat your fill,' and yet you do not supply their bodily needs, what benefit is that?"[72]

Admittedly, it is impossible to create a direct connection to Paul in these verses related to the naked and hungry. It is, however, much clearer that James is creating another hypothetical situation like he did in 2:2-7 to make another emphatic and similar point. In 2:1, James questions: "Do you really have the faith [ἔχετε τὴν πίστιν] of our glorious Lord Jesus Christ with your partiality?" Here he asks, what benefit is a faith that does not produce works? Possessing faith that only talks (cf. 1:26 and 3:1-12) and does not materialize into works is the same as being a wealthy oppressor (2:6-7). By not attending to the "necessities of the body" this kind of faith is not only dead to those who "possess" it, it is also disastrous to those who should benefit from it. In this way, "believers" are only the wealthy who pose as faithful. The rhetorical question indicates that the one who says,

71. Cf. Acts 24:17.

72. Both "stay warm" (θερμαίνεσθε) and "be filled" (χορτάζεσθε) are middle-voice imperatives that function as passive voice. This may indicate that the speaker of this hypothetical charge is commanding the naked and hungry brother and sister to rely on God for "the necessities of the body." This would render the verbs as divine passives. If this is the case, then James is harshly criticizing this kind of "faithful" response to poverty (cf. 2:2-7; 5:1-6).

"Go in peace, stay warm, and be filled," actually has the economic means to help, but only offers words. This kind of faith is a ruse. It sounds like faith, but does not look like faith. It is *not quite* faith. It is a hybrid faith that speaks like faith, but looks like wealthy oppression. Although they may sound different, the result is the same, that is, the poor are dishonored (2:6). James concludes this first section of his faith/works argument with verse 17 by calling a moratorium on this kind of faith: "Such faith by itself, if it has no works, is dead." This dead faith performs like the wealthy who "oppress you," "drag you to court," and "blaspheme the name that is invoked over you." This mimicry of the wealthy oppressors mentioned in the first half of chapter 2 violates the Law just as dead faith does: "You do well if you really perfect the imperial law" (v. 8). The works in 2:14-26, then, are precisely works of the imperial law.

Verse 18 reiterates James's position that faith *with* works is the ideal. This introduces the second section of James's faith/works binary. The construction of a straw figure to mouth the words of your opponents is typical of diatribe style. James uses diatribe throughout his letter as a means of argument. This is one of the reasons that explains the similarities between James and Paul, that is, both effectively use diatribe. James constructs a straw figure to speak the words of his adversary. The use of the future tense for λέγω anticipates this sort of reaction from those who have a dead faith. This shift from conditional sentences using the subjunctive in verse 14 places direct speech on the tongue of James's opponent: "You have faith and I have works" (σὺ πίστιν ἔχεις, καγὼ ἔργα ἔχω). Martin Dibelius pointed out the problem with this sentence decades ago: "*This protest, in which the speaker ascribes works to himself and faith to another, does not seem to come at all from one who is an opponent of our author.*"[73] Dibelius

73. Martin Dibelius, *James: A Commentary on the Epistle of James*, trans. Michael A. Williams, Hermeneia (Philadelphia: Fortress Press, 1976), 155 (emphasis original).

argues persuasively that the "you"/"I" pattern in the interlocutor's lips in verse 18a are there to express separation between James and his opponents, which is evidenced by James's opponent's insistence on the total separation of faith and works. "Therefore—to conclude from what can be seen in v. 18b—, the main point of the opponent in v. 18a is not the *distribution* of faith and works to 'you' and 'me,' but rather the *total separation* of faith and works in general."[74] In this line of argument, "Jas treats the interlocutor as if he had said, 'The one has faith, the other has works.' 'Quite wrong,' replies Jas, 'for works cannot be inferred from faith, but faith can be inferred from works.'"[75] Dibelius's persuasive interpretation is congruent with James's argumentation throughout 2:14-26, that is, faith and works cannot be separated. To separate faith from works renders faith dead. Bifurcating the two is indicative of a doubleness (δίψυχος, 4:8) that corrupts the purity that James champions throughout. From a postcolonial perspective this splitting is representative of hybridity. Hybridity is the paradoxical location of doubling and splitting. In the process of separating faith and works, James's interlocutor is a dangerous hybrid that threatens pure and unstained piety with this kind of bifurcation. Thus James responds to his opponent's doubleness in verse 18b, "Show me your faith without works, and I will show you my faith from works." In other words, it is impossible to make faith materialize without action and when faith does not materialize, the naked stay naked and the hungry stay hungry.

After this introduction, James uses the Shema (Deut. 6:4) in his argument, but in a very unusual manner. In verse 19, he says, "You believe that God is one [εἷς ἐστιν ὁ θεός]; you do well. Even the demons believe—and shudder." James constructs his argument by placing the Shema on the tongue of his adversary. Interestingly

74. Ibid. (emphasis original).
75. Dibelius, *James*, 156.

enough, Paul uses the Shema in his faith/works binary in Rom. 3:29-30: "Or is God the God of Jews only? Is he not the God of Gentiles also? Yes, of Gentiles also, since God is one [εἷς ὁ θεός]; and he will justify the circumcised on the ground of faith and the uncircumcised through that same faith." The irony of beginning verse 19 with πιστεύεις adds to the rhetorical force, that is, "You believe; so what?" The faith of verse 19 is no different than the "faith" of demons (δαιμόνια). This faith is less than demonic because demons understand enough to shudder. This faith in the Shema is, then, an arrogant faith that has less respect/fear for God than demons. The fact that this kind of faith—even in the Shema—does not produce fear of God evidences a faith that produces nothing; it is dead. For James, "faith in" the Shema demands some sort of response (demons shudder). James will repeat the use of a present, active, indicative, second-person singular verb in verses 20 (θέλεις) and 22 (βλέπεις), which rhetorically links these verses together as a concerted effort to discipline/educate/condemn James's interlocutor.

Similar to Paul's faith/works binary, James also uses Abraham as a proof text. For James, Abraham is the example that shows how faith cannot exist apart from works (vv. 20-24). In verses 20-21, James speaks to a single rhetorical individual saying, "Do you want to learn, O vain man, that faith apart from works is barren? Was not our ancestor Abraham justified by works when he offered his son Isaac on the altar?" In the same way that Paul used Abraham to prove his point about "being justified by faith," James now uses the Akedah (Gen. 22:1-19) to make the opposite point (justified by works), and by doing so, he attempts to make Paul's message impotent. James moves from the Shema to the Akedah, but heightens the offensive rhetoric by calling his interlocutor, "O vain man" (ὦ ἄνθρωπε κενέ). There is certainly a play on words between κενέ, here, and ἀργή at the end of the sentence, that is, vain and idle. This, however, is not the most important aspect of κενέ. Paul uses κενός repeatedly in his letters to describe his anguish and anxiety about proclaiming his gospel. As stated earlier, Paul speaks of presenting his gospel before James and other leaders in Jerusalem so that he "was not running, or had not run, in vain [κενὸν]" (Gal. 2:2). Again in 1 Corinthians 15, when Paul was describing how he received his gospel from God, he describes this bestowal of grace as not "in vain [κενὴ]" (v. 10). He goes on to compare himself with James, Cephas, and other apostles, but argues that "I worked harder than any of them" (v. 10). Combating another issue in the Corinthian gathering, Paul will ask, "then is our preaching in *vain* and your faith in *vain* [κενὸν ἄρα τὸ κήρυγμα ἡμῶν κενὴ καὶ ἡ πίστις ὑμῶν]?" Paul will end 1 Corinthians 15 with a similar usage of κενός. Paul uses κενός so often when he is speaking about "his gospel" it seems to be part of his rhetorical strategy when he proclaims his gospel (cf. 2 Cor. 6:1, twice in Phil. 2:16, and 1 Thess. 2:1, 3:5).[76] The "O vain man" in James 2:20 may well be aimed at Paul as one who has an arrogant and dead/idle faith.

James teaches this "vain man" that Abraham was "justified by works [ἐξ ἔργων ἐδικαιώθη]" in verse 21. Compared with Paul's faith/works binary in Romans where he says, "For we recognize that a person is justified by faith without works of the Law [δικαιοῦσθαι πίστει χωρὶς ἔργων νόμου]" (3:28), the division between James and Paul is clear. Paul will continue his faith/works binary in Romans by referencing Abraham and saying, "For if Abraham was justified by works [ἐξ ἔργων ἐδικαιώθη], he has something to boast about, but not before God." The words here are identical with James 2:21, but are used in a completely contrary way to show that Abraham was justified by faith. Both James and Paul (Rom. 4:3; cf. Gal. 3:6) then

76. Paul also uses other terminology within the same semantic domain (cf. εἰκῇ in Rom. 13:4 and 1 Cor. 15:2).

quote Gen. 15:6. Paul uses it to show Abraham's faith; James uses it (2:23) to show that it was fulfilled in Abraham's sacrifice of Isaac. These competing voices evidence a serious conflict between James and Paul. James's strict sense of the necessity of faith and works are exemplified in verse 22 where he says, "faith was *perfected* by works." James goes back to his central theme of purity and perfection in order to argue for the congruency of faith and works.

Before James concludes his faith/works binary, he uses another figure from Scripture. James uses Rahab, a female gentile, to provide another scriptural proof for his polemic. In a sentence that parallels the Abraham proof in verse 21 exactly, James shows that Rahab was also justified by works (ἐξ ἔργων ἐδικαιώθη). In her "works," she *received* (aorist participle) the messengers in the same way Abraham offered (aorist participle) Isaac. For James, both men and women and Judean and gentile are justified by works. Abraham and Rahab function to include the whole world. James finally concludes his faith/works binary by reminding his readers/listeners of what he had said before: "so faith without works is dead" (v. 26).

Postcolonial Interpretation of James 2:14-26

Throughout the letter, James exhorts his readers/hearers to follow a rigorous piety in an attempt to maintain purity and attain perfection. James 2:14-26 identifies the praxis of the *inside*. This functions as nativist rhetoric that supports James's ideology of otherness. Musa Dube grasps the impact of this nativist rhetoric: "New Testament texts, written under the domination of the Roman Empire, resisted the imperial oppression in their own ways but also articulated the right to propagate their own version of imperialism. Consequently, from Constantine's conversion, Christianity became 'unique in its imperial sponsorship' because its texts have always harbored an ideology of geographical expansion to foreign lands."[77] James sees a real threat from imperial assimilation (Paul) that would render his piety impotent. James calls out to his diasporic (1:1) audience to exhort them to maintain their boundaries with the world—to prove they belong. James demands that actions are the evidence of faith. His action-oriented faith creates boundaries that refuse bifurcated and doubled forms of existence. Bill Ashcroft, Gareth Griffiths, and Helen Tiffin describe this nativist desire (as well as its challenge) to maintain colonial boundaries: "The descendants of the diasporic movements generated by colonialism have developed their own distinctive cultures which both preserve and often extend and develop their originary cultures. . . . It also questions the simpler kind of theories of nativism which suggest that decolonization can be effected by a recovery or reconstruction of pre-colonial societies."[78] Pauline hybridity in the Diaspora threatens James in this same way. James understands "works" as a way to display faith, and this display would demarcate a follower from the "world." Faith that did not manifest itself in works, such as not giving a collection to the people that needed it, would indicate that that type of faith would make a follower indistinguishable from a nonfollower. The main threat James confronts is the compromising attitude found in statements like, "yet we know that a person is justified not by works of the law but through faith in Jesus Christ" (Gal. 2:16). For James, *works* are constitutive of his pious/political identity.

Paul, on the other hand, understood *faith* as constitutive of pious/political identity. Paul's faith could appropriate colonial culture as a way to transform it from within. Paul's gospel is, then, a hybrid that accepts diasporic identity as contradictory and ambivalent, which

77. Musa Dube, *Postcolonial Feminist Interpretation of the Bible* (St. Louis: Chalice, 2000), 18.

78. Bill Ashcroft, Gareth Griffiths, and Helen Tiffin, *Post-Colonial Studies: The Key Concepts* (London and New York: Routledge, 2000), 70.

makes claims of "purity" untenable. R. S. Sugirtharajah describes this type of hybridity as "not about the dissolution of differences but about renegotiating the structure of power built on differences. It is not synonymous with assimilation. Assimilation is something that the colonialists, and later the nativists advocated. Hybridity is a two-way process in which both parties are interactive so that something new is created."[79] Paul, at times, accepts the status quo of the world (empire) and his own piety (in-Christ Judeanness) and at other times adapts both. He will appropriate Greco-Roman household codes (1 Corinthians 7), yet will seemingly reject them in another setting (Gal. 3:28). Paul's piety mimics and mocks the Roman Empire, and, at the same time, he refuses nativist purity. Describing the threat of this type of mimicry/mockery, Bhabha says:

> It is from this area between mimicry and mockery, where the reforming, civilizing mission is threatened by the displacing gaze of its disciplinary double, that my instances of colonial imitation come. What they all share is a discursive process by which the excess or slippage produced by the *ambivalence* of mimicry (almost the same, *but not quite*) does not merely "rupture" the discourse, but becomes transformed into an uncertainty which fixes the colonial subject as a "partial" presence. By "partial" I mean both "incomplete" and "virtual." It is as if the very emergence of the "colonial" is dependent for its representation upon some strategic limitation or prohibition *within* the authoritative discourse itself. The success of colonial appropriation depends on a proliferation of inappropriate objects that ensure its strategic failure, so that mimicry is at once resemblance and menace.[80]

Ultimately, the hybrid is "uncontainable because it breaks down the symmetry and duality of self/other, inside/outside. In the productivity of power, the boundaries of authority—its reality effects—are always

79. R. S. Sugirtharajah, *Postcolonial Criticism and Biblical Interpretation* (Oxford: Oxford University Press, 2002), 191.
80. Homi K. Bhabha, *Location of Culture* (London and New York: Routledge, 1994), 86 (emphasis original).

besieged by 'the other scene' of fixations and phantoms."[81] Paul's ability to become "all things to all people" makes him a threat to the purity that James is trying to uphold; a purity that nevertheless finds its mirrored other in imperial constructs. Paul claims that his ability to morph into whatever he needs to in order to share his message is a direct result of his faith in Christ. Paul is a hybrid *because* of his identity in Christ. He uses his hybridity in order to transform the world. Paul's hybridity breaks down the distinctions constructed by his culture and begins to threaten both colonizer and native: "There is no longer Jew or Greek, there is no longer slave or free, there is no longer male and female; for all of you are one in Christ Jesus. And if you belong to Christ, then you are Abraham's offspring, heirs according to the promise" (Gal. 3:28-29).

The destruction of the duality, inside/outside, disrupts James's identity/ideology. James takes more seriously the effect of the empire on his (and his audience's) anguished and fragile position. In three different sections of his epistle (1:9-11; 2:1-13; and 5:1-6), he condemns those who are in positions of power and also condemns anyone that colludes with or shows partiality to those in power. Ania Loomba sympathetically narrates this nativist/nationalist reaction/resistance to colonial power:

> Nationalist struggles as well as pan-nationalist movements such as Negritude were fuelled by the alienation and the anger of the colonized, and cannot be understood, according to this view, within the parameters of current theories of hybridity. As mentioned earlier, many nationalists and anti-colonialists passionately, and often poetically appropriated the notion of a binary opposition between Europe and its others. Liberation, for them, hinged upon the discovery or rehabilitation of their cultural identity which European colonialism had disparaged and wrecked.[82]

81. Ibid., 116.
82. Ania Loomba, *Colonialism/Postcolonialism* (London and New York: Routledge, 1998), 181.

At least once, in Rom. 15:26 (cf. Gal. 2:10), the Christ followers in Jerusalem are explicitly described as poor. From this poverty, James confronts a hybridity that threatens to coalesce with the power that created the poverty portrayed in his letter. For James, his nativist identity cannot intermingle with Roman imperial power that so dominated the world. Pious identity could not be characterized as being friendly at all with the "world"; rather, it is characteristic of the faith/works of Abraham, who is considered a "friend of God." Paul represents everything that James stands against, that is, thoroughly hybridized identity. Seeing the poverty evidenced in his rhetorical refutations, James exhorts his readers/listeners to separate from the world.

Talk as Walk: Taming the Hybrid Tongue (James 3:1-12)

James 3:1-12 deals specifically with the power and poison of the teacher's tongue. Scholars debate whether this passage deals with censuring opponents or whether it reflects common notions regarding the need to control speech acts. In other words, the thrust of James's argument is either against the tongue or the teacher. I interpret the pericope as a rhetorical censure that is aimed at hybrid identity that coalesces with Roman imperial culture, that is, it is aimed at the teacher. James 3:1-12 fits within the overall project of the letter that simultaneously confronts Roman imperialism and any form of Judean, diasporic identity that absorbs or intermingles with imperial influence—especially anyone who would teach those in the Diaspora to assimilate imperial culture. This total rejection of empire reflects nativist identity negotiations that appropriate imperial binary ideology in order to combat imperialism. The hybrid native represents the deplorable degeneration and pollution of native culture, and disrupts the purist ideology espoused in nativist rhetoric. In this passage where James forcefully argues that words speak as loud as actions (cf. 2:14-26), "speech is an 'act' or 'work'" that ultimately reveals "the inner self and its dispositions."[83] Speaking with a forked tongue is evidence of a double mind (δίψυχος: 1:8; 4:8), which is tantamount to being an enemy of God (4:4). This type of rhetoric does not fit well within simple wisdom literature warnings against the terrible tongue. James confronts what he considers a threat to authentic pious identity by effectively silencing his hybrid opponents. James's penchant for purity makes it impossible for him to allow any spring to gush forth *both* sweet water and bitter water (3:12). This impossible piety is as ludicrous as faith without works (2:14-26). In fact, it resembles wisdom that is earthly, unspiritual, and demonic (3:13-18). James 3:1-12 is not a detached diatribe warning against tongue twisters; it is one part of a larger argument for pure and undefiled piety that stood against Roman imperialism and Pauline hybridity.

Teacher vs. Tongue

James 3:1-12 is a single pericope that is bracketed by direct discourse (ἀδελφοί μου) in both verses 1 and 12. The use of constant alliteration, repeated use of ἰδοὺ (behold), and the repeated use of participles all speak to the fact that, as Johnson says, "James is constructing an argument."[84] The argument focuses on the tongue of the teacher or, more specifically, pedagogical speech acts. The tongue is "a fire," "a *world* of iniquity," "a stain," and "untamable" (James 3:6-8). Since this is the fruit or result of James's argument, he begins this section with a negative statement about teachers (διδάσκαλοι): "Not many of you should become teachers, my brothers." The following tirade on the tongue gushes forth from this spring.

83. Johnson, *Letter of James*, 256.
84. Johnson, *Letter of James*, 254.

Narrowing the scope of this section to teachers specifically is important because it changes the nature of James's argument. James 3:1-12 is not a general warning about what one should say or how one should say it; rather, it is a warning against teachers who speak with a forked tongue. The first word of this section is the negative μὴ: Not or No! This is followed by the second-person plural imperative γίνεσθε: you all should become. James emphatically tells his audience not to become teachers because teachers "will receive a stricter judgment" (ὅτι μεῖζον κρίμα λημψόμεθα) and because "all of us stumble" (πολλὰ γὰρ πταίομεν ἅπαντες). The verbal shift in 3:1 from second person to first person clearly indicates that James places himself in the elite category of "teacher." Before James begins to talk about the tongue, he narrows his focus on teachers and emphatically tells his audience not to seek (t)his office.[85] It is a censure of *both* office and speech. The puppet opponent in 2:14-26, the "you who *say* 'I have faith,'" now materializes in teachers who cannot control their tongues and, in fact, should not be teachers at all because they speak with forked tongues. The conditional sentence that brings verse 2 to a close, however, opens a small window into which the audience can see what kind of teacher James is: "If someone does not stumble in word, this one is a *perfect man*, able to control even the whole body." James systematically limits the office of teacher based on how well one stands or stumbles in word.

From James's rhetoric, is it possible to identify a rival teacher or teachers that James is targeting with his tongue? If so, how does James characterize the speech of his interlocutor(s)? Johnson reads the

85. Cf. Peter H. Davids, *The Epistle of James: A Commentary on the Greek Text* (Grand Rapids: Eerdmans, 1982), 136. Here, Davids describes the difficulty in the early Jesus movement to identify "true" teachers from "false" teachers. It is interesting that he uses "Paul's struggles with the circumcision party in Galatians and elsewhere" as an example of one early contention between teachers, but never makes the connection between the "circumcision party" and "those from James." Because of this, Davids does not connect this antiteacher passage in 3:1-12 with Paul or Pauline thought.

negative command in 3:1 regarding the διδάσκαλοι in the gnomic sense, which would prevent this entire passage from being a pointed argument against opponents.[86] The term for teachers (διδάσκαλοι) is found most often in the New Testament in the canonical Gospels. These occurrences are all reflections of a later period than the Letter of James, but it is clear that the position of teacher, whether it was an office or function, operated at a high level of respect and had implications for the larger community. By using first-person verbs in 3:1, James gives us the first autobiographical information since he used δοῦλος in 1:1. As has been noticed above, James's authority is assumed in the nature of his rhetoric, quite *unlike* Paul's continual assertion of his own authority in his letters. By positioning himself as the "perfect man" (τέλειος ἀνὴρ) (3:2), James guides his writing utensil to censure would-be teachers. James seems fully confident that he can bear the stricter judgment of teachers even though he does not extend that confidence to the teacher who would "bless" the poor, saying, "Go in peace, stay warm, and be filled" (2:16).

Contrary to Johnson, Ralph Martin and François Vouga identify a real enemy here.[87] Martin locates James's rival teachers with those who disrupt worship in 1 Corinthians 12–14. Martin has James and Paul agreeing with each other while they both confront these charismatic disruptions. According to Martin, "James is directing his shafts of criticism against the misuse of the tongue *in worship*—in a manner that indirectly recalls 1 Cor. 12–14 . . . and is concerned for the 'good order' or οἰκοδομή of the church in a way akin to the Pauline maxim of 1 Cor. 14:40: 'let everything (you do) be done

86. Johnson, *Letter of James*, 255. Bauckham, *James*, 153, 203–5; Brosend, *James and Jude*, 91; Timothy B. Cargal, *Restoring the Diaspora: Discursive Structure and Purpose in the Epistle of James* (Atlanta: Scholars, 1993), 143–50, but specifically 144; and Sophie Laws, *A Commentary on the Epistle of James* (San Francisco: Harper & Row, 1980), 144, all agree with Johnson and argue that the main purpose in this passage is wisdom reflection on speech acts.

87. Ralph P. Martin, *James*, WBC, 48 (Nashville: Thomas Nelson, 1988), 106, 124; François Vouga, *L'Épître de Saint Jacques* (Genève: Labor et Fides, 1984), 94–97.

in a seemly manner and in good order.'"[88] Martin never gets any more specific regarding the identity of James's rival teachers than showing the similarities between James 3:1-12 and 1 Corinthians 12–14.[89] His analysis is indebted to Vouga's work, which I will address later, that gives a more exhaustive treatment to the parallels between James and Paul. Although Martin is instructive by showing how James 3:1-12 could be focusing on worship, he does not draw strong enough parallels between James and 1 Corinthians to warrant such a thesis—neither does Vouga. They both, however, read 3:1ff. as a polemic against other teachers and recognize a close connection to Pauline debates.[90]

Returning to the theme of perfection in 3:2, James describes the "perfect man" as one who "does not stumble in word" (λόγῳ). The use of "stumble" (πταίει) is peculiar because it is not the normal term used in moral discourse.[91] It literally means "to trip." Paul, however, uses the same term in Rom. 11:11 to describe how the Judeans' "stumbling" has provided a way for the inclusion of the gentiles. This is part of Paul's overall reinterpretation of the covenant between God and Israel and how the gentiles fit into it. Paul uses his faith/works binary in both Galatians and Romans to explicate this problem. The fact that Paul and James use the same terminology for "tripping" in the way they do in Rom. 11:11 and James 3:2 is instructive for any attempts to determine who James's interlocutor is in 3:1-12. The "stumbling" in 3:2 is directly related to teachers, James included, and echoes the way James uses the term specifically

88. Martin, *James*, 104 (emphasis mine).

89. Martin makes these connections due to the frequency with which γλῶσσα denotes ecstatic speech in 1 Cor. 12:10, 28, 30; 13:1, 8; 14:2, 4, 5, 6, 9, 13, 14, 18, 19, 22, 23, 26, 27, and 39.

90. Davids, *Epistle of James*, 135–49, agrees that this teaching on the tongue is being specifically applied to teachers, but does not follow Vouga's and Martin's argument regarding those in the Corinthian body that caused disruption in worship. He argues that this treatise is a general warning against people seeking the teaching office.

91. Johnson, *Letter of James*, 256.

related to the Law in 2:10: "For whoever keeps the whole Law but stumbles [πταίσῃ] on one part, has become guilty of them all." Paul uses a variety of language to describe "stumbling," and much of his "stumbling" language has to do with gentiles and the Law.[92] The constant occurrence of "stumbling" language in Paul may indicate that James is interpolating Paul into his argument about teachers from the beginning. Whether Paul is being interpolated or not, James makes a clear connection to the introductory chapter of his letter with the use of "bridle" (χαλιναγωγῆσαι). The "perfect man" is able to bridle "the whole body" by "not stumbling in word." The perfect man, who controls the tongue, is the absolute opposite of those who do "not bridle [χαλιναγωγῶν] their tongues but deceive their hearts, their piety is worthless" (1:26). This connection to 1:26 clearly highlights James's monstrous interlocutor(s)—those who say they are pious, but are pretenders with worthless piety, that is, those who stumble in word.

To illustrate the incredible responsibility of a teacher, James uses common rhetorical tropes: bits/horses, ships/rudders, and tongue/body (vv. 3-5a). The difficulty of the topoi is noticed by most commentators. Brosend, who understands the entirety of 3:1-12 as a treatise on the tongue, emphasizes the incapacity of the illustrations to perform their duties to illustrate the point of the argument. Since he focuses on the tongue rather than the teacher, Brosend misses the obvious parallel between charioteer/captain/*teacher*, chariot/ship/*body*, and bit/rudder/*tongue*.[93] Indeed, if this pericope only concerns

92. Paul uses σκάνδαλον and σκανδαλίζω to refer to the same type of "moral" stumbling in Rom. 9:33, 11:9, 14:13, 16:17; 1 Cor. 1:23, 8:13 (twice), 2 Cor. 11:29, and Gal. 5:11. Paul also makes extensive use of the derivative of πταίω: παράπτωμα [transgression] in his faith/works binary in Rom. 4:25, 5:15 (twice), 16, 17, 18, 20 (cf. Rom. 11:12; Gal. 6:1; 2 Cor. 5:19). Again, Paul uses προσκόπτω and πρόσκομμα to describe stumbling blocks or causes of stumbling (Rom. 9:32, 33; 14:13, 20, 21; 1 Cor. 8:9; and 2 Cor. 6:2). The overlapping semantic domains of these terms add to the possibility of a link here between James and Paul.

93. Brosend, *James and Jude*, 89. Cf. Davids, *Epistle of James*, 139, as a correction to Brosend.

speech-acts, then the illustrations are wanting. The point of the illustrations, however, is to show the power of the tongue *as it relates to a teacher*. This functions to intensify the warning in verse 1: "Not many should be teachers." The power of the teacher's tongue guides the corporate body just as a captain steers a ship with a rudder and a charioteer guides a chariot with a bit. Davids is certainly correct: "It is not that the tongue steers the ship, but that the proper helmsman is often not in control."[94] After acknowledging the power of the position, James turns to the enormous evil that can be generated by a deviant teacher.

Before we focus on the most negative section of this pericope (vv. 5b-6), we should note Martin's insights regarding verses 9-12. As he exegetes verses 9-12, Martin inadvertently raises a strong possibility about whom James's interlocutor(s) may have been. Referencing the impossibility of one spring producing two types of water and a certain kind of fruit tree bearing a different kind of fruit, Martin eloquently restates James's point: "The monstrous phenomenon contradicting the natural order of the orchard is one of a hybrid plant that is designated at one and the same time a fig-bearing tree and an olive bush, or a plant that yields simultaneously grapes and figs. It is ludicrous to imagine such a case. No more so, says the text, than to justify the action of the double-tongued person who speaks out of a 'divided soul' (*dypsuchos*, in 1:7-8; 4:8)."[95] It is helpful to read verses 5b-12, then, with this "monstrous phenomenon" in front of us.

James changes tone in verse 5b when he negatively exclaims: "How a small flame sets ablaze a great forest!" Concentrating on the influence of teachers, this exclamation highlights the destruction of teachers who do not teach correctly—or, at least teach contrary to James. Although Hartin sees James's argumentation in 3:1-12

94. Davids, *Epistle of James*, 140.

95. Martin, *James*, 106.

as being "like a spiral"[96] that implies both teacher and tongue, he acknowledges that the pericope "was concerned above all with the divisions which arose within the community and the author feared that teachers could inspire and fuel these divisions."[97] For James, the whole Diaspora is being jeopardized by this fire. James begins to criticize such double-teaching as "the world of injustice," "polluting the whole body," "setting fire to the course of nature," and "being set on fire by Gehenna" (v. 6). The nominative construct of "the world of injustice" coupled with the nominative ἡ γλῶσσα has troubled scholars due to its awkward grammar. The two nominatives should be placed in apposition to each other where "the world of injustice" describes the tongue. As I discussed in the last chapter, "the world" carries the full weight of the empire and James does not deviate here. The tongue of the poisonous (v. 8) teacher *is* complicit with the unjust [ἀδικία] empire—"der gottwidrigen Welt" (the anti-God world), as Manabu Tsuji puts it.[98] There is broad consensus among scholars regarding "the world of injustice," which is summarized by Robert W. Wall:

> According to 1:27, the "world" is where anti-God values and sentiment are found, which contaminate life purified by obedience to "the perfect law of liberty" and ultimately undermine the prospect of divine blessing in an age to come. It is out of this evil world order that God calls the pious poor to be rich in faith and heirs of the promised kingdom (2:5). These prior meanings of "world" are retained here. The evils of the tongue are in kind with the evils found within the anti-God world; the peril of human speech is that it can verbalize and mobilize all that opposes God in the world.[99]

96. Hartin, *James*, 189.
97. Patrick J. Hartin, *James and the Q Sayings of Jesus* (Sheffield: Sheffield Academic Press, 1991), 98.
98. Manabu Tsuji, *Glaube zwischen Vollkommenheit und Verweltlichung: Eine Untersuchung zur literarischen Gestalt und zur inhaltlichen Koharenz des Jakobusbriefes* (Tübingen: Mohr Siebeck, 1997), 80.
99. Robert W. Wall, *Community of the Wise: The Letter of James* (Valley Forge, PA: Trinity Press International, 1997), 169.

The tongue is not just "the world of injustice," but it is "set in" (καθίσταται) your members in exactly the same way one "sets him/herself" (καθίσταται) as an enemy of God by desiring friendship with "the world" in 4:4—the next antihybrid pericope. This looks forward to calling the forked-tongue teacher a "friend of the world."

The tongue of the teacher is then described in perfect parallel with three present participles: σπιλοῦσα, φλογίζουσα, φλογιζομένη. The polluting power of the teacher is set in opposition to the thesis of the entire letter: "and keep oneself unpolluted [ἄσπιλον] by the world" (1:27). In other words, "polluting the whole body" (v. 6) is the "monstrous phenomenon" that is completely contrary to being "unpolluted by the world" (1:27). Again, this indicates that James has the whole Diaspora in mind by "the whole body," a phrase he repeats three times in this pericope. The next two participial phrases show how this tongue moves feverishly beyond the Diaspora to the entire "course of nature" and ultimately is indicative of "pure" evil. "Setting on fire the course of nature" is problematic on a topical level. Since the phrase is a *hapax legomenon* in the New Testament, and not that well attested in other literature, the phrase is difficult to translate. The "wheel" or "cycle" is understood as "course" (τροχὸν). This construction with ethnic language (γενέσεως) may indicate what Denise Kimber Buell calls "ethnic reasoning."[100] Instead of "course of nature," one can translate this construction as "course of the generations." By doing so, this concentrates on the "natural" (or, more accurately, naturalizes) genealogical connections among those scattered in the Diaspora. By "setting on fire the course of the generations," the teacher's tongue threatens naturalized ethnic boundaries within Judeanness. This not only pollutes the whole

100. Buell, *Why This New Race?* Buell defines ethnic reasoning as argumentation that "refers to the modes of persuasion that may or may not include the use of a specific vocabulary of peoplehood," 2.

body, but is set on fire, or better initiated, by Gehenna. Here, James uses a Jesus tradition that emerges in the canonical Gospels—the only other place where Gehenna is used in the New Testament. In the Gospel contexts, Gehenna is "a place of punishment."[101] By using Gehenna, Johnson argues that James "does more than evoke the symbolic world of Judaism. He points to the cosmic dualism underlying the 'two ways' of disposing human freedom. The rule of God in the world is opposed by the work of the devil."[102] Using Johnson's argument, the teacher is in direct disagreement not only with James, but with God. Johnson correctly describes James's "two ways." James creates rigid boundaries that this teacher threatens with the tongue. Destroying the genealogy that provides the Diaspora with its "natural," nostalgic, and native identity is, for James, "the world of injustice."

James turns to an illustration of the created world (v. 7) to emphasize the trouble of the untamed tongue (v. 8). Verse 8 stresses the point that all of creation can be tamed, but not the tongue. The tongue (of the teacher) is "unstable evil" and full of "deadly poison." The word "unstable" (ἀκατάστατον) is important because it terminologically links this untamed tongue with the ultimate mimetic monster, that is, the *dypsuchos*—"double-minded." James 1:8 says that the "double-minded" (δίψυχος) is "unstable [ἀκατάστατος] in every way"—especially in actions and speech. The *dypsuchos didaskalos* is full of deadly poison (ἰοῦ), which looks forward to the "rust" that will be evidence against the wealthy and "will eat [their] flesh like fire" (5:3). The total condemnation of the wealthy is prefigured here in the poison of the *dypsuchos didaskalos*. It is also evidence that the teacher is analogous to the wealthy. This hybrid *dypsuchos*'s instability and evil stand in stark distinction from "the

101. Johnson, *Letter of James*, 260.
102. Ibid., 265.

perfect man" in verse 2 and the purity to which James calls the Diaspora.

James brings this section to a close by disclosing the double-minded dialogue of the forked-tongue teacher. With a surprising turn back to the first person, James places himself beside the teacher. He may recognize his own invective as somewhat "slanderous" and "poisonous." The duplicity of the teacher's tongue is evidenced from the fact that the same tongue "blesses the Lord and Father," and "curses people made in the likeness of God." James again returns to Gen. 1:26-28 to show the inconsistency in his opponent's politics. It is not clear if James is refuting an antagonistic teacher who may have been "cursing" him, but Manabu Tsuji calls this issue "innergemeindliche Streitigkeiten."[103] Tsuji sees the "cursing of the people made in the image of God" in verse 9 by other teachers/leaders ("Leute in führender Position") as the main "Problem innergemeindlicher Konflikte" (problem of inner-community conflicts). This inner-community problem has to do with rogue teachers, who James discredits as those with "Doppelheit der Zunge" (duality of the tongue).[104] Might James be refuting a rival teacher who was cursing him? Davids sees a liturgical setting for these blessings and curses, and shows that "Paul certainly expressed at least curse like formulas (e.g. 1 Cor. 5; 15:22; Gal. 1:1)."[105]

Galatians makes it abundantly clear that Paul had an ambivalent relationship with the Jerusalem leaders. When describing his experience with the leaders in Jerusalem, Paul, in spite of going to seek their commission (Gal. 2:2), denies them the authority that he

103. Tsuji, *Glaube zwischen Vollkommenheit und Verweltlichung*, 79.

104. Ibid., 82. Tsuji interprets the reference to "teachers" in 3:1 as controlling the entire section from 3:1 to 4:12 (79–88). Davids, *Epistle of James*, 146, agrees with Tsuji, arguing: "What James appears to be referring to is the use of a curse in anger, especially in inner-church party strife."

105. Davids, *Epistle of James*, 146. Nowhere does Davids argue for an anti-Pauline polemic in James 3:1-12. He is here only referencing several occasions in the New Testament where other authors used blessing/curse formulas.

desires from their approval: "And from those who were supposed to be acknowledged leaders (what they actually were makes no difference to me; God shows no partiality)—those leaders contributed nothing to me" (Gal. 2:6). Paul also recounts his Antioch experience with Cephas by saying that "those from James" came and "led astray" the rest of the Judeans (Ἰουδαῖοι) and even Barnabas into what Paul calls "hypocrisy" (both the verb συνυποκρίνομαι and the noun ὑπόκρισις, Gal. 2:13). After stating that "those from James" were "not acting consistently with the truth of the gospel," Paul launches into his faith/works binary and repeats three times in one verse: "one is not justified by works of the Law" and twice that "a person is justified by the faith of Jesus Christ" (2:16). The imperative force at the end of verse 10 summarizes the way James responds to the criticism: "This should not happen, my brothers!" Johnson rightly comments that "This is the only example of the usage in the NT and wonderfully captures the moralist's sense of outrage at 'what ought not to be.'"[106] James refers back to the Jesus tradition in order to illustrate his outrage at this hybrid hyperbole. Starting with a spring (v. 11) and moving to plants (v. 12a), then back to water (v. 12b), James shows the utter impossibility of double-speak. The *same* spring cannot "gush forth both sweet and bitter water." This line of argument is close thematically to the Jesus tradition in Matt. 7:16/Luke 6:44, where Jesus says, "You will know them by their fruits. Are grapes gathered from thorns or figs [σύκα] from thistles?" In the same way, James asks, "My brothers, is a fig tree [συκῆ] able to make olives or a vine figs [σῦκα]?" With the strength of the Jesus tradition, James chastens the teacher as a hybrid that renders pure and unpolluted piety impossible. For James, "This should not happen!"

106. Johnson, *Letter of James*, 262.

The Mimetic Monster in 3:1-12

What teacher could be so ambiguous in his or her teaching that this monstrous double message could be taught? François Vouga, in an attempt to show parallelism between James and Paul, sheds light on this shameful hybrid. Vouga finds parallels between James 2:1-13 and 1 Cor. 11:17-34 regarding the wealthy and poor; James 3:14-18 and 1 Cor. 1:17—2:16 regarding wisdom; James 2:14-26, Romans 14–15, and 1 Corinthians 8 regarding consistency in faith; and finally James 3:1-13 and 1 Corinthians 12–14 regarding orderly worship.[107] Rather than a criticism of charismatic speaking, however, James 3:1-12 deals with inconsistency in speech or hypocrisy in speech—in a similar fashion to the faith/works argument that immediately precedes this pericope. This hybrid tongue is utterly contradictory to James's understanding of perfection and purity. In verse 6, it "pollutes the whole body." As stated earlier, this pollution (the present active participle of σπιλόω) is also found, although in negative form, in what makes the thesis statement for the entire Letter of James: "If any think they are pious, and do not bridle their tongues but deceive their hearts, their piety is worthless. Piety that is pure and undefiled before God, the Father, is this: to care for orphans and widows in their distress, and to keep oneself unstained [ἄσπιλον] by the world" (1:26-27). The connection between James's thesis statement in 1:26-27 and James 3:1-12 only strengthens the potential for 3:1-12 being a pointed passage against a hybrid opponent.

In James's strict nativist binary system there is absolutely no room for intermingling with the world. The empire of God, which is governed by imperial law (2:8), stands in direct opposition to this "world" (κόσμος) and against a forked-tongued teacher. As is the case in nativist rhetoric, empire is never the only opponent. Within

107. Vouga, *L'Épître de Saint Jacques*, 94–95.

this universe, there is good and bad—for James it is the pure and the impure. Any semblance of transgressing this boundary and befriending the world is completely contradictory to pure and undefiled piety. Those who would transgress that boundary and "teach" others to do so would be characteristic of double-mindedness and exhibit worthless piety.

An example of piety that *could* be characterized in this light can be found in passages such as Romans 14 and 1 Corinthians 8 in Paul's discussion of food laws. In both passages, Paul ultimately argues that his readers should not eat anything that could potentially cause another to stumble (cf. "stumbling block"—πρόσκομμα—in 1 Cor. 8:9 and Rom. 14:13 and "stumble"—προσκόπτω—in Rom. 14:21, and compare πταίω in James 3:2). Paul argues that there are circumstances in which Jesus' followers should not eat meat that has been sacrificed to idols. At these points in his discussion, Paul coincides with the nativist/rigorist standpoint of James, and so to that extent these two would agree. The way in which Paul arrived at his conclusions, however, would have certainly put him at odds with James's conception of "friendship with the world," that is, hybridity. Paul's hybridity would have confronted James's nativism in at least two ways.

First of all, Paul flatly states that there is absolutely nothing wrong with eating anything whatsoever. In 1 Cor. 8:8b, Paul says, "We are no worse off if we do not eat, and no better off if we do." He says the same thing about circumcision in 7:19a, "Circumcision is nothing, and uncircumcision is nothing." In Rom. 14:14a, Paul goes so far as to argue that nothing at all is unclean: "I know and am persuaded in the Lord Jesus that nothing is unclean in itself." Later in the chapter Paul insists that "everything is indeed clean [καθαρός]" (v. 20b).[108]

108. Contrast James 4:8: "Cleanse [καθαρίσατε] your hands, Sinners!"

In every one of these instances, Paul qualifies his radical statements. At each turn, he tells his readers that they should lay aside their freedoms and rights to partake in these practices "for the sake of the weak." In Rom. 14:20, Paul qualifies his statement about everything being clean with "Do not, for the sake of food, destroy the work of God." He adds in verse 21, "it is good *not* to eat meat or drink wine or do anything that makes your brother [or sister] stumble." Likewise, in 1 Cor. 8:9, Paul again qualifies his statements: "But take care that this liberty of yours does not somehow become a stumbling block to the weak." Paul only agrees with James in the end, and it seems difficult to imagine a scenario where James would accept many of the statements that Paul makes on the way to that end. Most commentators who argue that James and Paul are not responding to each other in their letters point out that James never explicitly mentions either the food laws or circumcision. All commentators, however, understand James as a rigorist when it comes to piety. James's constant use of purity and impurity clearly indicates that his nativist position cannot allow for Paul's line of argumentation even when the results would be something similar to his own piety. This would transgress the boundaries that James stringently polices. Paul's capacity to *teach* that there is really no boundary for those with a "strong" conscience except for their consideration for the weak would, for James, slide down a slippery slope of hypocritical hybridity. This type of "friendship with the world" equals being at "enmity with God."

The second reason why James and Paul would be at odds with each other is based on Paul's use of the term "weak" in 1 Corinthians 8 and Romans 14. Although Paul never uses this term in Romans 14, the concept is certainly there. The qualifications that Paul uses as reasons why his readers should abstain from certain food are that others would be influenced by the use of their freedoms. Paul, however, repeats this theme of weakness five times in 1 Corinthians 8 (vv. 7, 8, 10, 11, and 12). Unless Paul is being unduly sarcastic when referring to the weak, he seems to seriously consider those with a rigorist position against eating meat sacrificed to idols as those who have weak consciences. Those who know that food laws and circumcision are actually meaningless are those who have strong consciences. A rigorist/nativist position is characterized as weak according to Paul's argumentation. The rhetoric of weakness that Paul uses would place him in opposition to any nativist conceptions of self. There is no way to read the Letter of James and imagine that James would consider his nativist position as one of weakness. Paul's assertions beg a question to which there is no possible answer: How would someone from a rigorist position respond to being called weak? Better yet, can we imagine how James would have responded to this line of argumentation? Is this a small fire that sets a whole forest ablaze? Would James consider Paul's rhetoric a "monstrous phenomenon," to use Martin's words again? Paul's capacity to live out his hybrid identity in a way that negotiates a space for his readers to acknowledge that there is nothing unclean, and, yet, live as if there were unclean things, gets very close to James's inconceivable idea of a fig tree producing olives.

Throughout James 3:1-12, James argues that talk is as important as walk. In doing so, he attempts to tame the hybrid tongue that is so loud in Paul's writings. Paul's letters thoroughly exhibit colonial hybridity. James's letter thoroughly exhibits nativism. Both confront empire and negotiate an identity that inevitably puts them at odds with each other. James's notion of purity and impurity could never account for Paul's statement that "everything is clean," no matter where Paul finishes his thought. It is clear that this kind of imperfect stumbling on Paul's part would completely disqualify him as a *didaskalos*; however, it would surely qualify him as a *dypsuchos*.

Martin may miss the mark in identifying the *dypsuchos didaskalos*, but his identification of the antagonistic teacher as a hybrid interlocutor is helpful when reading Paul as the mimetic monster. In fact, Martin's "monstrous phenomenon" of a hybrid fig/olive tree/bush symbolizes exactly the kind of inconsistency that James's previous argument denounced in relation to faith and works. In 3:1-12, James gets more specific in identifying his interlocutor—one who would just as easily believe that faith alone could save you.

An edited version of a portion of this chapter ("Actions as Evidence [2:14-26]" section) was published as K. Jason Coker, "Nativism in James 2.14-26: A Post-Colonial Reading," in *Reading James with New Eyes: Methodological Reassessments of the Letter of James*, ed. Robert L. Webb and John S. Kloppenborg (New York: T. & T. Clark, 2007), 27–48.

6

Identifying the Mimetic Monster, Part 2

James 4:1-12 is the most aggressive antihybrid passage in the letter. In the opening verse, James begins with military language to describe the problem in the Diaspora. These "wars" (πόλεμοι) and "battles" (μάχαι) are the result of their desire (ἡδονή) for empire, which is evil (κακῶς). This desire for empire among the Diaspora is evidenced in their urge to "spend freely" on their pleasures. This, in effect, makes them as bad as the wealthy/worldly, or, even worse, it makes them a "friend of the world" (ἡ φιλία τοῦ κόσμου/φίλος τοῦ κόσμου). At this point, James uses the most incendiary language for insiders in his entire letter. In the language and tone of a prophet, James calls those in the Diaspora "whores" (μοιχαλίδες). The sexually provocative language in the previous verses leads to this denunciation of infidelity. Setting the "world" in direct opposition to God, James forces the Diaspora to choose. Friendship, as I will show below, was an important social factor in Greco-Roman culture. There were certain privileges and responsibilities that came with friendship, so choosing a friend was critical for social status.

Duality as Difference: *Dypsuchos* Dichotomy and Pauline Thought (James 4:1-12)

Still within a military framework, James argues that "friendship with the world is enmity with God." True to nativist form, the separation is absolute; the boundary between purity and pollution is drawn down this axis. James then uses a scriptural citation peppered with Jesus tradition to ground his argument: "God opposes the arrogant but gives grace to the humble [ταπεινοῖς]" (cf. Prov. 3:34). After this reference to Scripture, James issues a string of imperatives that demand the Diaspora's allegiance to the empire of God and denunciation of the empire of this world, that is, the Roman Empire: "Therefore, subject yourselves to God and oppose the Devil and he will flee from you." Rather than fighting an internal war of compromise, assimilation, and hybridity, James argues that this is the "war" and "battle" that the Diaspora should be fighting—the war between God and the devil/world. James returns to the prophetic vocative. In the same way he calls those who desire the world "whores," he now calls them "sinners" (ἁμαρτωλοί) and "double-minded" (δίψυχοι). The call to purity, here, is accompanied by the call to "be miserable" (ταλαιπωρήσατε), "mourn" (πενθήσατε), and "weep" (κλαύσατε), which are the correct responses to God's discipline according to the ancient prophets. This mourning, paralleled in the prophets, is due to infidelity to the covenant. According to the prophetic literature, because of Israel's mixture with other empires (usually described in sexual terms), God has judged and punished or will judge and punish them (cf. Hos. 10:2; Mic. 2:4; Joel 1:10; Zech. 11:2-3).

As James has recourse to the prophetic tradition, he corrects the Diaspora's desire for empire and commands them with an echo of the Jesus tradition: "Be humble before the Lord and he will exalt you" (cf. Matt. 18:4; 23:12; Luke 18:14). James ends his most aggressive pericope concerning hybridity by warning the Diaspora not to slander one another because "There is only one Lawgiver and Judge, who is able to save and destroy." Throughout this section, James violently condemns hybrid arrogance that lusts after empire. As we now move to a closer reading of this passage, it will be important to notice how this nativist call to purity militarily positions hybrid identity as whorish, sinful, and double-minded—all synonymous with "friendship with the world." An accompanying question to this analysis is: Could the "forked-tongue teacher" of 3:1-12 embody such a hybrid identity?

Military Language

With the use of military language and several binary constructions, James thoroughly splits the universe between God and "world" in 4:1-12. In a world dominated by imperialism, and James's context in Jerusalem as a tenuous and contested place in relation to Rome, one should pay close attention when James begins to use militaristic language. Rather than using the *topos* of envy, which was common among other Hellenistic writers and included militant language to describe internal conflicts within individuals, James is making a more forceful argument about cultural hybridity. His militaristic imagery is responding to what Ngũgĩ wa Thiong'o calls the cultural bomb:

> The effect of a cultural bomb is to annihilate a people's belief in their names, in their languages, in their environment, in their heritage of struggle, in their unity, in their capacities and ultimately in themselves. It makes them see their past as one wasteland of non-achievement and it makes them *want* to distance themselves from that wasteland. It makes them *want* to identify with that which is furthest removed from themselves; for instance, with other peoples' languages rather than their own. It makes them identify with that which is *decadent* and reactionary, all those forces which stop their own springs of life.[1]

Envy alone is not in James's scope. The "pleasures that make war" (στατευομένων) in their "members" (μέλεσιν) is as dangerous as the destructive tongue (γλῶσσα) in 3:6. These pleasures are the desire for empire—the "wanting" of the decadence of empire. This is a war that James wants to fight and win! James engages this battle against the culture bomb with bombs of his own: whores (μοιχαλίδες), sinners (ἁμαρτωλοί), the double-minded (δίψυχοι).

By relegating this passage to an ordinary Hellenistic *topos*, Johnson (as well as Hartin and Laws) defuses James's weapons as rhetorical flourishes about individual, internal conflict—that *can* lead to social unrest.[2] In this pericope, according to Johnson, James is one ancient moralist among others with the same sort of message. In spite of arguing that the "level of contentiousness" in 4:1-12 is "previously unknown in the letter," Brosend then renders this invective impotent by saying that the *topos* of envy is "about the pull and tug of competing desires within the hearts of members of the community."[3] Johnson argues that "envy is constantly associated with wars and battles, as with social upheaval," but never attributes James's use of this rhetoric as evidence for any *real* social situation.[4] In fact, Brosend critiques Martin's overcontextualization of James where "rhetoric is mistaken for evidence of historical context."[5] Resisting Martin's reading that situates James in Roman Palestine during severe social unrest, Brosend proposes that James's intense imperatives and name-calling are directed against the "have-nots," who want what the

1. Ngũgĩ wa Thiong'o, *Decolonizing the Mind: The Politics of Language in African Literature* (Harare, Zimbabwe: Zimbabwe Publishing House, 1987), 3 (emphasis mine).
2. Luke Timothy Johnson, *The Letter of James: A New Translation with Introduction and Commentary* (New York: Doubleday, 1995), 267–90; Patrick J. Hartin, *James*, Sacra Pagina, 14 (Collegeville, MN: Liturgical, 2003), 190–217; Sophie Laws, *The Epistle of James*, Harper's New Testament Commentary (San Francisco: Harper & Row, 1980), 166–85.
3. William F. Brosend II, *James and Jude*, The New Cambridge Bible Commentary (Cambridge: Cambridge University Press, 2004), 105, 107.
4. Johnson, *Letter of James*, 276.
5. Brosend, *James and Jude*, 113.

"haves" have *in the community*. "Yes, there is ample blame and condemnation for those who have and do not share faithfully or treat equitably those who have not. But there is no sense of 'It's all *their* fault.' Rather, those who do not have are also held accountable for the quality of their lives and the faithfulness of their practice."[6] It is worth noting that no other commentator shares Brosend's interpretation regarding the "have nots" as the culprits of desire. Johnson shows the cultural weight that the *topos* of envy had in the Hellenistic world, when he argues that

> [t]he ancient moralists were precise in their dissection of vices and virtues. When they considered the logic of envy as it was displayed in real human behavior, they saw that it lay behind every sort of rivalry, party spirit, and competition. In the moral literature, envy is consistently associated with hatred, boorishness, faithlessness, tyranny, malice, hubris, ill will, ambition, and above all, arrogance (*hyperēphania*). It is envy that creates desires to have and possess (see 4:2). And envy recognizes no bounds to its ambition. The result? Social upheaval and unrest, battles and wars (3:16; 4:1).[7]

Johnson, however, cannot account for James's vitriolic rhetoric, which distinguishes 4:1-12 from other "ancient moralists." Envy in 4:1-12 is more than internal agony that, left unchecked, leads to social upheaval. These pleasures (ἡδονή) are James's battleground where he goes to war with hybridity, that is, double-mindedness.

Ralph Martin's optic on James's location in Jerusalem during the tumultuous period between 40 and 62 CE reads the military language of 4:1-12 as historical rather than metaphorical. "The fighting, in our interpretation, is not 'within the body of the individual Christian,' but within the life of James' church relating to societal and political issues."[8] Martin (re)constructs James's situation in Roman Palestine as

6. Ibid., 114.
7. Johnson, *Letter of James*, 288.
8. Ralph P. Martin, *James*, WBC, 48 (Nashville: Thomas Nelson, 1988), 140.

one with "the presence of a disadvantaged and disgruntled peasant population" and a highly assimilated "Jewish ruling class."[9] This class division was exacerbated by "the Romans, whose presence in Israel ever since Pompey's invasion in 63 B.C. was a sore spot on the body of Israel's theocratic life."[10] According to Martin, a social and political environment such as this gave rise to revolutionary causes into which James was drawn: "James' sympathies would certainly have lain with the peasant people and the lower priests."[11] Rather than interpreting James as a revolutionary, Martin argues that James was only "sympathetic" to the cause and this was misunderstood by the high priest Ananus as complicity, which is why Ananus had James killed.[12] With this as his historical framework, Martin argues that James's community "wavered in their allegiance to God and were tempted to be drawn away to false hopes and into 'diabolic' paths led by Zealot factionalists."[13] The "wars and battles" of 4:1, then, are not internal conflicts within individuals or internal conflicts within the community. These are the "wars and battles" that were taking place all through Roman Palestine that were a prelude to the Jewish-Roman War in 66–70 CE. In this view, James rebukes would-be Zealots from his community "who were ready to fight to the death in the interests of national freedom"[14] because they pursued war rather than peace. Martin ultimately argues that James is caught between the Zealots and the imperial collaborationists (the Sadducees) in his views against Rome. For Martin, it is this environment that produces James's military language in 4:1-12.

9. Ibid., lxiv.
10. Ibid.
11. Ibid., lxvi.
12. Ibid., lxvii.
13. Ibid., 143.
14. Ibid., 145.

Contrary to Martin, Peter Davids sees the military language as indicative of "inner-community conflicts occasioned by the party spirit of the teachers in the previous section."[15] It is insightful of Davids to connect the *didaskalos* of 3:1-12 with the *dypsuchos* of 4:1-12 precisely because double-mindedness is the result of the teaching—a point many commentators miss due to their insistence on the *topos* of envy. Although Martin's analysis is important, the text argues for more of an internal issue related to Judeanness. Specifically, the use of ἐν ὑμῖν (4:1) to describe the location of the "wars and battles" strongly indicates that James is referencing an inner-community problem. Additionally, James describes "your pleasures" as "making war in your members [μέλεσιν]" (4:1). James uses the same terminology to describe the problem of the tongue in 3:6: "The tongue is placed among our members [μέλεσιν]." The pleasures/hedonism in 4:1 is connected to the tongue in 3:6, and both are happening, to James's dismay, *within the community*. The pleonastic use of πόθεν illustrates that these "wars and battles" are actively happening in the present. The ultimate enemy is found in the most vitriolic verse in the entire passage (4:4): "Do you not know that friendship with the world is hatred/hostility/enmity toward God? Therefore, if someone wants to be a friend of the world, he is established as a hater/hostile/enemy of God." The term "enemy/hostile/hater" (ἐχθρὸς) is used in military discourse to describe opposition and is synonymous with πολέμιος, *one who is at war*. It is the opposite of friendship. This militant hostility between God and the world disrupts the argument that this pericope is indebted to a *topos* of envy, as Johnson himself recognizes: "There is no such proverb in the Greco-Roman moral literature, or in Hellenistic

15. Peter H. Davids, *The Epistle of James: A Commentary on the Greek Text* (Grand Rapids: Eerdmans, 1982), 156.

Jewish writings."[16] The militant language, then, goes beyond the *topos* of envy.

In verses 6-7, James uses "oppose/resist/range in battle" to describe God's position against "the arrogant" (ὑπερηφάνοις) and the Diaspora's position against "the devil" (διαβόλῳ). James quotes Proverbs 3:34 as a proof text that brings the first part of this pericope to a close and bases his argument against "pleasures" in Scripture: "God battles the arrogant, but gives grace to the humble [ταπεινοῖς]." James takes the vocabulary of militant opposition between God and the arrogant and turns it into an imperative for the Diaspora when he begins his next argument in verse 7: "Therefore, subject yourselves to God; go to battle [ἀντίστητε] with the devil [διαβόλῳ], and he will flee from you." As God battles the arrogant, so should the Diaspora battle the devil. The "definite military nuance" here is not within the rubric of envy and is hardly nuanced.[17] It is overt military language as is evidenced in a passage from Josephus's *Jewish War*, where Josephus describes a meeting between Petronius and Judean (Ἰουδαῖοι) leaders to discuss the reasons why Roman statues should not be erected in Roman Palestine:

> The Jews assembled with their wives and children in the plain of Ptolemais and implored Petronius to have regard first for the laws of their fathers, and next for themselves. Yielding so far to this vast multitude and their entreaties, he left the statues and his troops at Ptolemais and advanced into Galilee, where he summoned the people, with all persons of distinction, to Tiberias. There he dwelt upon the power of the Romans and the emperor's menaces, and, moreover, pointed out the recklessness of their request; all the subject nations [τῶν ὑποτεταγμένων], he urged, had erected in each of their cities statues of Caesar, along with those of their other gods, and that they alone should oppose [ἀντιτάσσεσθαι] this practice amounted almost to rebellion, aggravated by insult.[18]

16. Johnson, *Letter of James*, 279.
17. Johnson, *Letter of James*, 283.

In an attempt to reason with these leaders, Petronius replies, "But I too must obey the law of my master; if I transgress it and spare you, I shall be put to death, with justice. War will be made [πολεμήσει] on you by him who sent me, not by me; for I too, like you, am under orders."[19] Using similar military language, James commands the Diaspora to "subject" (ὑποτάγητε) themselves to God and go to battle with the devil. Subjection to God contrasts with Josephus's portrayal of "subject nations" (τῶν ὑποτεταγμένων ἐθνῶν) and, more importantly, with Paul's command that "Every soul should submit [ὑποτασσέσθω] to governing authorities" (Rom. 13:1). James demands militant subjection to God and militant resistance to the devil/slanderer/accuser.

The final use of military language in this pericope comes in verse 12, where James chastises the "slanderer" (καταλαλῶν) and, with an allusion to the Shema, decries, "There is one Lawgiver and Judge, who is able to save [σῶσαι] and destroy [πλησίον]." James references a common notion from Scripture that God was able to save Israel and also destroy them, but this verse also has strong echoes in the Jesus tradition (cf. Matt. 8:25; 16:25; Luke 6:9, 19:10). Within the LXX, God's act of saving is always within a military setting, for example, "Blessed are you, O Israel! Who is like you, a people saved [σῳζόμενος] by the Lord, the shield of your help and the sword of your triumph. Your enemies [οἱ ἐχθροί] will lie to you and you will put your foot on their necks" (Deut. 33:29). Salvation here is from enemies (οἱ ἐχθροί) rather than some eschatological moment. Likewise, destruction is usually a result of breaking the covenant with God. James reminds the one who would slander that this action amounts to breaking covenant with God. The specific use of

18. Josephus, *JW.* 2.192–94 (trans. Thackery, LCL). Cf. Herodotus, *The Histories* 5.72.2, 6.117.3; Dionysius of Halicarnassus, *Roman Antiquities* 2.42, 6.8, 9.5.

19. Josephus, *J.W.* 2.195 (trans. Thackery, LCL).

"neighbor" (πλησίον) reminds one of 2:8, where love of neighbor is considered the imperial law (νόμον βασιλικόν). This transgression of the covenant amounts to hostility toward the God who is able to "save and destroy."

It is clear from the constant uses of military language throughout this pericope that James had more in mind than a treatise on envy. While the *topos* of envy may be used by James, he is not simply arguing for the Diaspora to be careful in regard to immoral desires. There is a specific desire that James is violently opposing—the desire for empire. This is the threat that should be understood as hatred toward God and friendship with the world. In this war between God and the world, those who would transgress this boundary or blur the boundary are traitors, and this is exactly who James is targeting in his polemic. The cultural differences that James has constructed and reified throughout his letter are being jeopardized by one who takes no account of the "cultural bomb" that has hegemonically waged war against James's Judeanness. "What is irremediably estranging in the presence of the hybrid—in the revaluation of the symbol of national authority as the sign of colonial difference—is that the difference of cultures can no longer be identified or evaluated as objects of epistemological or moral contemplation: cultural differences are not simply *there* to be seen or appropriated."[20] For James, hybridity, understood as friendship with the world, is exactly the problem against which he militates. The desire for empire melts differences that James aggressively reifies in his harshest attack against hybridity.

Absolute Binary

James's constant use of various conflicting binaries also evidences his rhetorical drive to separate/purify, that is, separate the Diaspora from

20. Homi K. Bhabha, *Location of Culture* (London and New York: Routledge, 1994), 114.

the world. This division between the bad and the good operates in nearly every verse of this pericope. Working in tandem with his military language, James clearly creates two sides of the conflict. God/world (v. 4), God/arrogant (v. 6), God/devil (v. 7), cleanse/sinners and purify/double-minded (v. 9), humble/exalted (v. 10), and save/destroy (v. 12) all conspire to divide and separate James, and those who would follow his instructions, from those who would complicate these boundaries. The repetition of division cumulatively creates one major division on which the entire letter is based: God/world. The equation, used twice in 4:4, defines this section: friendship with the world = enemy of God. Here, James reflects Bhabha's "process of identification."[21] First, "It is always in relation to the place of the Other that colonial desire is articulated: the phantasmic space of possession that no one subject can singly or fixedly occupy, and therefore permits the dream of the inversion of roles."[22] Bhabha argues that "[t]he fantasy of the native is precisely to occupy the master's place while keeping his place in the slave's *avenging* anger."[23] James's insistence on the God/world binary compels him to use militant language of resistance that betrays his own call for purity. Purity is only comprehensible within a binary system of purity/pollution. In this sense, James's call to purity is seemingly betrayed in the act of annunciation. Bhabha continues: "[I]dentification is never the affirmation of a pre-given identity, never a *self*-fulfilling prophecy—it is always the production of an image of identity and the transformation of the subject in assuming that image."[24] James's insistence on God/world entangles the identity he is producing within a colonial framework that is inescapable. By using this binary, however, and framing his argument on a "pre-given identity," James

21. Ibid., 44.
22. Ibid.
23. Ibid. (emphasis original).
24. Ibid., 45 (emphasis original).

seeks to transform the Diaspora in his call to repentance in 4:1-12. The friendship *topos* functions, for James, as the site of his identity production. The social contract of friendship is important in this equation and deserves attention, especially since James has previously critiqued the social system of patronage (2:1-13). This social contract with the world threatens to nullify the covenant with God, which is the reason for James's prophetic denunciation.

Friendship was an important and complex social phenomenon in the Greco-Roman world. Like patronage, it was a social system of exchange, but ideologically, friendship existed between two people of equal social status. Peter Garnsey and Richard Saller recognize at least three "categories of exchange relationships" in the Roman Empire: patron/clients, superior/inferior friends (patrons/protégés), and equal friends.[25] Although friendship was unlike the asymmetrical system of patronage, it was still governed by a "reciprocity ethic."[26] When a friend gave a favor, it was expected that a reciprocal favor would be given. Ideologically, this was not the intent of favors, but could certainly affect the (dis)continuity of friendship if reciprocity was not shown. This amounted to ungratefulness, which was a terrible vice within both the system of patronage and friendship. According to Saller, friendship had specific technical ideals:

> [A] friend should be forgiving but frank in advice and criticism; a man has an obligation to spread his friend's fame and reputation (an obligation which also carries interesting implications for the objectivity or otherwise of *commendationes*); a man should attend to a friend when ill and look after his family, interests and reputation after his death; on the one hand, friends should attend to petty formalities and expressions of affection such as *vota* on birthdays, congratulations on reaching office,

25. Peter Garnsey and Richard Saller, *The Roman Empire: Economy, Society and Culture* (Berkeley and Los Angeles: University of California Press, 1987), 149.
26. Richard P. Saller, *Personal Patronage under the Early Empire* (Cambridge: Cambridge University Press, 1982), 14.

> and letter writing; on the other hand, close friends may be allowed the liberty of dispensing with the formalities.[27]

Friends are one soul (μιᾶς ψυχῆς)[28] and are considered a "second self" (*alter idem*).[29] Friends were also important "because in the Roman view a man's character was reflected in his friends."[30] According to one ancient author, "perhaps the tightest bond for keeping friendships [*amicitias*] united is similar manners [*morum similitudo*]."[31]

James's binary between God and world is illustrated in the social contract of friendship; that is, friendship with the world is hostility with God. Garnsey and Saller make an important contribution to our understanding of the *topos* of friendship in showing that "the exchange of services was a foundation for friendship."[32] It was a social contract among equals, but the contract came with obligations. Friendship with the world, for James, meant that one had serious obligations to the world under the contract of friendship. These obligations were in direct conflict with God's claim on the Diaspora. In Luke Timothy Johnson's illuminating essay "Friendship with the World and Friendship with God: A Study of Discipleship in James," he argues that the "world" is "a measure of reality, or a system of meaning."[33] According to Johnson, James is dramatically calling his listeners/hearers to follow God's measure rather than the world's measure: "What makes someone double-minded is precisely the

27. Saller, *Personal Patronage*, 13.
28. Plutarch, *De amicorum multitudine* 96f. The whole passage accentuates the equality of friends: "to be together and to deliberate together and to agree perfectly and be affected the same way, even as one soul—even more, being divided from a single body."
29. Cicero, *De Amicitia* 21.80.
30. Saller, *Personal Patronage*, 109.
31. Pliny the Younger, *Epistles* 4.15.2
32. Garnsey and Saller, *Roman Empire*, 154.
33. Luke Timothy Johnson, "Friendship with the World and Friendship with God: A Study of Discipleship in James," in *Brother of Jesus, Friend of God: Studies in the Letter of James* (Grand Rapids/Cambridge: Eerdmans, 2004), 213.

desire to live by both measures at once, to be friends with everyone."[34]

The world, however, as I have described earlier, carries more meaning than a simple "measure." As we have seen in James's condemnation of the patronage system in 2:1-13, his insistence on wisdom from above in 3:13-18, and his condemnation of the wealthy in 5:1-6, James has the Roman Empire in view when he speaks of "the world." His anti-imperial arguments now concentrate on those who would be friends with Rome. The arrogance ("God goes to battle with the arrogant," 4:6) and pleasures ("that you might spend freely on your pleasures," 4:3) involved in this type of friendship diametrically opposes the empire of God. The obligations to empire that friendship requires, that is, μιᾶς ψυχῆς (one soul) and *alter idem* (second self), make those who "desire to be a friend of the world" enemies of God. They cannot be μιᾶς ψυχῆς with the world and μιᾶς ψυχῆς with God; this would make them δίψυχοι (double-minded). The *dypsuchoi* desire to be a friend of the world takes no account for the oppression experienced by those suffering under Roman imperialism. Ngũgĩ wa Thiong'o speaks to this violence:

> Colonialism imposed its control of the social production of wealth through military conquest and subsequent political dictatorship. But its most important area of domination was the mental universe of the colonized, the control, through culture, of how people perceived themselves and their relationships to the *world*. . . . To control a people's culture is to control their tools of self-definition in relationship to others.[35]

James then is calling the Diaspora to a "self-definition" that is controlled by the covenant with God rather than the social contract of friendship with the world. It should be noted that James does not

34. Ibid., 219.
35. Ngũgĩ wa Thiong'o, *Decolonizing the Mind*, 16 (emphasis mine).

recommend "friendship with God" as an alternative. He only states that friendship with Rome makes one an enemy of God. Nowhere does James implore his readers/hearers to seek friendship with God. Although Abraham, who James specifically calls a "friend of God [φίλος θεοῦ]," is offered as an example of faith-in-action, James commands the Diaspora to "subject" (ὑποτάγητε) themselves to God—a total break with the *topos* of friendship. In fact, this central binary places friend in opposition to enemy in the same way the world is opposed to God. In this way, James may be subtly critiquing the social practice of friendship in similar fashion to the way he explicitly criticized the patronage system. The nativist Manicheism that James exerts throughout this pericope seeks no Hegelian sublation. James's binary is absolute and he rigidifies it throughout. Here, James is reminiscent of an agonized Fanon:

> [W]hen students from the Antilles meet in Paris, they have the choice of two possibilities: —either to stand with the white *world* (that is to say, the real *world*), and since they will speak French, to be able to confront certain problems and incline to a certain degree of universality in their conclusions; —or to reject Europe, "Yo," and cling together in their dialect, making themselves quite comfortable in what we shall call the *Umwelt* of Martinique.[36]

It is clear from James's rhetoric which choice would be "pure and unstained by the world." In James's rigid system of identification, there is no room for hybridity. What Stephen D. Moore said of the Revelation rings true here in the Letter of James: "[T]he distinction between the agents of empire, on the one hand, and the victims of empire, on the other, must be asserted at an absolute, and hence metaphysical, level, and such a distinction is necessarily menaced by any manifestation of Christian hybridity, however innocuous."[37]

36. Frantz Fanon, *Black Skin, White Masks*, trans. Charles Lam Markmann (New York: Grove, 1967), 37 (emphasis mine).

Paradoxically, it is at this precise moment in his argument where James resembles, rather than resists, empire the most. It is in the binarisms themselves and the way James totalizes and essentializes them that his "pure identity," or at least the pure identity that he demands of the Diaspora, is inextricably linked to the world. If Bhabha's work applies to the "colonized no less than the colonizer,"[38] then nativist aggression—like James's—begins to double as empire. James's nativist rhetoric of essentialized binary opposites negatively reflects what David Huddart says about the colonizer: "The colonizer aggressively states his superiority to the colonized, but is always anxiously contemplating his own identity, which is never quite as stable as his aggression implies."[39] As he waxes militant in his anxious binaries, James resorts to name-calling regarding those who would venture into the liminal space between God and world.

Name-Calling

The vocative use of "whores" (μοιχαλίδες), "sinners" (ἁμαρτωλοί), and "two-faced"/"double-minded" (δίψυχοι) deserves special attention. Name-calling is not new to the reader/hearer of James at this point in the letter, but the intensity of James's rhetoric focused on "insiders" makes 4:1-12 unique. The only place where James is more absolutely condemnatory is when he condemns the wealthy (πλούσιοι) in 5:1-6; however, the similarity in the language James uses in these two pericopae does not go unnoticed among commentators. If 5:1-6 is the total denunciation of the wealthy, then 4:1-12 is James's *near*-total condemnation of hybridity. The three terms James uses in 4:1-12 to (pro)vocatively illuminate hybridity

37. Stephen D. Moore, *Empire and Apocalypse: Postcolonialism and the New Testament* (Sheffield: Sheffield Phoenix Press, 2006), 117–18.
38. Ibid., 115.
39. David Huddart, *Homi K. Bhabha* (London and New York: Routledge, 2006), 43.

all exemplify the worst forms of mixing, that is, sexual infidelity, cultic infidelity, and psychic infidelity. The "beloved brothers" (1:2, 16, 19; 2:1, 5, 14; 3:1, 10; 4:11; 5:7, 9, 12, 14, and 19) of the "twelve tribes of the diaspora" (1:1) disappear as James unleashes his prophetic voice. Using prophetic stereotypes, James "pushes 'sinners' to the periphery and jeopardizes their social relations with the ingroup. . . . The naming transforms them into a subordinate type, serviceable for the discourse of identity."[40] For James, the Diaspora's identity within Judeanness is in jeopardy by assimilating the Roman world.

James's discourse on the "desire for empire" in verses 1-3 sets up his most vicious vocative: Whores/Adulteresses (μοιχαλίδες)! This feminine plural noun is firmly rooted in the prophetic tradition, specifically Hosea and Ezekiel. The feminine gender of this noun caused trouble for early transcribers who tried to make it work with James's constant use of "brothers" [ἀδελφοί]. Later scribes included the masculine μοιχοι in an attempt to resolve the perceived problem. In this context, however, the first referent would be James's argument against empire in 2:1-13 where he references the Decalogue: "For the one who said, 'Do not commit adultery [μοιχεύσῃς],' also said, 'Do not kill'; but if you do not commit adultery [μοιχεύεις], but kill, you have become a transgressor of the Law" (2:11). Transgressing the Law, then, is the same as "wanting to be a friend of the world," that is, hybridity. The stereotype of μοιχαλίδες, however, conjures up more than James's reference to the Decalogue. The vocative use of μοιχαλίδες coupled with the language of "be miserable, weep, mourn" in verse 9, pushes the referent beyond the Decalogue to the prophetic calls for destruction in Hosea and Ezekiel. It is a common motif in Jewish Scripture for God to be Israel's groom. In the

40. Minna Shkul, "Religious Identity and Power of Naming—Saints and Sinners in Ephesians," a paper delivered in the Early Jewish Christian Relations Section at the annual meeting of the Society of Biblical Literature, Philadelphia, 2005, 4. Quoted with the permission of the author.

prophetic tradition, Israel's betrayal of God as evidenced in coalitions with foreign empires is considered adultery.[41] While idolatry is certainly a part of the adulterous equation, it was the worst form of mixing because it involved foreign nations. The charge of adultery against Israel is always due to Israel's "desire" for political/military help from foreign nations, specifically Assyria and Babylon. In this way, idolatry is always linked to foreign empires that are prophetically pitted against the God of Israel. Even in these various prophetic texts, adultery is more than idolatry. It is trusting in foreign powers rather than in the God of Israel. In these cases, Israel "turns her back" on her lover (God) and chases after the Assyrians and Babylonians. The charge of adultery, then, functions as anti-imperial rhetoric in these prophetic texts.

Hosea and Ezekiel exemplify this form of anti-imperial prophecy against Israel/Ephraim and Judah/Jerusalem. Throughout the prophecies of Hosea, he uses whoring (πορνείαν) and adultery (μοιχείω) interchangeably: "Let her remove her whoring [πορνείαν] from before me and her adultery [πορνείαν] from between her breasts" (Hosea 2:4 LXX; cf. Hosea 4:13 LXX). Likewise, Ezekiel uses πορνεία/πορνεύω throughout his prophetic denunciation of Jerusalem that culminates in the charge of adultery: "For they have committed adultery [ἐμοιχῶντο] and blood is on their hands; they have committed adultery [ἐμοιχῶντο] with their idols" (Ezek. 23:37 LXX). Due to the way Hosea and Ezekiel use μοιχαλίδος in conjunction with πορνεία coupled with James's use of these Scriptures as the substance of his stereotype, I translate μοιχαλίδες as

41. Johnson, *Letter of James*, 278; Peter H. Davids, *The Epistle of James: A Commentary on the Greek Text* (Grand Rapids: Eerdmans, 1982), 160; Laws, *Epistle of James*, 174; and François Vouga, *L'Épître de Saint Jacques* (Genève: Labor et Fides, 1984), 115, all point to the referent of μοιχαλίδες as idolatry rather than political impropriety that countered the ideological theocratic monarchy. This is due to reading the clean separation of religion and politics onto ancient texts. None of them describe idolatry as the "fruit" of making alliances with foreign powers.

"Whores!" in order to capture the force of James's rhetoric. In Hosea's prophetic context, Israel/Ephraim is being judged by God due to her unfaithfulness to her bridal obligations. Israel is described as "going after" her "lovers," who are none other than the Assyrians (Hosea 2:7 LXX). By seeking provisions from Assyria, Israel has "forgotten the Law [νόμον] of God" (4:6) and "transgressed my covenant and acted impiously [ἠσέβησαν] against my Law" (8:1). Due to Israel's constant whoring with Assyria, "the land mourns [πενθήσει]" (4:3), "its people shall mourn [ἐπένθησεν]," and "the idolatrous priests shall wail [παρεπίκραναν]" (10:5). Throughout Hosea's prophecy against Israel, adultery is the charge that causes this wailing and is identified with Israel's alliance or desire for an alliance with Assyria.

Ezekiel's prophetic denunciation of Jerusalem echoes Hosea's use of adultery language. In spite of Jerusalem's original hybridity (16:1 LXX), God makes a marriage covenant (διαθήκῃ) with "her" (16:8 LXX). Jerusalem is then depicted as a whore (πορνεία) who chases after Egypt (16:26), Assyria (16:28), and Chaldea/Babylon (16:29). Ezekiel ultimately condemns Jerusalem as an "adulterous wife" (ἡ γυνὴ ἡ μοιχωμένη) in 16:32 (cf. 16:38). Ezekiel levels the same charge against Jerusalem as Hosea did against Israel, that is, "transgressing the covenant [παραβῆναι την διαθήκην]" (16:59). With intensified language, Ezekiel revisits his condemnation of Jerusalem as adulterous in chapter 23. Jerusalem has whored and committed adultery with Babylon, who "came to her sex bed" and "defiled her" (23:17). Twice in this pericope, Jerusalem's adultery is considered lawless (ἀνομίας) (23:36, 44).

It is clear that James has this prophetic tradition in view when he uses the vocative μοιχαλίδες. The weeping and mourning imperatives in James 4:9 are a part of this prophetic tradition that recalls how both Israel/Ephraim and Judah/Jerusalem broke their covenant with God and attempted to make treaties with the empires of Assyria and Babylon (cf. Hosea 12:1). What is unavoidable in Hosea and Ezekiel's prophecies is their explicit anti-imperial stance. They utterly lampooned Assyria and Babylon and considered "mixing" with them an abomination that rendered Israel/Jerusalem's covenant with God invalid. As James brings this tradition to bear on the Diaspora, he systematically condemns "mixing" with empire. Sleeping with the enemy/desiring friendship with the world seriously compromises the covenant with God and makes their actions lawless. This nativist call to denounce imperialism for a pure native identity recalls the poetry of Aimé Césaire, where he criticizes those who would pander to Europe:

> And there are those who will never get over not being made in the likeness of God but of the devil, those who believe that being a nigger is like being a second-class clerk; waiting for a better deal and upward mobility; those who beat the drum of compromise in front of themselves, those who live in their own oubliette; those who say to Europe: "You see, I *can* bow and scrape, like you I pay my respects, in short I am not different from you; pay no attention to my black skin: the sun did it." And there is the nigger pimp, the nigger askari, and all the zebras shaking themselves in various ways to get rid of their stripes in a dew of fresh milk.[42]

James's other two vocative pronouncements are similar in scope but add another dimension to his antihybrid hyperbole. Unlike his use of the vocative in 4:4, James provides an imperative that coincides with each name: "Cleanse your hands, Sinners! Purify your hearts, Two-faced!" Again, "saints and sinners are stereotypical codes that convey central values and paradigms, and provide prototypes and antitypes for social orientation."[43] The "sinners" and "two-faced" are clearly antitypes that have already hybridized; thus their need to

42. Aimé Césaire, *Notebook of a Return to the Native Land*, trans. and ed. Clayton Eshleman Annette Smith (Middletown, CT: Wesleyan University Press, 2001 [French original 1947]), 45.
43. Shkul, "Religious Identity," 1.

"cleanse" and "purify." Johnson sees these imperatives to "cleanse" and "purify" as directly connected to the first part of 4:8, "Come near to God and God will come near to you." Approaching God has cultic value, according to Johnson, which is why James commands them to wash their hands and purify their hearts. These imperatives—come near, cleanse, and purify—have "ritual overtones" regarding "moral purity."[44] By concentrating on the moral nature of these imperatives, Johnson misses their ideological nature. The cultic language involved in these imperatives is based on the boundary between purity and pollution, that is, a boundary that James insists on policing. According to Christine E. Hayes, "Purity terminology is repeatedly employed to both inscribe and police the boundary between Israelite and alien."[45] Paul, himself, makes this clear in Gal. 2:15: "We are Judeans by nature [φύσει Ἰουδαῖοι] and not sinners of the gentiles [ἐξ ἐθνῶν ἁμαρτωλοί]." Paul, however, makes this statement only to transgress the boundary rather than uphold it. Rather than making *and keeping* a clear distinction between Ἰουδαῖοι and ἐξ ἐθνῶν ἁμαρτωλοί, he systematically blurs this boundary in the next verse by arguing that "a person is justified not by the works of the Law but through the faith of Jesus Christ" (Gal. 2:16). In what may be an answer to his opponents' accusations, Paul continues with a rhetorical question: "But if, in our effort to be justified in Christ, we ourselves have been found to be sinners [ἁμαρτωλοί], is Christ a servant of sin [ἁμαρτίας]? Certainly not!" (Gal. 2:17). It is not clear whether Paul's use of ἁμαρτωλοί in verse 17 is directly related to his equation in verse 15 regarding gentiles, but this may indicate that Paul is being accused of sinning due to his transgression of the

44. Johnson, *Letter of James*, 284.
45. Christine E. Hayes, *Gentile Impurities and Jewish Identities: Intermarriage and Conversion from the Bible to the Talmud* (Oxford: Oxford University Press, 2002), 7.

Judean/alien boundary—the very boundary that James prophetically rigidifies: "Cleanse your hands, Sinners!"

The other vocative in this couplet is the notorious "Two-faced"/"Double-minded" [δίψυχοι]! The term is unattested in literature before James, which has led some scholars to posit that James coined the term.[46] Laws argues that the term was an "idiom current in Greek-speaking Judaism" and probably had a Roman provenance.[47] James's continual use of traditional Scriptures makes it more likely that he coins the term based on his reading of Scripture, where one is to "love the Lord your God with your whole heart [ὅλης τῆς καρδίας], and with your whole soul [ὅλης τῆς ψυχῆς], and with all of your power" (Deut. 6:5 LXX). James has already referenced the Shema (2:19), so this passage would help James formulate the concept of δίψυχος in contrast to "the whole soul." There are also various passages from the LXX that describe a divided/doubled heart (Sirach 1:28, καρδίᾳ δισσῇ) and a divided tongue (Sir. 5:9, 15, ἁμαρτωλὸς ὁ δίγλωσσος) as well as the commonly quoted passage from the Testament of Asher 2:25 describing a two-faced person as διπρόσωπος. James uses this tradition to create a word that is "one of the most expressive words in the letter."[48]

Laws shows that "The *double-minded* are the archetypal *sinners*; for James doubleness is of the essence of human sin, seen in the divisive desires of the individual (iv.1) and the 'adulterous' attempts to combine prayer to God and a quest for the friendship of the world (iv.3f.)."[49] To capture the depth of this vocative, the colloquial "two-faced" captures both the idea behind the term and the rhetorical force. Laws is correct to see in this term an archetypal sinner. Already, James

46. Johnson, *Letter of James*, 181; Hartin, *James*, 61; and Martin, *James*, 20, all postulate this possibility.
47. Laws, *Epistle of James*, 60.
48. Martin, *James*, 20.
49. Laws, *Epistle of James*, 184.

has described the two-faced as one who is "unstable [ἀκατάστατος] in all his ways" (1:8). The instability of the two-faced is referenced again by James when he describes the tongue in 3:8 as "unstable/ restless evil [ἀκατάστατον κακόν]." Here the tongue of the teacher is connected to the two-faced one. The term, then, carries the full weight over everything that James stands against and represents in one term everything that the Diaspora should avoid. Using similar imaginative vocabulary, Ngũgĩ wa Thiong'o describes postcolonial natives as having "vacillating mentality, the evasive self-contemplation, the existential anguished human condition, or the man-torn-between-two-worlds-facedness of the petty-bourgeoisie."[50] Ngũgĩ's anguished description captures the thrust of James's invective. Putting on the clothes of empire, the two-faced masquerades as a Christ follower, but this masquerade, for James, is a mockery of Judeanness. The imperatival "purify" (ἁγνίσατε) demands turning away from this insidious hybridity.

James positively affirms his Judean identity as expressed through fidelity to the covenant with God. The Two-faced threatens the fixity of James's identity. This is true for all nativist movements. Léon Damas, one of the three originators of the Negritude movement, sought to reject "Western civilization on one hand and on the other" affirm "his own black identity."[51] Damas evidences the nativist dual attack against empire and hybridity in his poetry: "So / I will put my foot down / or simply / [grab] the collar / of everything that annoys me in larger letters / colonization / civilization / assimilation / and more / in the meantime / you will often hear me / slamming the door."[52] In his rage of "slamming the door," Damas clearly states

50. Ngũgĩ wa Thiong'o, *Decolonizing the Mind*, 22.
51. Mamadou Badiane, *The Changing Face of Afro-Caribbean Cultural Identity: Negrismo and Négritude* (Lanham, MD: Lexington, 2010), 127.
52. Léon-Gontran Damas, *Pigments Nevraldies* (Paris: Gallimard, 1956), 53 (my translation): "Alors / je vous mettrai les pieds dans le plat / ou bien tout simplement / la main au collet / de tout

his anger toward "colonization, civilization, assimilation, and more." Reacting to Western civilization, Damas asserts his identity as negritude—blackness—and he challenges his followers to do the same without shame. In his analysis of negritude and negrismo, Mamadou Badiane describes both Damas's and Césaire's desire to rigidify the boundaries of native identity:

> Not only does Damas claim his black identity without any problems, but he also whips those who flee from this identity. This is the backbone of the conflict between members of Négritude and Créolité. Cultural identity does not present ambiguities for him like Negrismo and Créolité. Both Césaire and Damas know how to define themselves and they do it without hesitating. Essence for these two poets is undoubtedly African. They are two rebels against French cultural hegemony.[53]

Those who would assimilate the colonial culture, for both Damas and Césaire, are traitors. There is no room in their cultural negotiation for hybridity. The Two-faced is the quintessential native assimilationist—one who would befriend the world. This desire for empire simply has no place in James's identity negotiation. The Two-faced functions as an archetype, or antitype, that represents pollution and impurity—the ultimate boundary transgressor. For James, this threatens the stability that he attempts to create throughout his letter.

Paul as Hybrid Whore

How closely can we read James's antihybrid rhetoric in 4:1-12 as directed at Pauline thought, or the Pauline "gospel"? The militant language within this passage explicitly references "battles and wars" related to cultural assimilation with the "world," that is, the Roman Empire. The primary binary that James constructs is based on

ce qui m'emmerde en gros caractères / colonisation / civilisation / assimilation / et la suite / En attendant / vous m'entendrez souvent / claque la porte."

53. Badiane, *Changing Face*, 128.

friendship and hatred between the world and God. In the process of constructing this binary James uses the harshest language in the letter referring to "insiders": Whores, Sinners, and Two-faced. The severity of his invective shows how important this boundary, God/world, is for James. What, or who, has put the Diaspora at such risk? How have those in the Diaspora transgressed the Law in such a way that would compel James to imperatively command them to "cleanse" and "purify" themselves?

John M. G. Barclay's article regarding Paul as a diasporic Jew, to which I have already referred, is helpful in identifying Pauline hybridity in relation to James's nativism. Barclay argues that

> Paul counts as a Diaspora Jew inasmuch as he spent nearly all the last thirty years of his life in the Diaspora and it is in this geographical and social context that his mission and his new theological reflection took place. . . . For all their diversity, spread in their millions around the Mediterranean basin, Jews in the western Diaspora faced in common the necessity to define their identity in a social environment shaped by non-Jewish cultural norms.[54]

In Barclay's analysis, Paul ranks low on the scale of acculturation and accommodation. He defines acculturation as the "non-material, and especially educational, aspects of cultural exposure,"[55] and accommodation as the use of this nonmaterial aspect of another culture to "express the essence of one's Judaism."[56] There are two forms of cultural accommodation, according to Barclay. An "integrative" accommodation merges "Judaism with the Hellenistic tradition to the extent of submerging it," whereas a "purely oppositional" accommodation uses this knowledge in "virulent antagonism to Graeco-Roman culture."[57] Barclay understands Philo

54. John M. G. Barclay, "Paul among Diaspora Jews: Anomaly or Apostate?," *Journal for the Study of the New Testament* 60 (1995): 90.
55. Ibid., 95.
56. Ibid., 97.

as a diasporic Jew who is highly acculturated but moderately accommodating—somewhere between integrative and oppositional—because he uses Hellenism as a vehicle for his Judeanness. Assimilation, however, is distinct from both acculturation and accommodation because it deals with "*social integration* (becoming similar to one's neighbours)."[58] A diasporic Judean, according to Barclay, could be highly acculturated and yet negotiate his/her identity in such a way that would evidence low assimilation. Barclay uses Philo again as an example of this type of cultural negotiation because "Philo considers the Jewish tradition superior to all others in the quality of its piety and virtue."[59] In contrast to Philo, Barclay argues that "[t]he intimate associations which Paul enjoyed with Gentiles who were not, in Jewish terms, law-observant set him high on the [assimilation] scale, not indeed fully assimilated, but certainly higher than Philo."[60] Paul, then, is a highly assimilated diasporic Judean; however, he is very low on the acculturation and accommodation scales.[61] Even Paul's accommodation of Greco-Roman culture would be oppositional rather than integrative. This amounts to an "anomalous combination," as Barclay concludes:

> The great anomaly here is the way Paul combines this culturally conservative form of Judaism with a social policy which seemed to his contemporaries dangerously assimilative. In his conceptual world Paul is most at home among the particularistic and least Hellenized segments of the Diaspora, yet in his social behaviour he shatters the ethnic mould in which such concepts were formed. He shows relatively limited acculturation and minimal accommodation, yet he applies the

57. Ibid., 98.
58. Ibid., 93 (original emphasis).
59. Ibid., 100.
60. Ibid., 104.
61. Barclay, "Paul among Diaspora Jews," 106, argues that Paul's use of Scripture was much more influential than common Greco-Roman topoi. Paul's acculturation is "merely superficial" due to the fact that most of the topoi Paul uses exercise the "forms but little if any of the contents."

> language of the most defensive Diaspora Jews to a Gentile mission which threatens their identities![62]

Barclay's insight into Paul's cultural negotiation as a diasporic Judean sheds light on how Paul functioned as an enigmatic hybrid. Although he does not use Barclay's categories of assimilation, acculturation, and accommodation, Christopher D. Stanley mistakenly reads Paul's low ranking in acculturation and accommodation as evidence for Paul's conservatism. Because Paul's thought-world is indebted to Judean scriptural binaries that Paul uses throughout his letters, Stanley argues that the term "hybridity" is misapplied to Paul.[63] Stanley argues that scholars should not mistake Paul's rhetoric—rhetoric that can be interpreted as anti-*Ioudaioi*—with Paul's more ambiguous self-perception.[64] What Stanley never recognizes, and what Barclay emphasizes, is how Paul's rhetoric would have been received by other Judeans (whether diasporic or not). Barclay is quite right to recognize that Paul's rhetoric—if not his gospel—put him at odds with contemporary Judeans even among Judean Christ-followers.[65] Regarding Paul's self-assessment in Phil. 3:2-11, where Paul describes his Judeanness as "loss" and "dung," Barclay asks, "How would he have gone down in the synagogue if he had presented himself as of the people of Israel, of the tribe of Benjamin, a Hebrew born of Hebrews, but then declared that he now considered such things 'shit' (3:8)?!"[66] Stanley, however, misses this aspect of Paul's hybridity—the key aspect against which James's invectives of 4:1-12 are directed.

62. Barclay, "Paul among Diaspora Jews," 110.
63. Christopher D. Stanley, "Paul the Ethnic Hybrid? Postcolonial Perspectives on Paul's Ethnic Categorizations," in *The Colonized Apostle: Paul through Postcolonial Eyes*, ed. Christopher D. Stanley (Minneapolis: Fortress Press, 2011), 125.
64. Ibid., 124.
65. Barclay, "Paul among Diaspora Jews," 103, specifically references Peter and Barnabas's disagreement with Paul in Antioch, where they agreed and followed "those from James."
66. Barclay, "Paul among Diaspora Jews," 113.

It is clear in the way James constructs and polices pure, nativist Judean identity—specifically in the invectives of 4:1-12—that he would not consider such an identity "shit" no matter the comparison. One clear example of where "friendship with the world" would collide with Pauline thought is in 1 Corinthians. Within the broader argument concerning the consumption of meat that had been sacrificed to idols (cf. 1 Cor. 8:7-13), Paul begins to expound on his rights as an apostle. In 1 Cor. 9:19-23, Paul tells the Corinthians that he becomes all things to all people in order to convince them of the message that he preaches. He says this in relation to his apostleship and his right to eat the food that he just warned the Corinthians not to eat. In 9:20, Paul says, "To the Judeans ['Ιουδαίοις] I became as a Judean ['Ιουδαῖος], in order to win Judeans ['Ιουδαίους]; to those under the Law [νόμον] I became as one under the Law (although I, myself, am not under the Law), so that I may win those under the Law," and in verse 21, he continues, "To the lawless [ἀνόμοις] ones I became as a lawless one (although I am not lawless before God but lawful [ἔννόμος] before Christ) so that I might win the lawless." He finishes in verse 23 saying, "I do it all for the gospel, so that I may share in its blessings." In other words, Paul will become anybody he needs to be in order to win others for Christ: "I have become [γέγονα] all things to all people, so that I might by all means [πάτως] save [σώσω] some" (v. 22). To Paul's opponents, this might simply have seemed wishy-washy as Gordon D. Fee acknowledges: "[O]n the matter of marketplace food he had been known to be of two minds. He ate such food in Gentile settings, but declined when among Jews (vv. 19-22). Such vacillation does not seem worthy of an apostle."[67] Although James never speaks about food sacrificed to idols explicitly, such vacillation would certainly have been indicative

67. Gordon D. Fee, *The First Epistle to the Corinthians* (Grand Rapids: Eerdmans, 1987), 393.

to him of a Two-faced person (1:8; 4:8), who must purify his/her heart. Paul's hybridity here gives his opponents a nice opportunity to ridicule him as being hypocritical. Later in 1 Cor. 10:23—11:1, Paul will explicitly tell his readers/listeners that they may eat "idol meat" during certain times. Again, this reveals Paul's hybrid nature and clearly distinguishes him from someone like James.

Besides 1 Corinthians 8–10, there is an interesting contrast between 1 Cor. 5:9-10 and James 4:4:

> I wrote to you in my letter not to associate with sexually immoral persons—*not at all meaning the immoral of this world*, or the greedy robbers, or idolaters, *since you would then need to go out of the world.* (1 Cor. 5:9-10)

> Adulterers! Do you not know that friendship with the world is enmity with God? Therefore whoever wishes to be a friend of the world becomes an enemy of God. (James 4:4)

Road to Conflict: Intersecting Pauline Itineraries

The main problem, for James, was not that a Roman had gotten off the "ship" in Jerusalem, but that a "Roman" had been traveling all over the empire/diaspora doing business as an itinerant minister/apostle. James 4:13-17 criticizes those who would travel from one city to another for employment opportunities without paying proper attention to God's will and human limitation. The disregard for God's will amounts to an arrogance of evil boasting. The congruency between arrogance and sin here recalls James's previous antihybrid rhetoric in 4:1-12 where James quotes Proverbs 3:34: "God goes to battle against the arrogant [ὑπερηφάνοις] but gives grace to the humble" (4:6). James, then, retorts: "Cleanse your hands, Sinners [ἁμαρτωλοί]!" (4:8). In 4:13-17, the arrogance (ἀλαζονείαις) that is sin (ἁμαρτία) is shown in travel plans that do not include divine guidance. Reading Paul's travel itineraries in light of James's critical stance against such itineraries in 4:13-17 reveals an intersection between competing forms of identity negotiation within Judeanness under Roman Imperialism. It is at this level of cultural negotiation where James's and Paul's itineraries intersect.

Travel in the Roman Period

The Roman technology of paving roads dramatically increased the capacity for mobility previously unmatched by other empires. Additionally, sea travel was a major economic factor between Rome and sites in the Eastern Mediterranean, specifically Egypt where grain was a major import to Rome. Due to the economic factors related to sea trade/travel, Rome increased maritime security, which decreased piracy and made sea travel safer.[68] Due to increased mobility, "inns" and "hostels" became important parts of land routes. By their very nature, "these hostels were cross-cultural institutions" and "were often held in ill-repute."[69] Increased mobility, then, caused significant difficulties for Judeans who attempted to remain Law observant while traveling. The capacity to travel also evidenced social status, as Catherine Hezser explains: "Similarly, Jewish, just like Roman, travelers would have been required to plan their trips carefully to ensure that they carried the necessary provisions. . . . The chosen means of transport will have depended on the type of journey, the geography, the infrastructure of the area, and the wealth and social status of the person travelling."[70] Issues of piety and economics, then, were important factors in any travel itineraries for Judeans and, according to Hezser, this gave rise to "[a] whole series of legal traditions [that] deal with family members who travel overseas. The

68. See John E. Stambaugh and David L. Balch, *The New Testament in Its Social Environment* (Philadelphia: Westminster, 1986), 37–39.
69. Catherine Hezser, "Travel and Mobility," in *The Oxford Handbook of Jewish Daily Life in Roman Palestine*, ed. Catherine Hezser (Oxford: Oxford University Press, 2010), 214.
70. Ibid., 212.

overseas death of a husband, wife, or son posed a variety of legal problems as far as remarriage, inheritance, and property ownership were concerned."[71] For "those ancient Jews who tried to participate in the Roman culture of mobility, while at the same time leading a Torah-observant life,"[72] hybridity—whether based on assimilation, acculturation, or accommodation—was an inevitable outcome. While mobility was more available for those who could afford it, it is important to remember that "the primary purpose of these roads was the movement of Roman administrative and military officials" that enabled "Roman access and control over distant conquered regions."[73] Considering the greater capacity to travel under Roman imperialism, and why this was possible, Musa Dube's question "Does this text encourage travel to distant and inhabited lands, and, if so, how does it justify itself?" is critically important for a postcolonial reading of James 3:13-17 since this passage specifically deals with travel.[74]

James 4:13-17

The ἄγε νῦν that begins this passage separates verses 13-17 from the verses that precede them, and the reiteration of this phrase in 5:1 establishes 4:13-17 as a unit. The frozen imperative ἄγε with the temporal adverb νῦν functions as direct speech from James to the wayward traveler: "Now you listen!" The force of this imperative recalls the vocative in 4:8: Sinners! Two-faced! Unlike 5:1, where the same construction is used to open another pericope, James does not name his opponents in this passage; rather, he puts words in their mouths in an attempt to identify them. The opponents are

71. Ibid., 213.
72. Ibid., 219.
73. Ibid., 211.
74. Musa W. Dube, *Postcolonial Feminist Interpretation of the Bible* (St. Louis: Chalice, 2000), 57.

"you who say [οἱ λέγοτες]," which is reminiscent of the way James rhetorically represents his interlocutors in 2:14 (λέγῃ), 16 (εἴπῃ), and 18 (ἐρεῖ)—the first antihybrid pericope. The content of the opponents' speech is business; more specifically, business plans that require future travel, that is, a business itinerary. James structures their speech with four rhythmic future-tense verbs: πορευσόμεθα, ποιήσομεν, ἐμπορευσόμεθα, and κερδήσομεν (v. 13). "Today or tomorrow *we will go* to this or that city and *we will work* one year and *we will do business* and *we will win some*." This is the only information that is given by James regarding the identity of these people. Commentators agree that these opponents are "merchants" of some nature, but that is the *only* consensus regarding their identity. The primary scholarly debate has to do with these merchants' position in relation to James's audience. Were they a part of the communities to whom James wrote? Arguing for their presence among James's recipients, most scholars point to the *conditio Jacobaea*: "If the Lord wills" in verse 15.[75] This condition allows for the possibility that the merchants can *reform* or *repent* at some level from their arrogance and autonomy from God in similar fashion to the imperatives in 4:8, that is, "cleanse" and "purify." This would make "you should say [λέγειν]" in verse 15 a corrective to "you who say [λέγοντες]" in verse 13. It would translate as follows, as Johnson acutely recognizes: "You who say . . . instead should say. . . ."[76] Other scholars, arguing for the absence of the merchants from the addressees' communities, point to the lack of ἀδελφοί in verse 13, which characterizes James's speech to the "inside" throughout most of his letter. Additionally, Patrick Hartin understands the invective to

75. See Peter H. Davids, *The Epistle of James: A Commentary on the Greek Text* (Grand Rapids: Eerdmans, 1982), 171; William F. Brosend II, *James and Jude*, The New Cambridge Bible Commentary (Cambridge: Cambridge University Press, 2004), 125–26.

76. Johnson, *Letter of James*, 296.

be likened "to the way the prophets singled out nations around Israel for condemnation."[77] Luke Timothy Johnson takes a compromise position by seeing a progression from the ἀδελφοί, addressed in verses 11-12, and the πλούσιοι, addressed in 5:1-6: "The examples move progressively from 'the brothers,' whom we assume to be within the community, to 'the rich' who are quintessentially the outsiders for this community (2:2-7)."[78] Johnson's observation is important because "the merchants" in verses 13-17 represent those who are in the liminal space between inside and outside in James's nativist discourse. These are the Roman-road-hybrids, which is one reason why there has been so much scholarly debate regarding their identity. The cultural hybridity represented in verses 13-17 does not necessarily reflect either "the world" or James's ideal. "The merchants" are both insiders and outsiders and simultaneously neither insiders nor outsiders. The root of their problem according to James, as Johnson correctly identifies, is their arrogance.[79]

Verse 14 immediately begins to correct the mentality of the merchants with the uncertainty of the future and the frailty of life. James takes αὔριον (tomorrow) out of the mouths of the merchants and uses it as a foil. The uncertainty of "tomorrow" reproves future plans and holds an abrupt stop sign in the middle of their itinerary. Life itself is uncertain and unpredictable. James plays with the words φαινομένη/ἀφανιζομένη (appear/disappear) in a rhetorical attempt to emphasize how fleeting life is. The imagery James employs in verse 14 is similar to, and may be a fulfillment of, 1:10-11 where he speaks specifically about the plans of the wealthy. Using the same vocabulary for boasting in 1:10 and 4:16, James commands the wealthy to "boast in their humiliation" (1:10). Their wealth is compared to a blade

77. Hartin, *James*, 223. See also Laws, *Epistle of James*, 190; Martin, *James*, 159.
78. Johnson, *Letter of James*, 306.
79. Ibid., 292; Hartin, *James*, 232.

of grass that passes away. "For the sun rises with burning heat and dries up the grass and its flower falls away and the beauty of its presence perishes. So also, the wealthy will die out [μαρανθήσεται: future tense] in their journeys [πορείαις]" (1:11). What is true of the wealthy in their "travels" in 1:10–11 is also true for the hybrids in 4:13–17. Their similarity to the condemned wealthy threatens their status among the faithful.

As previously stated, James offers a corrective to the "you who say" (v. 13) in verse 15 where we find the *conditio Jacobaea*: "*If the Lord should want* [ἐὰν ὁ κύριος θελήσῃ], we will live and we will do this or that." The future tense of the verbs in the apodosis logically corresponds to the future travel plans of those in verse 13. The protasis, "If the Lord should want," is the condition for all travel plans. By creating the *conditio Jacobaea*, James is not simply providing a corrective to travel plans, he is systematically casting the plans themselves in doubt. James would certainly want those in the Diaspora to seek the Lord's desires in their travel plans, but that's not the full weight of this condition. The condition basically says that the travel plans of James's interlocutor(s) are not commissioned by God. This is self-evident due to the boasting and arrogance that James describes in the next verse. The travel itineraries of "you who say" exemplify a kind of arrogance that James opposed throughout his letter. James ends the pericope with a verse that recalls both the faith/works binary and the sinners of 4:8: "Therefore, to the one who knows [εἰδότι] to do [ποιεῖν] good and does not do it [ποιοῦντι], sin [ἁμαρτία] is to him!" The cumulative effect of so much of James's terminology here reflecting back on James's previous antihybrid critiques indicates that this passage is also directed at the same type of hybridity James has consistently opposed. Specifically, this word of caution against business itineraries creates an interesting intersection with certain Pauline travel plans regarding money.

Intersecting Itineraries

In at least three different letters, Paul expects his addressees to house him and send him to his next destination (see Rom. 15:17-33; 1 Cor. 16:1-7; and 2 Cor. 1:12-18). Joseph Marchal recognizes that "[i]n fact, the conditions for Paul's letters all involve traveling across some distance to address an audience in often densely inhabited, colonized locales."[80] Using his relationships would have been a common way to avoid inns and hostels. "Unless one had relatives or friends to stay with, however, the only alternative to hostels would have been to spend the night outdoors."[81] In his letter to the Romans, Paul expects hospitality from a congregation that he has never previously visited. In return, Paul would gift them with his presence and preaching, that is, his gospel. Marchal describes a similar hegemonic move in Paul's letter to the Philippians: "The letter depicts Paul as the bringer of 'progress' to the communities he visits, while casting the audience as in need of his unique authority and model."[82] In this way, for Marchal, Paul answers Dube's haunting question in the affirmative: Yes, this text encourages travel to a distant land, that is, Rome itself, and justifies it due to the need they have for Paul's gospel ("progress," for Marchal). This certainly could be interpreted by some as arrogant. In Rom. 15:23-24, Paul says, "And I desire [ἐπιποθίαν ἔχων—same term as in James 4:5] to come to you, as I have for many years, when I go [πορεύωμαι—same as James 4:13] to Spain. For I hope to visit you when I travel [διαπορευόμενος] through and be *sent by you* [προπεμφθῆναι]." He continues in verse 25, "But now, I am going [πορεύομαι] to Jerusalem on a ministry to the saints."[83] Traveling to

80. Joseph A. Marchal, *The Politics of Heaven: Women, Gender, and Empire in the Study of Paul* (Minneapolis: Fortress Press, 2008), 45.
81. Hezser, "Travel and Mobility," 114.
82. Marchal, *Politics of Heaven*, 47.
83. It is worth noting that this collection has already been amassed in Macedonia and Achaia and its purpose is for "the poor [τοὺς πτωχοὺς]" in Jerusalem (Rom. 15:26).

Jerusalem, presumably to present the saints in Jerusalem with a large sum of money (15:26), and then to Spain via Rome, could certainly constitute the kind of planning that James criticizes in 4:13-17—a type of travel more suited for imperial agents. According to his letter to the Philippians, "[Paul] shows his elevated influence or power as a result of his contact with imperial authorities, speaking about or even for the entire praetorian guard (1:13) and some from the household of Caesar (4:22)."[84] Interestingly, Paul uses the *conditio Jacobaea* in Rom. 15:32: "so that I may come to you by God's will [διὰ θελήματος θεοῦ]."[85] Even using this condition for his itinerary, Paul still has reason for anxiety as he asks his audience in Rome to pray fervently for him so that his "ministry to Jerusalem may become acceptable" and so that he might be "rescued from the unbelievers [ρυσθῶ ἀπὸ τῶν ἀπειθούντων]" (Rom. 15:31).

Paul has additional business/ministry itineraries in 1 and 2 Corinthians. First Corinthians 4:19 uses the exact phrase found in James 4:15—the *conditio Jacobaea*: "If the Lord should want [ἐὰν ὁ κόριοςθελήσῃ], I *will come* (future tense) to you soon and I will know (future tense) not the word of these arrogant [πεφυσιωμένων] people but their power!" This is a strong connection with James 4:15, where James offers the ultimate correction to arrogant planning: "Instead you should say, 'If the Lord should want [ἐὰν ὁ κόριος θελήσῃ], we will live [future tense] and we will do [future tense] this or that.'" Does this lexical connection indicate that Paul has heard of the *conditio Jacobaea* and begun to put it into action? Or, is this evidence of an active debate among these two titans?[86] It is clear that Paul uses

84. Marchal, *Politics of Heaven*, 98.

85. Also found in Rom. 1:10, "I will succeed in coming to you by the will of God [τῷ θελήματι τοῦ θεοῦ]."

86. Martin Dibelius, *James: A Commentary on the Epistle of James*, trans. Michael A. Williams, Hermeneia (Philadelphia: Fortress Press, 1976), 233–34, points out that the *conditio Jacobaea* is not uniquely Christian and is found in many classical texts like Plato, *Phaedo* 80d; Epictetus,

this phrase in relation to his opponents who have undermined his authority and possibly his message. By using the *conditio Jacobaea*, is Paul rhetorically using these words in jest? Bringing James's critique of travel itineraries into dialogue with Paul's writings evidences some of Paul's anxieties about traveling and destabilizes Paul as a "central" authority. It also offers a counter-narrative to Marchal's insight:

> Too often, because there are few resources besides Paul's letters to develop concepts of these first-century communities in various imperial cities, most malestream Pauline scholars have rhetorically acquiesced and operated as if there were not community outside of what Paul describes. When and if other participants are considered, they are treated as "bit players" to our main character, the missionary adventure hero Paul.[87]

In the closing chapter of 1 Corinthians (16:1-9), Paul revisits his itinerary in relation to the Jerusalem collection, "I will come to you (future tense) after I go through Macedonia. For I will go [future tense] through Macedonia and perhaps I will stay [future tense] with you or I will spend [future tense] the winter, so that you might send me wherever I may go [πορεύωμαι] . . . if the Lord allows it [ἐὰν ὁ κύριος ἐπιτρέψῃ]" (vv. 5-7). Here again, Paul is planning to go through Macedonia to Corinth after spending time in Ephesus, stay in Corinth for a possible extended period, and then have them financially support him in his next endeavor/business trip. And again, he uses a close derivation of the *conditio Jacobaea*. Within this pericope, Paul speaks of his collection activities for Jerusalem (vv. 3-4) and closes by referencing his "many adversaries" in Ephesus.

Discourses 1.1.17, 3.21.12, 3.22.1. It is also found elsewhere in the New Testament; cf. Acts 18:21 and Heb. 6:3. See also Johnson, *Letter of James*, 297; Davids, *Epistle of James*, 173; Brosend, *James and Jude*, 124; Martin, *James*, 166–67. While the *conditio Jacobaea* is not unique to James and Paul, it is important to notice that they are using the stock phrase specifically related to business travel.

87. Marchal, *Politics of Heaven*, 105–6.

In his second letter to the Corinthians, Paul is on the move again and expecting the Corinthians to pay for his expenses: "Through you [I wanted] to go through Macedonia and come to you again from Macedonia then have you send me to Judea" (2 Cor. 1:16). There is no *conditio Jacobaea* in this passage; however, the following verse recalls James's insistence on making a "Yes" a "Yes" and a "No" a "No" in James 5:12—only a few verses beyond our passage in 4:13-17. Paul's questioning in 2 Cor. 1:17-18 indicates that he is combating charges of insincerity in speech. He argues, "Therefore, when I was planning this, was I vacillating [ἐλαφρίᾳ]? Do I make my plans [βουλεύομαι] according to flesh, ready to say 'Yes, yes' and 'No, no' at the same time? But as God is faithful, our word to you is not 'Yes and No.'" These charges of inconsistency between speech and action can certainly be found in James 2:14-26 and 3:1-12. The closest parallel in the Letter of James, however, is in the closing imperatives on 5:12b, "But let your 'Yes' be 'Yes' and your 'No' be 'No,' so that you might not fall under judgment." Paul's reaction to certain criticism in 2 Corinthians certainly sounds like a response to something like that found in James 5:12b. Paul constantly defends himself in 2 Corinthians with regard to the Jerusalem collection (2 Cor. 8:1—9:15) and how he was supported financially while among the Corinthians (2 Cor. 11:7-9a). Do the charges of wavering or vacillating come from a nativist strategy of identity formation that has no room for cultural hybridity?

In his correspondence between Rome and Corinth, Paul requests and expects these addressees to financially help him in his business travels. In every case, there are close lexical affinities with the letter of James. In every case, Paul is defending himself against accusations from some unknown opponent or opponents. In many of these cases, the imperatives in James closely match the accusations against Paul. If James criticizes itinerant ministers/businesspeople, then Paul embodies an itinerant businessperson. The *conditio Jacobaea* was more than a simple condition in James 4:15; it was an indictment against arrogant boasting regarding various travel plans all over the Roman Empire. Paul may be sent [ἀποστέλλω], but it seems as though James questions the cosmic origin of Paul's sender. Paul has lost his roots while in route (to Rome). Paul Gilroy, however, problematizes James's/nativist concentration on roots: "Dealing equally with the significance of roots and routes . . . should undermine the purified appeal of either Africentrism or the Eurocentrisms it struggles to answer."[88] The battle between nativism and hybridity is never as simple as God versus the world.

Boasting in Arrogance

Besides the intersecting itineraries, James 4:13–17 also evidences other strong connections between this pericope and Pauline vocabulary. In 4:16, James makes his final verdict on the travelers: "But now, you boast [καυχᾶσθε] in your arrogance [ἀλαζονείαις]; every such boasting [καύχησις] is evil." Commentators point out that the term for arrogance only occurs one other time in the New Testament;[89] however, the terms James employs for boasting are fairly common. What is striking about the terms καυχάομαι and καύχησις is the fact that besides their use in James, they only occur in Pauline writings. Even the derivatives of this word (καύχημα and κατακαυχάομαι) are found only in James's and Paul's writings, apart from one occurrence in Hebrews.[90] In other words, James may be using a recognizable Pauline term to oppose such business

88. Paul Gilroy, *The Black Atlantic: Modernity and Double Consciousness* (Cambridge, MA: Harvard University Press, 1993), 190.

89. See 1 John 2:16. The derivative ἀλαζών is found in Rom. 1:30.

90. κατακαυχάομαι: James 2:13; 3:14; Rom. 11:18 (twice); καυχάομαι: James 1:9; 4:16; Rom. 2:17, 23; 5:2, 3, 11; 1 Cor. 1:29, 31 (twice); 4:7; 13:3; 2 Cor. 5:2; 9:2; 10:8, 13, 15, 16, 17 (twice); 11:12, 16, 18 (twice), 30 (twice); 12:1, 5 (twice), 6, 9; Gal. 6:13, 14; Phil. 3:3; καύχημα: Rom. 4:2; 1 Cor. 5:6; 9:15, 16; 2 Cor. 1:14; 5:12; 9:3; Gal. 6:4; Phil. 1:26; 2:16 (and in Heb. 3:6);

itineraries—a term Paul would have used in his preaching as much as in his writing. Commentators who imagine this passage to be an attack on a hypothetical merchant miss this important link. Johnson only sees a "stock character, expressing an empty arrogance" while Martin finds this invective "clearly attributed to the godless who devise future plans without reference to faith in God."[91] The terminology suggests that James's choice of vocabulary is dramatically pointed at those whose cultural hybridity reflects the arrogance of empire. Laws correctly points to James 1:9 and 2:13 as instances where boasting is positive: "the poor may boast . . . and mercy boasts in the face of judgment"; but, she adds, "the boasting of the tongue . . . and of human presumption . . . are to be deplored."[92]

As Hezser makes clear, traveling for Judeans in particular was fraught with difficulties related to Law observance and issues of purity. The careful Judean traveler would have to pay close attention to diet, space, and place, if she/he had any desire to be Law observant. James certainly does not add this concern for the Law to his adversaries' itinerary. The omission of these concerns compounds the arrogance of James's rhetorical other—an arrogance in which they boasted. In addition, Hezser reminds us of who the primary travelers would be during the Roman period.

> Official travel for communal and administrative purposes, and business travel for local, regional, and international trade relations and the control of one's estates were probably the main causes of mobility in the Roman Empire at large. Accordingly, public officials, businessmen, and landowners will have been the most mobile members of society. . . . One can only surmise that officers such as tax collectors, as well as various types of intermediaries between the Roman government and the local Jewish communities, would have to travel for professional reasons.[93]

καύχησις: James 4:16; Rom. 3:27; 15:17; 1 Cor. 15:31; 2 Cor. 1:12; 7:4, 14; 8:24; 11:10; 11:17; 1 Thess. 2:19.

91. Johnson, *Letter of James*, 297; Martin, *James*, 161.

92. Laws, *Epistle of James*, 192–93.

From Hezser's analysis, then, travel in itself represented a form of assimilation not simply because of the cross-cultural contact that it inevitably entailed, but because it was associated with Roman collaboration. James's condemnation of the wealthy would certainly support this critical stance against travel because it is part of their luxurious living (5:5). Boasting, then, about travel—tantamount to being a Roman collaborator—would be the height of absurdity, and, in fact, evil. Paul, the self-proclaimed "*apostle*, sent by Jesus Christ and God, to the gentiles" (Gal. 1:1; 2:7-9), whose "business" trips took him to Damascus, Jerusalem, Antioch, Galatia, Ephesus, Miletus, Philippi, Thessalonica, Macedonia, Achaia, Corinth, and Rome (to name but a few destinations), certainly felt as if he had reason to boast in his "work" (cf. Rom. 15:17).

Paul vacillates much more than James in the way he uses the terms for boasting. Boasting is rarely acceptable to Paul except when he is the one who is boasting. In Rom. 15:17, Paul emphatically announces, "Therefore, I have reason to boast [καύχησιν] in Christ Jesus for my work/ministry for God." This "boasting" comes just before he outlines his travel itinerary in verses 22-33. His opponents, however, have misplaced pride according to his faith/works binary in Rom. 3:27: "Then what becomes of boasting [καύχησις]? It is excluded. Through what Law? Through works? No, but by the Law of faith." This theme of appropriate and inappropriate boasting is common throughout Paul's writings. Inappropriate boasting, for Paul, has to do with the works of the Law in Rom. 3:27ff. and the flesh in his other writings—specifically circumcision in Gal. 6:13-14 and Phil. 3:3.

Boasting becomes a buzzword for Paul in 2 Corinthians, where he uses it twenty-one times from chapter 9 through 12. In 9:1-5, Paul

93. Hezser, "Travel and Mobility," 215.

boasts to the Macedonians about the Corinthians' eagerness to give to the Jerusalem collection. He encourages them to give generously so that "our *boasting* about you may not prove to have been empty in this case, so that you may be ready, as I said you would be; otherwise, if some Macedonians come with me and find that you are not ready, we would be humiliated—to say nothing of you—in this undertaking." Paul's crafty use of "boasting" here functions to shame the Corinthians into giving "generously." In 2 Corinthians 10, when Paul defends his ministry at Corinth, he proclaims, "Now, even if I boast somewhat excessively about our authority, which the Lord gave for building you up and not for tearing you down, I will not be ashamed of it" (10:8). He states twice in the following verses that he will not "boast beyond his limits" (vv. 13, 15) and that he would not boast in someone else's work (v. 16). He ends this chapter with a quote from Jer. 9:23-24, "Let the one who boasts, boast in the Lord" (v. 17). Apparently, this is what Paul has been doing. In chapters 11 and 12, Paul takes his opponents to task by comparing their capacity to boast with his. Eventually, Paul settles for boasting only in his weakness (2 Cor. 12:9). Could James's chastisement of the boastful fit into what has just been detailed in Paul's writings? "As it is, you boast in your arrogance; all such boasting is evil" (James 4:16). I am not suggesting that James had a copy of Paul's Corinthian correspondence, or any other Pauline letters, but it is clear that "boasting" played a major role in Paul's preaching and may have functioned to rhetorically establish Paul's authority as one "sent to the gentiles." It seems that James has carefully chosen a familiar Pauline theme to use against him in an attempt to show the absurdity, or even the evilness, of Paul's hybridity. James is condemning Paul's Roman routes/roots.

Winning/Gaining

I do not want to overstate this point, but there is another important terminological connection between James 4:13-17 and certain Pauline writings. In James's rhetorical construction of his adversaries' travel plans (4:13), the last future active indicative verb that he uses is usually translated as "we will make money [κερδήσομεν]."[94] This translation fits conceptually within the context and adds strength to the argument that James is criticizing general merchant behavior. Within the New Testament, the term is used in the Jesus tradition found in Mark 8:36/Matt. 16:26/Luke 9:25 where Jesus rhetorically asks, in language reminiscent of James 2:14, "What does it profit a man to gain [κερδῆσαι] the whole world [κόσμον ὅλον] and lose his soul [ψυχὴν]?" (Mark 8:36). This close terminological and thematic connection may indicate that James is again using the strength of the Jesus tradition to counter Pauline hybridity. However important this link is to the Jesus tradition, the connection to Paul is greater still. In key passages in two of Paul's letters he uses the same language of "winning/gaining" that James puts on the lips of his travelers. In his opening to the Letter to the Philippians, Paul emphatically states: "For to me to live is Christ, and to die is gain [κέρδος]" (1:21). Paul makes this bold statement after defending himself against opponents who preach Christ out of "envy and rivalry [φθόνον καὶ ἔριν]" (1:15). Paul returns to his language of "winning/gaining" after he warns the Philippians to "beware of the dogs, beware of those who work evil, beware of the mutilators!" (3:2). At the end of his autobiographical flourish, where he proudly describes his Judeanness, Paul says, "But whatever these gains [κέρδη] had been to me, these I have come to regard as loss because of Christ. But on the contrary, I regard all things to be loss because of the surpassing knowledge of Christ Jesus

94. NRSV has "making money." See Johnson, *Letter of James*, 295; Martin, *James*, 165.

my Lord, for whom I suffered the loss of all things and regard [them] as shit [σκύβαλα],[95] in order to gain [κερδήσω] Christ" (3:7-8). I have mentioned the scandal of this impurity previously, but here I want to show the "winning/gain" terminology that is crucial for Paul's argument about his own identity—and how Judeanness ranks in his identity.

The Pauline passage, however, that is closest to James 4:13 regarding "win/gain" language is 1 Cor. 9:19-22. I have previously used this passage from Paul to describe Paul's strategic hybridity, which would have incensed James. It is important to revisit because Paul uses "win/gain" terminology as the rationale for his hybridity. Paul repeatedly uses the subjunctive of κερδαίνω throughout this passage and it is the controlling theme: "that I might win [κερδήσω] many" (v. 19), "that I might win [κερδήσω] Judeans" (v. 20), "that I might win [κερδήσω] those under the Law" (v. 20), "so that I might win [κερδάνω] the lawless" (v. 21), "so that I might win [κερδήσω] the weak" (v. 22). These "winnings/gains" all culminate with a switch in vocabulary at the end: "so that I might save [σώσω] some by any means" (v. 22). It is clear from this self-described hybridity that Paul would be willing to become almost anything while he traveled around the Roman world in order to "win/gain" people. Paul's emphatic use of κερδαίνω in 1 Corinthians, coupled with the way he used the term in Philippians, indicates that it was an important term for his "gospel" and/or self-description. James's use of the term in 4:13, then, is probably no coincidence. In relation to Paul's rhetoric, κερδήσομεν in James 4:13 should be translated "we will win/gain [some]" in order to emphasize the antihybrid/anti-Pauline polemic in this passage. Such hybrid arrogance has no place in James's nativist rhetoric. In this way, James counters Paul's

95. See Barclay's "translation" of this term in "Paul among Diaspora Jews," 113.

rationale for travel to, in Dube's words, "distant and inhabited lands."[96]

Even if the Apostle Paul is not the direct target of James's invectives in 4:13–17, it is not hard to imagine that someone like Paul would hear James's letter as a corrective. Likewise, it is hard to imagine that James would have been completely ignorant of Paul's travel itineraries given the fact that many of those itineraries had something to do with the offering that Paul was collecting for "the saints in Jerusalem," not to mention his various travels to Jerusalem to meet with James specifically. In Paul's movements, and those of others like him, James saw too much of the world. The capacity to travel from one place to the next without tremendous difficulty was only possible because of the contours of empire. Itinerant "ministry" began to look too much like the travels of the mercantile class of the Greco-Roman world. This cultural hybridity blurred the boundaries that James wrote to reify. Within the realm of nativism, there is no space for hybridity. Itinerant ministry/business slid somewhere in the liminal space between the ἀδελφοί in verses 11–12 and the πλούσιοι in 5:1–6. These merchant ministers were monstrous mimics of empire, or to use James's terminology, they were becoming a friend of the world. Brosend offers an insightful interpretation of these intersecting itineraries between James and the travelers (possibly Paul):

> These verses reveal a good deal about the community for and to which James writes, about the values at work, prominent or dominant, in that community, and James's attitude toward both. In this sense it reveals both a greater diversity than is often admitted for the early Church and *competing ideologies* that are, finally, *mutually exclusive*. This assumes that "you who say" are members of James's community. Certainly they are members of his intended audience, or at the very least the attitude expressed is present among members of the audience, otherwise the

96. Dube, *Postcolonial Feminist Interpretation*, 57.

> inclusion of the verses makes no sense. To propose that the verses target hypothetical persons who have a hypothetical attitude about a hypothetical trip to engage in hypothetical trade is an inadequate hypothesis.[97]

Does James, then, in his disciplining of Paul, avoid falling prey to Dube's empire-critical question? It is clear that James criticizes the itineraries of his interlocutors, but does James resist the neocolonial tug to recolonize? Yes and no. James clearly discourages the kind of travel that involved boasting and arrogance. In fact, James's argument may indicate that he regarded ambitious travel in general as an imperialist enterprise that should be avoided in order to keep oneself "unstained by the world." The slippage from nativism into neocolonialism is not necessarily in the rhetoric of 4:13-17. The slippage is in the letter itself. This letter, in the end, is a *Diasporabriefe*, written with the authority of a central figure in Jerusalem. The letter *is sent* to the Diaspora with more imperatives and invectives than nearly any other letter in the New Testament. The letter may not be "encouraging travel to distant and inhabited lands," but it is, in fact, *traveling* to distant and inhabited lands. And if a letter represented the sender, then the Letter of James functioned as James's absent-presence in the Diaspora. James's correction, not only to the hybrid traveler of 4:13-18, but to the entire Diaspora, comes in the form of his presence and preaching via his letter. This inadvertent, yet inescapable, neocolonial move is the constant outcome of nativist/essentialist movements according to Paul Gilroy's scathing, yet important, critique:

> The Africentric movement appears to rely upon a linear idea of time that is enclosed at each end by the grand narrative of African advancement. This is momentarily interrupted by slavery and colonialism, which make no substantial impact upon African tradition or the capacity of black

97. Brosend, *James and Jude*, 125–26 (emphasis mine).

> intellectuals to align themselves with it. The anteriority of African civilisation to western civilisation is asserted not in order to escape this linear time but in order to claim it and thus subordinate its narrative of civilisation to a different set of political interests without even attempting to change the terms themselves. The logic and categories of racial metaphysics are undisturbed but the relationship between the terms is inverted. Blacks become dominant by virtue of their biology or culture; whites are allocated a subordinate role. The desperate manner in which this inversion proceeds betrays it as merely another symptom of white supremacy's continuing power.[98]

Conclusion

The dangers of this type of nativist/nationalist reaction/resistance are also recognized by Bill Ashcroft, Gareth Griffins, and Helen Tiffin: "The dangers of a national bourgeoisie using nationalism to maintain its own power demonstrates one of the principal dangers of nationalism—that it frequently takes over the hegemonic control of the imperial power, thus replicating the conditions it rises up to combat."[99] This danger is extremely potent in nativism and is one of the reasons nativism is so harshly criticized. The rhetoric that James employs throughout the epistle simply does not allow room for any opposing position. James attacks his opponents with such vigor that he undermines his own call for ethics/works that should characterize faith. Indeed, if James actually practiced what he preached in James 3:1-12, a passage concerning how a follower should handle his or her tongue, he could hardly be so bold as to call people whores (4:4). In other words, the polemical rhetoric James uses effectively undermines his argument about works and faith. The way in which he addresses the threat of hybridity destroys his own call for faith with actions.

98. Gilroy, *The Black Atlantic*, 190–91.

99. Bill Ashcroft, Gareth Griffins, and Helen Tiffin, "Introduction" to "Part V: Nationalism," in *The Post-Colonial Studies Reader*, ed. Bill Ashcroft, Gareth Griffins, and Helen Tiffin (London and New York: Routledge, 1995), 151.

These two early leaders of the Jesus movement, James and Paul, were on the road to conflict at a very early stage in the development of nascent Christianity. Both sought the allegiance of their constituents and both struggled vehemently with the power and pressure of empire. According to Josephus, James was killed around 62 CE in Jerusalem, and tradition has Paul being killed in Rome not long afterwards. Ultimately, what is at stake when we read James and Paul as adversaries? What is lost and what is gained? Reading James as nativist and Paul as cultural hybrid offers a new itinerary for scholarship interested in this intersection.

7

Conclusion

While reading James as a form of first-century, anti-imperial, Judean nativism, it is important to remember that James lost. He was killed, according to Josephus, just before the outbreak of the Jewish-Roman war. In fact, the Letter of James was never commonly circulated until it was championed by Origen in the third century, which is why some scholars argue that it is a pseudonymous work written later in the first or second century.[1] Was James an "intercepted letter" as Elsa Tamez suggests?[2] She argues that the Letter would have been "branded as subversive because of the paragraphs that vehemently denounce the exploitation by landowners (5:1-6) and the carefree life of the merchants (4:13-17)."[3] Because of the subversive nature of the Letter and its late addition to the New Testament canon, Tamez understands James as a document that authorities (both Roman and ecclesiastical) attempted to intercept throughout its history. While

1. See Origen, *In Librum Jesu Nave* VII.I (PG 12:857).
2. Elsa Tamez, *The Scandalous Message of James: Faith without Works Is Dead*, revised edition (New York: Crossroad, 2002 [original 1985]), 1–5.
3. Ibid., 1.

the Letter of James has survived and remains in the canon, Tamez suggests that it still faces an "unconscious 'interception'" due to its place in current biblical scholarship.[4] With the wide circulation of the Pauline letters and the rise of the "Pauline School," it certainly appears that this is the case. Pauline hybridity would become more definitive for the Jesus movement than James's nativism; however, it is worth remembering that Paul was also killed, according to tradition. Paul's predominance in subsequent Christianity is not an expression, however, of his vision having succeeded in his own time, any more than did James's.

Eventually, in the view of later Christians like Eusebius, the Roman Empire became the empire of God, something James could not have imagined. Friendship with Rome was tantamount to being an enemy of God, for James, so it would be inconceivable to him for the two to become one. Regardless of James's capacity to conceive it, however, the unlikely eventually happened and Rome became Christian, which provides ample reasons to caution against an unnuanced endorsement of a nativist reading of James. In other words, when the empire of Rome becomes the empire of God, James's nativist use of purity provides the powerful with the capacity to foreignize the other from the top down rather than from the bottom up. This turns the Letter of James upside down and becomes very similar to the way nativism is defined by John Higham and Tyler Anbinder in their assessment of American nativism.[5] Here, nativism as a means to resist imperial power is reversed and becomes a nativism that supports oppressive

4. Ibid., 4–5. She argues that more "theological" letters like Paul's have a privileged position in the Western academy due to its priority of abstract thought. Tamez also criticizes Martin Dibelius's work for making the Letter of James wholy incomprehensible based on literary style.

5. See John Higham, *Strangers in the Land: Patterns of American Nativism, 1860–1925* (New Brunswick, NJ and London: Rutgers University Press, 2002 [1955 original]) and Tyler Anbinder, *Nativism and Slavery: The Northern Know Nothings and the Politics of the 1850s* (Oxford: Oxford University Press, 1992). I describe in detail their conception of American nativism in chapter 2, "Nativism."

authority. In spite of Paul's dominance early on (which has become even more significant in the wake of the Protestant Reformation), the Letter of James was incorporated into the body of the New Testament, and its emphasis on purity and perfection became elements in the larger construction of now-dominant Christianity. There are clear dangers when the empire uses nativism to argue for purity and perfection. As we learned, nativism was used by American politicians in the nineteenth century to discriminate against immigrants and minorities. When nativism moves from the margins to the center, there is reason for caution.

It is obvious that the Letter of James is a case of nativism from the margins, but Christian history is full of crusades and pogroms that reinforced cultural essentialist ideas. This is one of the reasons postcolonial theory challenges nativism so forcefully. But as a marginal negotiating tool, nativism provides a strong sense of belonging and place—a home for the Diaspora. Providing an identity of hope and resistance to a dominating empire inspires adherents to "endure," thus James's final insistence: "Indeed we bless those who endure" (James 5:11a).

Bibliography

Ashcroft, Bill, Gareth Griffiths, and Helen Tiffin, eds. *The Post-Colonial Studies Reader.* London and New York: Routledge: 1995.

———. *Post-Colonial Studies: The Key Concepts.* London and New York: Routledge, 1998.

Avemarie, Friedrich. "Die Werke des Gesetzes im Spiegel des Jakobusbriefs: A Very Old Perspective on Paul." In *Zeitschrift fur Theologie und Kirche* 98, no. 3 (2001): 282–309.

Badiane, Mamadou. *The Changing Face of Afro-Caribbean Cultural Identity: Negrismo and Négritude.* Lanham, MD: Lexington, 2010.

Barclay, John M. G. *Jews in the Mediterranean Diaspora: From Alexander to Trajan (323 BCE–117 CE).* Edinburgh: T. & T. Clark, 1996.

———. "Paul among Diaspora Jews: Anomaly or Apostate?" *Journal for the Study of the New Testament* 60 (1995): 89–120.

Barclay, John M. G., ed. *Negotiating Diaspora: Jewish Strategies in the Roman Empire.* London and New York: T. & T. Clark International, 2004.

Batten, Alicia. "God in the Letter of James: Patron or Benefactor?" Pages 49–61 in *The Social World of the New Testament.* Edited by Jerome H. Neyrey and Eric C. Stewart. Peabody, MA: Hendrickson, 2008.

Bauckham, Richard. *James: Wisdom of James, Disciple of Jesus the Sage.* New Testament Readings. London and New York: Routledge, 1999.

Becker, Adam H., and Annette Yoshiko Reed, eds. *The Ways That Never Parted: Jews and Christians in Late Antiquity and the Early Middle Ages.* Minneapolis: Fortress Press, 2007.

Betz, Hans Dieter. *Galatians: A Commentary on Paul's Letter to the Churches in Galatia.* Hermeneia. Philadelphia: Fortress Press, 1979.

Bhabha, Homi K. *The Location of Culture.* London and New York: Routledge, 1994.

———, ed. *Nation and Narration.* London and New York: Routledge, 2000.

Boyarin, Daniel. *Border Lines: The Partition of Judeo-Christianity.* Philadelphia: University of Pennsylvania Press, 2004.

———. *Dying for God: Martyrdom and the Making of Christianity and Judaism.* Stanford: Stanford University Press, 1999.

———. *A Radical Jew: Paul and the Politics of Identity.* Berkeley: University of California Press, 1994.

Braziel, Jana Evans, and Anita Mannur. "Nation, Migration, Globalization: Points of Contention in Diaspora Studies." Pages 1–22 in *Theorizing Diaspora: A Reader.* Edited by Jana Evans Braziel and Anita Mannur. Oxford: Blackwell, 2003.

Brosend, William F., II. *James and Jude.* New Cambridge Bible Commentary. Cambridge: Cambridge University Press, 2004.

Burchard, Christoph. *Der Jakobusbrief.* Handbuch zum Neuen Testament 15/1. Tübingen: Mohr Siebeck, 2000.

Buell, Denise Kimber. *Why This New Race: Ethnic Reasoning in Early Christianity.* New York: Columbia University Press, 2005.

Buell, Denise Kimber, and Caroline Johnson Hodge. "The Politics of Interpretation: The Rhetoric of Race and Ethnicity in Paul." *Journal of Biblical Literature* 123, no. 2 (2004): 235–51.

Byron, John. "Living in the Shadow of Cain: Echoes of a Developing Tradition in James 5:1-6." *Novum Testamentum* 48, no. 3 (2006): 261–74.

Cargal, Timothy B. *Restoring the Diaspora: Discursive Structure and Purpose in the Epistle of James*. Atlanta: Scholars, 1993.

Carter, Warren. *John and Empire: Initial Explorations*. London: T. & T. Clark, 2008.

———. *Matthew and Empire: Initial Explorations*. Harrisburg, PA: Trinity Press International, 2001.

———. *The Roman Empire and the New Testament*. Nashville: Abingdon, 2006.

Césaire, Aimé. *Discourse on Colonialism*. Translated by Joan Pinkham. New York: Monthly Review Press, 1976. French original, 1955.

———. *Notebook of a Return to the Native Land*. Edited and translated by Clayton Eshleman and Annette Smith. Middletown, CT: Wesleyan University Press, 2001. French original, 1947.

Chevrier, Jacques. "Des formes variées du discours rebelle." *Notre Librairie* 148 (July–September 2002): 64–70.

Childs, Brevard S. *The New Testament as Canon: An Introduction*. Valley Forge, PA: Trinity Press International, 1994.

Chow, Rey. *The Protestant Ethnic and the Spirit of Capitalism*. New York: Columbia University Press, 1989.

Cohen, Shaye. *The Beginnings of Jewishness: Boundaries, Varieties, and Uncertainties*. Berkeley: University of California Press, 2001.

Coker, K. Jason. "Calling on the Diaspora: Nativism and Diaspora Identity in the Letter of James." In *The T. & T. Clark Handbook for Social Identity and the New Testament*. Edited by J. Brian Tucker and Coleman A. Baker. London: Bloomsbury, 2014.

———. "Nativism in James 2.14-26: A Post-Colonial Reading." Pages 27–48 in *Reading James with New Eyes: Methodological Reassessments of the Letter of James*. Edited by Robert L. Webb and John S. Kloppenborg. New York: T. & T. Clark, 2007.

Conti, Cristina. "James" in *Global Bible Commentary*. Edited by Daniel Patte. Nashville: Abingdon, 2004.

Conzelmann, Hans. *1 Corinthians*. Hermeneia. Philadelphia: Fortress Press, 1975.

———. *Acts of the Apostles: A Commentary on the Acts of the Apostles*. Hermeneia. Philadelphia: Fortress Press, 1987.

Crossan, John Dominic. *The Greatest Prayer: Rediscovering the Revolutionary Message of the Lord's Prayer*. New York: HarperCollins, 2010.

———. *Jesus: A Revolutionary Biography*. San Francisco: HarperSanFrancisco, 1995.

Damas, Léon-Gontran. *Pigments. Nevraldies*. Paris: Gallimard, 1956.

Davids, Peter H. *The Epistle of James: A Commentary on the Greek Text*. New International Greek Testament Commentary. Grand Rapids: Eerdmans, 1982.

De Lacy, Douglas R. "Paul in Jerusalem." *New Testament Studies* 20, no. 1 (1973): 82–86.

Deppe, Dean B. *The Sayings of Jesus in the Epistle of James*. Chelsea, MI: Bookcrafters, 1989.

Dibelius, Martin. *James: A Commentary on the Epistle of James*. Translated by Michael A. Williams. Hermeneia. Philadelphia: Fortress Press, 1976.

Dufoix, Stéphane. *Diasporas*. Translated by William Rodarmor. Berkeley: University of California Press, 2008. French original, 2003.

Dunn, James D. G. *The New Perspective on Paul*. Revised Edition. Grand Rapids: Eerdmans, 2005.

———. *Romans 1–8*. WBC, 38A. Dallas: Word, 1988.

———. *Romans 9–16*. WBC, 38B. Dallas: Word, 1988.

———. *The Theology of Paul the Apostle*. Grand Rapids: Eerdmans, 1998.

———. *The Theology of Paul's Letter to the Galatians*. Cambridge: Cambridge University Press, 1993.

Dube, Musa W. *Postcolonial Feminist Interpretation of the Bible*. St. Louis: Chalice, 2000.

Dube, Musa W., Andrew M. Mbuvi, and Dora Mbuwayesango, eds. *Postcolonial Perspectives in African Biblical Interpretations*. Global Perspectives on Biblical Scholarship, 62. Atlanta: Society of Biblical Literature, 2012.

Edgar, David Hutchinson. *Has God Not Chosen the Poor?: The Social Setting of the Epistle of James*. Sheffield: Sheffield Academic Press, 2001.

Edmondson, Jonathan, and Allison Keith, eds. *Roman Dress and the Fabrics of Roman Culture*. Toronto, Buffalo, and London: University of Toronto Press, 2008.

Eichholz, Georg. *Glaube und Werk bei Paulus und Jakobus*. Munich: Chr. Kaiser, 1961.

Elliott, John Hall. "The Epistle of James in Rhetorical and Social Scientific Perspective: Holiness-Wholeness and Patterns of Replication." *Biblical Theology Bulletin* 23 (Summer 1993): 71–81.

Elliott, Neil. *The Arrogance of Nations: Reading Romans in the Shadow of Empire*. Minneapolis: Fortress Press, 2008.

Fanon, Frantz. *Black Skin, White Mask*. Translated by Charles Lam Markmann. New York: Grove, 1967. French original, 1952.

———. *Toward the African Revolution: Political Essays*. Translated by Haakon Chevalier. New York: Grove, 1967. French original, 1964.

———. *Wretched of the Earth*. Translated by Constance Farrington. New York: Grove, 1963. French original, 1961.

Fee, Gordon D. *The First Epistle to the Corinthians*. NICNT. Grand Rapids: Eerdmans, 1987.

Ferris, Iain M. *Enemies of Rome: Barbarians through Roman Eyes*. Thrupp, Stroud, Gloucestershire, UK: Sutton, 2000.

Fiensy, David A. "Ancient Economy and the New Testament." Pages 194–206 in *Understanding the Social World of the New Testament*. Edited by Dietmar Neufeld and Richard E. DeMaris. London and New York: Routledge, 2010.

Fitzmyer, Joseph A. *The Acts of the Apostles: A New Translation with Introduction and Commentary*. Anchor Bible 31. New York: Doubleday, 1998.

Friesen, Steven J. "Injustice or God's Will? Early Christian Explanations of Poverty." Pages 17–36 in *Wealth and Poverty in Early Church and Society*. Edited by Susan R. Holman. Grand Rapids: Baker Academic, 2008.

Frilingos, Christopher A. *Spectacles of Empire: Monsters, Martyrs, and the Book of Revelation*. Divinations: Rereading Late Ancient Religion. Philadelphia: University of Pennsylvania Press, 2004.

Garnsey, Peter, and Richard Saller. *The Roman Empire: Economy, Society and Culture*. Berkeley and Los Angeles: University of California Press, 1987.

Gaston, Lloyd. *Paul and the Torah*. Vancouver: University of British Columbia Press, 1987.

Gilroy, Paul. *The Black Atlantic: Modernity and Double Consciousness*. Cambridge, MA: Harvard University Press, 1993.

Gruen, Erich S. *Diaspora: Jews amidst Greeks and Romans*. Cambridge, MA and London: Harvard University Press, 2002.

Guha, Ranajit. "On Some Aspects of the Historiography of Colonial India." In *Selected Subaltern Studies*. Edited by Ranajit Guha and Gayatri Chakravorty Spivak. Oxford: Oxford University Press, 1988.

Haber, Susan. *"They Shall Purify Themselves": Essays on Purity in Early Judaism*. Edited by Adele Reinhartz. Atlanta: Society of Biblical Literature, 2008.

Hall, Stuart. "Cultural Identity and Diaspora." Pages 223–24 in *Identity: Community, Culture, Difference*. Edited by Jonathan Rutherford. London: Lawrence & Wishart, 1990.

Hanson, K. C., and Douglas E. Oakman. *Palestine in the Time of Jesus: Social Structures and Social Conflicts*. Minneapolis: Fortress Press, 2008.

Hardin, Justin K. *Galatians and the Imperial Cult: A Critical Analysis of the First-Century Social Context of Paul's Letter.* Tübingen: Mohr Siebeck, 2008.

Harland, Philip A. "The Economy of First-Century Palestine: State of the Scholarly Discussion." Pages 511–27 in *Handbook of Early Christianity: Social Science Approaches*. Edited by Anthony J. Blasi, Jean Duhaime, and Paul-André Turcotte. Lanham, MD: Altamira, 2001.

Hartin, Patrick J. *James*. Sacra Pagina 14. Collegeville, MN: Liturgical, 2009.

———. *James and the Q Sayings of Jesus.* Sheffield: JSOT Press, 1991.

———. "The religious context of the letter of James." Pages 203–31 in *Jewish Christianity Reconsidered*. Minneapolis: Fortress Press, 2007.

———. *A Spirituality of Perfection: Faith in Action in the Letter of James.* Collegeville, MN: Liturgical, 1999.

Hayes, Christine E. *Gentile Impurities and Jewish Identities: Intermarriage and Conversion from the Bible to the Talmud*. Oxford: Oxford University Press, 2002.

Hengel, Martin. *The "Hellenization" of Judaea in the First Century after Christ.* Translated by John Bowden. London: SCM, 1989.

———. "Der Jacobusbrief als antipaulinische Polemik." In *Tradition and Interpretation in the New Testament.* Edited by Gerald F. Hawthorne and Otto Betz. Grand Rapids: Eerdmans, 1987.

Hezser, Catherine. "Travel and Mobility." In *The Oxford Handbook of Jewish Daily Life in Roman Palestine*. Edited by Catherine Hezser. Oxford: Oxford University Press, 2010.

Hodge, Caroline Johnson. "Apostle to the Gentiles: Constructions of Paul's Identity." *Biblical Interpretation* 13, no. 3 (2005): 270–88.

———. *If Sons, Then Heirs: A Study of Kinship and Ethnicity in the Letters of Paul*. Oxford: Oxford University Press, 2007.

Holman, Susan R., ed. *Wealth and Poverty in Early Church and Society*. Grand Rapids: Baker Academic, 2008.

Hopkins, Keith. "Élite Mobility in the Roman Empire." *Past and Present* 32 (1965): 12–26.

Horsley, Richard. *Jesus and Empire: The Kingdom of God and the New World Disorder*. Minneapolis: Fortress Press, 2003.

———, ed. *Paul and Empire: Religion and Power in Roman Imperial Society*. Harrisburg, PA: Trinity Press International, 1997.

Huddart, David. *Homi K. Bhabha*. London and New York: Routledge, 2006.

JanMohamed, Abdul R. "The Economy of Manichean Allegory: The Function of Racial Difference in Colonialist Literature." *Critical Inquiry* 12, no. 1 (1985): 59–87.

Jenkins, C. Ryan. "Faith and Works in Paul and James." *Bibliotheca Sacra* 159, no. 633 (January–March 2002): 62–78.

Johnson, Luke Timothy. *The Acts of the Apostles*. Sacra Pagina 5. Collegeville, MN: Liturgical, 1992.

———. *Brother of Jesus, Friend of God: Studies in the Letter of James*. Grand Rapids: Eerdmans, 2004.

———. *The Letter of James: A New Translation with Introduction and Commentary*. Anchor Bible 37A. New York: Doubleday, 1995.

Joy, David. *Mark and Its Subalterns: A Hermeneutical Paradigm for a Postcolonial Context*. London: Equinox, 2008.

Keith, Pierre. "Les destinataires de l'épître de Jacques." *Foi et Vie* 102, no. 4 (2003): 19–27.

Klein, Martin. *"Ein vollkommenes Werk": Vollkommenheit, Gesetz und Gericht als theologische Themen des Jakobusbriefes*. Stuttgart, Berlin, Köln: Kohlhammer, 1995.

Kloppenborg, John. "The Reception of the Jesus Traditions in James." Pages 91–139 in *The Catholic Epistles and the Tradition*. Edited by Jacques Schlosser. Leuven: Peeters, 2004.

Kloppenborg, John. *Q, the Earliest Gospel: An Introduction to the Original Stories and Sayings of Jesus.* Louisville and London: Westminster John Knox, 2008.

Krüger, René. *Jakobusbrief als prophetische Kritik der Reichen: Eine exegetische Untersuchung aus lateinamerikanischer Perspektive.* Münster: Lit, 2005.

Kvammen, Ingeborg A. K. *Imperial Presence in the Assembly: An Interpretation of Jas 2:1-13 with a Postcolonial Optic.* Ph.D. diss., School of Mission and Theology, 2008.

Kümmel, Werner Georg. *Introduction to the New Testament.* Revised English Edition. Translated by Howard Clark Kee. Nashville: Abingdon, 1975.

Laws, Sophie. *The Epistle of James.* Harper's New Testament Commentary. San Francisco: Harper & Row, 1980.

Levine, Amy-Jill, ed. *A Feminist Companion to the Catholic Epistles and Hebrews.* London and New York: T. & T. Clark International, 2004.

Liew, Tat-siong Benny. *Politics of Parousia: Reading Mark Inter(con)textually.* Biblical Interpretation Series 42. Leiden: Brill, 1999.

Lockett, Darian. *Purity and Worldview in the Epistle of James.* London: T. & T. Clark, 2008.

Loomba, Ania. *Colonialism/Postcolonialism.* London and New York: Routledge, 1998.

Lopez, Davina C. *Apostle to the Conquered: Reimaging Paul's Mission.* Minneapolis: Fortress Press, 2008.

Luangphinith, Seri Inthava Kau'ikealaula. "Nativism." Pages 321–22 in *Encyclopedia of Postcolonial Studies.* Edited by John C. Hawley. Westport, CT and London: Greenwood, 2001.

MacMullen, Ramsay. *Roman Social Relations: 50 B.C. to A.D. 284.* New Haven: Yale University Press, 1974.

Maier, Gerhard. *Der Brief des Jakobus.* Historische Theologische Auslegung. Markgröningen: R. Brockhaus Verlag Wuppertal, 2004.

Marchal, Joseph A. *The Politics of Heaven: Women, Gender, and Empire in the Study of Paul.* Paul in Critical Contexts. Minneapolis: Fortress Press, 2008.

Martin, Ralph P. *James.* WBC 48. Nashville: Thomas Nelson, 1988.

Martyn, J. Louis. *Galatians: A New Translation with Introduction and Commentary.* Anchor Bible 33A. New York: Doubleday, 1997.

Maxwell, David R. "Justified by Works and Not by Faith Alone: Reconciling Paul and James." *Concordia Journal* 33, no. 4 (October 2007): 375–78.

Maynard-Reid, Pedrito U. *Poverty and Wealth in James.* Maryknoll, NY: Orbis, 1987.

Memmi, Albert. *The Colonizer and the Colonized.* Translated by Howard Greenfeld. Boston: Beacon, 1965. French original, 1957.

Mitchell, Margaret M. "The Letter of James as a Document of Paulinism?" In *Reading James with New Eyes: Methodological Reassessments of the Letter of James.* Edited by Robert L. Webb and John S. Kloppenborg. London: T. & T. Clark, 2007.

Moore, Stephen D. *The Bible in Theory: Critical and Postcritical Essays.* Atlanta: Society of Biblical Literature, 2010.

———. *Empire and Apocalypse: Postcolonialism and the New Testament.* The Bible in the Modern World 12. Sheffield: Sheffield Phoenix Press, 2006.

———. "Situating Spivak." In *Planetary Loves: Spivak, Postcoloniality, and Theology.* Edited by Stephen D. Moore and Mayra Rivera. New York: Fordham University Press, 2011.

Moore, Stephen D., and Fernando F. Segovia, eds. *Postcolonial Biblical Criticism: Interdisciplinary Intersections.* The Bible and Postcolonialism Series. London and New York: T. & T. Clark International, 2005.

Moore, Stephen D., and Mayra Rivera, eds. *Planetary Loves: Spivak, Postcoloniality, and Theology.* Transdisciplinary Theological Colloquia. New York: Fordham University Press, 2011.

Morton, Stephen. *Gayatri Chakravorty Spivak.* Routledge Critical Thinkers. London and New York: Routledge, 2003.

Nanos, Mark. *The Mystery of Romans: The Jewish Context of Paul's Letter*. Minneapolis: Fortress Press, 1996.

———, ed. *The Galatians Debate: Contemporary Issues in Rhetorical and Historical Interpretation*. Peabody, MA: Hendrickson, 2002.

Ndlovu-Gatsheni, Sabelo J. "Nativism and the Debate on African Public Sphere in Postcolonial Africa: Reflections on a Problematic 'Reverse-Discourse.'" Paper presented under a panel called "Nationalism, Public Sphere and Citizenship in Africa" at the Council for the Development of Social Science Research in Africa (CODESRIA)'s Twelfth General Assembly: Governing the African Public Sphere. Yaoundé, Cameroon, December 7–11, 2008.

Ngũgĩ wa Thiong'o, *Decolonizing the Mind: The Politics of Language in African Literature*. Harare, Zimbabwe: Zimbabwe Publishing House, 1987.

Neusner, Jacob. "Sin, Repentance, Atonement and Resurrection: The Perspective of Rabbinic Theology on the Views of James 1–2 and Paul in Romans 3–4." Pages 409–34 in *Missions of James, Peter, and Paul*. Leiden and Boston: Brill, 2005.

Noreña, Carlos F. *Imperial Ideals in the Roman West: Representation, Circulation, Power*. Cambridge: Cambridge University Press, 2011.

Oakman, Douglas E. "Jesus and Agrarian Palestine: The Factor of Debt." Pages 65–82 in *The Social World of the New Testament: Insights and Models*. Edited by Jerome H. Neyrey and Eric C. Stewart. Peabody, MA: Hendrickson, 2008.

Painter, John. *Just James: The Brother of Jesus in History and Tradition*. 2nd edition. Columbia: University of South Carolina Press, 2004.

Parry, Benita. *Postcolonial Studies: A Materialist Critique*. London and New York: Routledge, 2004.

Pearce, Sarah, and Siân Jones, eds. *Jewish Local Patriotism and Self-Identification in the Graeco-Roman Period*. Sheffield: Sheffield Academic Press, 1998.

Popkes, Wiard. "Two Interpretations of 'justification' in the New Testament: Reflections on Galatians 2:15-21 and James 2:21-25." *Studia Theologica* 59, no. 2 (2005): 129–46.

Porter, Stanley E., ed. *Paul and His Opponents.* Atlanta: Society of Biblical Literature, 2005.

Porter, Stanley E., and Cynthia Long Westfall, eds. *Empire in the New Testament.* McMaster New Testament Studies Series. Eugene, OR: Pickwick, 2011.

Punt, Jeremy. "Empire as material setting and heuristic grid for New Testament interpretation: Comments on the value of postcolonial criticism." *HTS Teologiese Studies/Theological Studies* 66, no. 1, Art. #330, 7 pages, 2010. DOI: 10.4102/hts.v66i1.330.

———. "Towards a Postcolonial Reading of Freedom in Paul." In *Reading the Bible in the Global Village: Cape Town.* Atlanta: Society of Biblical Literature, 2002.

Reinhartz, Adele. "The Colonizer as Colonized: Intertextual Dialogue between the Gospel of John and Canadian Identity." In *John and Postcolonialism: Travel, Space and Power.* Edited by Musa W. Dube and Jeffrey L. Staley. The Bible and Postcolonialism 7. London and New York: Sheffield Academic Press, 2002.

Rhoads, David, David Esterline, and Jae Won Lee, eds. *Luke-Acts and Empire: Essays in Honor of Robert L. Brawley.* Princeton Theological Monograph Series. Eugene, OR: Pickwick, 2011.

Richardson, Peter. *Herod: King of the Jews and Friend of the Romans.* Minneapolis: Fortress Press, 1999.

Ringe, Sharon H. "The Letter of James." Pages 369–79 in *A Postcolonial Commentary on the New Testament Writings.* Edited by Fernando F. Segovia and R. S. Sugirtharajah. New York: T. & T. Clark International, 2007.

Rocca, Samuel. *Herod's Judea: A Mediterranean State in the Classical World.* Tübingen: Mohr Siebeck, 2008.

Runions, Erin. *Changing Subjects: Gender, Nation and Future in Micah.* Playing the Texts 7. Sheffield: Sheffield Academic Press, 2002.

Said, Edward W. *Culture and Imperialism.* New York: Vintage, 1993.

———. *Orientalism.* New York: Vintage, 1978.

Saldarini, Anthony J. *Matthew's Christian-Jewish Community.* Chicago and London: University of Chicago Press, 1994.

Saller, Richard P. *Personal Patronage under the Early Empire.* Cambridge: Cambridge University Press, 1982.

Sanchez, David. *From Patmos to the Barrio: Subverting Imperial Myths.* Minneapolis: Fortress Press, 2008.

Schwartz, Seth. *Imperialism and Jewish Society: 200 bce to 640 ce.* Princeton: Princeton University Press, 2001.

Seesengood, Robert Paul. *Competing Identities: The Athlete and Gladiator in Early Christianity.* London: Continuum, 2007.

———. "Hybridity and the Rhetoric of Endurance: Reading Paul's Athletic Metaphors in a Context of Postcolonial Self-Construction." *Bible and Critical Theory* 1, no. 3 (2005): 1–14.

Segovia, Fernando F. *Decolonizing Biblical Studies: A View from the Margins.* Maryknoll, NY: Orbis, 2000.

———, ed. *Interpreting Beyond Borders.* The Bible and Postcolonialism 3. Sheffield: Sheffield Academic Press, 2000.

Sevenster, Jan Nicolaas. *Do You Know Greek? How Much Greek Could the First Jewish Christians Have Known?* Supplements to Novum Testamentum 19. Leiden: Brill, 1968.

Shkul, Minna. "Religious Identity and Power of Naming—Saints and Sinners in Ephesians." A paper delivered in the Early Jewish Christian Relations Section at the Annual Meeting of the Society of Biblical Literature, Philadelphia, 2005.

Spivak, Gayatri Chakravorty. "Can the Subaltern Speak? Speculations on Widow Sacrifice." *Wedge* 7/8 (Winter/Spring 1985).

———. *A Critique of Postcolonial Reason: Toward a History of the Vanishing Present*. Cambridge, MA and London: Harvard University Press, 1999.

———. *The Post-Colonial Critic: Interviews, Strategies, Dialogues*. Edited by Sarah Harasym. London and New York: Routledge, 1990.

Stanley, Christopher D., ed. *The Colonized Apostle: Paul through Postcolonial Eyes*. Paul in Critical Contexts. Minneapolis: Fortress Press, 2011.

Stambaugh, John E., and David L. Balch. *The New Testament in Its Social Environment*. Philadelphia: Westminster, 1986.

Stowers, Stanley K. *A Rereading of Romans: Justice, Jews, & Gentiles*. New Haven and London: Yale University Press, 1994.

Sugirtharajah, R. S. *The Bible and the Third World: Precolonial, Colonial and Postcolonial Encounters*. Cambridge: Cambridge University Press, 2001.

———. *Exploring Postcolonial Biblical Criticism: History, Method, Practice*. Oxford: Wiley-Blackwell, 2012.

———. *Postcolonial Criticism and Biblical Interpretation*. Oxford: Oxford University Press, 2002.

Tamez, Elsa. *The Scandalous Message of James: Faith Without Works Is Dead*. New York: Crossroad, 1990.

Tate, Shirley Anne. *Black Skins, Black Masks: Hybridity, Dialogism, Performativity*. Hants, UK: Ashgate, 2005.

Taylor, N. H. "Apostolic Identity and the Conflicts in Corinth and Galatia." Edited by Stanley E. Porter. *Paul and His Opponents*. Pauline Studies 2. Atlanta: Society of Biblical Literature, 2005.

Theissen, Gerd. "Éthique et communauté dans l'épître de Jacques: réflexions sur son Sitz im Leben." *Études théologiques et religieuses* 77, no. 2 (2002): 157–76.

Thurman, Eric. "Looking for a Few Good Men: Mark and Masculinity." In *New Testament Masculinities*. Edited by Stephen D. Moore and Janice

Capel Anderson. Semeia Studies 45. Atlanta: Society of Biblical Literature, 2003.

Tsuji, Manabu. *Glaube zwischen Vollkommenheit und Verweltlichung: Eine Untersuchung zur literarischen Gestalt und zur inhaltlichen Koharenz des Jakobusbriefes.* Tübingen: Mohr Siebeck, 1997.

Van de Sandt, Huub, and Jurgen K. Zangenberg, eds. *Matthew, James, and Didache: Three Related Documents in Their Jewish and Christian Settings.* Symposium Series 45. Atlanta: Society of Biblical Literature, 2008.

Verseput, Donald J. "Genre and Story: The Community Setting of the Epistle of James." *CBQ* 62 (2000): 96–110.

Viviano, Benedict. "La Loi Parfaite de Liberté: Jacques 1.25 et la Loi." Pages 213–26 in *The Catholic Epistles and the Tradition.* Edited by J. Schlosser. Leuven: Leuven University Press, 2004.

Vouga, François. *L'Épître de Saint Jacques.* Genève: Labor et Fides, 1984.

Wachob, Wesley Hiram. *The Voice of Jesus in the Social Rhetoric of James.* Cambridge: Cambridge University Press, 2000.

Wall, Robert W. *Community of the Wise: The Letter of James.* Valley Forge, PA: Trinity Press International, 1997.

Wallerstein, Immanuel. "Reading Fanon in the 21st Century." *New Left Review* 57 (May/June 2009): 117–25.

Webb, Robert L., and John S. Kloppenborg, eds. *Reading James with New Eyes: Methodological Reassessments of the Letter of James.* London: T. & T. Clark International, 2007.

Wheatley, Alan B. *Patronage in Early Christianity: Its Use and Transformation from Jesus to Paul of Samosata.* Eugene, OR: Pickwick, 2011.

West, Gerald, ed. *Reading Other-Wise: Socially Engaged Biblical Scholars Reading with Their Local Communities.* Semeia Studies 62. Atlanta: Society of Biblical Literature, 2007.

Young, Robert. *Postcolonialism: An Historical Introduction.* Oxford: Blackwell, 2001.

———. *White Mythologies: Writing History and the West.* London and New York: Routledge, 1990.

Index of Subjects and Names

Index of Scripture and Ancient Literature References

New Testament

Ancient Authors